STUDY GUIDE TO ACCOMPANY

CORLEY • REED • SHEDD

THE LEGAL ENVIRONMENT OF BUSINESS

EIGHTH EDITION

O. LEE REED
Professor of Legal Studies, University of Georgia

McGraw-Hill Publishing Company

New York St. Louis San Francisco Auckland Bogotá Caracas Hamburg Lisbon London Madrid Mexico Milan Montreal New Delhi Oklahoma City Paris San Juan São Paulo Singapore Sydney Tokyo Toronto

Study Guide to accompany Corley • Reed • Shedd: The Legal Environment of Business

1234567890 SEMSEM 8932109

ISBN 0-07-013290-9

The editor was Johanna Schmid; the production supervisor was Leroy A. Young. Semline, Inc., was printer and binder.

CONTENTS

PREFACE

For most of you studying The Legal Environment of Business, this will be your first law-related course. Because the basic tool of law is words, this course requires much reading and a great deal of thinking about words. In preparing your text, the authors realized that a guide to help direct student reading and study in law would be especially important. The publisher agreed, which led to preparation of the following study guide.

Many student study guides are written by someone other than a text author. However, as co-author of The Legal Environment of Business, I am proud to bring to bear on the study guide knowledge gained from research and writing of the text. I believe that students will benefit more from a text author's personal attention to this important guide than if its preparation were left to someone substantially unfamiliar with the writing of the text.

The guide does not replace a thorough reading of the text, but if used to assist your reading and study, it can prove a very valuable tool. Each study guide chapter corresponds to a text chapter. It contains an outline that summarizes principal points of each chapter, using the same section headings found in the chapter. Major terms and concepts are underlined to highlight them.

Following the outline are completion exercises, true-false choices, multiple choice selections, and a discussion analysis. At the end of the study guide are answers to the various exercises. Also included is a suggested development for the discussion analysis. Careful attention to the exercises and discussion analysis should aid self-measurement and exam preparation significantly.

Woodrow Wilson noted, "Every citizen should know what law is, how it came into existence, what relation its form bears to its substance, and how it gives to society its fibre and strength and poise of frame." For the business professional, whose decisions are heavily influenced by legal considerations, an understanding of the legal environment of business is especially important. This study guide, used along with your text, can make a significant contribution to that understanding.

O. Lee Reed

Chapter 1

Introduction to Law

STUDY GUIDE AND OUTLINE

I. The Law and Business

A. The law guides and limits business decisions.

B. Since the 1960s there has been an explosion in the laws regulating business, the number of lawsuits against businesses, and the number of lawyers.

II. Definitions of Law

A. There are many definitions of law.

B. Criminal law commands individuals, telling them what they may or may not do. Civil law (for example, the law of contracts) does not usually command. Instead, it imposes liability and damages for failing to comply with the law.

C. Law is made up of three elements:

1. Formal legislation, including constitutions, statutes, and treaties.
2. Rules of law announced by the courts in deciding cases.
3. The system of legal concepts which forms the basis of judicial action.

D. Oliver Wendell Holmes defined law as "a statement of the circumstances in which the public force will be brought to bear through courts." The statement illustrates the importance of the courts to the legal system.

E. Law may also be regarded as a scheme of social control. Thus judges are in a sense social engineers.

F. Roscoe Pound defined law in terms of justice. He said that law is "that organized body of knowledge that has to do with the administration of justice by public or regular tribunals in accordance with principles or rules of general character and more or less uniform application."

III. Schools of Legal Thought

A. The various schools of legal thought have helped to shape development of legal principles.

B. The historical school gives great weight to custom and history as a source of law.

C. The analytical school of legal thought focuses on logic as the basis of law. Social order logically requires definite rules for governing human conduct.

D. The natural school of legal thought sees law as arising from right, reason, and the intelligence of man as coming from God.

E. The sociological school of legal thought recognizes that law is a scheme of social control and that it may change to meet changing needs in society.

F. The realist school of legal thought sees law as coming from experience. Realists recognized that law is constantly changing. What officials do about the law, rather than just say about it, is important.

G. Appreciate that these schools of law are philosophies about law. They are not law itself.

IV. The Rule of Law

A. John Adams described our political system as "a government of laws and not of men."

B. Lincoln described law as the "political religion" of our country.

C. The study of law essentially concerns "rules of law." A rule of law is a statement that if certain facts exist, the courts will take action or refuse to take action at the request of someone involved. Facts create legal issues that are resolved by using rules of law. Be aware of the tremendous importance of facts to the law. The usual function of the jury is fact finding.

V. Lawyers

A. The number of lawyers in the legal profession has doubled since 1970.

B. A lawyer serves in three capacities: counselor, advocate, and public servant.

C. The attorney-client privilege ensures that communications between a lawyer and client are confidential.

D. Legal codes of ethics maintain high professional standards for the legal profession and help to eliminate "ambulance chasing" and other unethical conduct by lawyers.

VI. General Classification of Legal Subjects

A. There are several ways of classifying legal subjects.

B. Public law and private law.

1. Public law includes constitutional law, administrative law, and criminal law. In public law the interests of society are represented by the state.
2. Private law involves those legal problems which exist between individuals, as contrasted with those in which society is concerned. Private law is divided into the law of contracts, the law of torts, and the law of property.

C. Substantive law and procedural law.

1. Substantive law defines legal relationships between people or between individuals and the state. The rules of contract law and statutes prohibiting possession of drugs are examples of substantive law.
2. Procedural law deals with the means by which substantive law is made and administered. Rules involving the method of conducting trials, appeals, and enforcement of judgments are examples of procedural law.

D. Civil law and criminal law.

VII. The Criminal Law

A. Criminal law involves wrongs against society that the state punishes.

B. Criminal law is generally divided into felonies and misdemeanors.

1. Felonies are punishable by fine or imprisonment of one year or more.
2. Misdemeanors are punishable by a fine or imprisonment of less than one year.
3. Violations of traffic ordinances, building codes, and other local ordinances are sometimes called petty offenses.

C. White-collar crime is on the increase. There have been many proposals made for reducing crime in general and white-collar crime in particular.

D. The Racketeer Influenced and Corrupt Organizations Act (RICO) was passed by Congress in 1970. It gives private persons the right to sue for triple damages and attorneys' fees when federal laws dealing with various forms of fraud have been violated by someone twice within a ten year period.

1. Over three-fourths of all RICO suits involve securities or other business frauds.
2. There are numerous proposals before Congress to change RICO.

VIII. The Law of Contracts

A. A contract is a legally binding agreement between persons. Courts recognize that persons have a duty to live up to their contracts, and the law provides remedies for breach of contracts.

B. The subject of contracts is the subject of Chapter 9.

IX. The Law of Torts

A. A tort is a non-contractual civil wrong for which the law gives a right to recover damages. The same act may be both a tort and a crime, e.g., an assault.

B. Tort liability assumes that in a civilized society people will not intentionally injure others or their property, and that all persons will exercise reasonable care in their activities.

1. Intentional torts include assault and battery, false imprisonment, libel, trespass and conversion.
2. Negligence liability arises from an injury caused by a failure to exercise the duty of reasonable care.

C. There are separate chapters on torts and products liability .

X. The Law of Property

A. In a legal sense property is a bundle of rights. The primary rights are title (ownership) and possession.

B. Property is usually classified as either real or personal.

1. Real property is land or any interest in land, including things attached to the land, such as buildings, which are called fixtures.
2. Personal property includes all other tangible or intangible interests. For example, you have intangible personal property when you have accounts receivable.

C. Fundamental to the concept of property is the right to exclude others from its possession and use.

XI. Sources of Law

A. Our law comes from four basic sources:

1. Constitutions (state and federal)
2. Legislation (state and federal)
3. Judicial decisions (state and federal)
4. Rules, regulations and decisions of administrative agencies (state and federal)

B. Constitutions are the basic and supreme law.

C. Most of our laws are found in some form of legislation.

D. Judge-made law is often called <u>common law</u>. Common law has its origins in England. Common law is based on the principle <u>stare decisis</u>, which means that in present cases courts follow decisions (precedents) laid down in prior cases. In a sense, courts also "make law" when they interpret constitutions, statutes, and regulatory rules and decisions.

XII. Other Influences on Behavior

A. The law interacts with economics, ethics, and social responsibility to influence decisions and shape society. Appreciate that these forces overlap and affect each other.

B. To examine the trends in the law requires that we consider contemporary ethical standards that may some day become law.

XIII. Law and Ethics

A. If the goal of law is justice, including social justice, then the ethics of society plays a major role in the search for that goal.

B. Many businesses have adopted codes of ethics. Throughout your textbook, many references are made to the code of ethics of the Caterpillar Tractor Company.

COMPLETION EXERCISES

1. Holmes said "Law is a statement of the circumstances in which the public force will be brought to bear through ________________."

2. ________________ defines those legal problems and relationships which exist between individuals.

3. ________________ deals with the method and means by which substantive law is administered.

4. Law may be divided into criminal law and ________________.

5. Criminal law is generally divided into ________________ and ________________.

6. Non-violent business crime is generally referred to as ________________.

7. ________________ concerns the legal relationships created between individuals by their own agreement.

8. A non-contractual civil wrong is a ________________.

9. ________________ is a breach of the duty to use reasonable care.

10. Property is subdivided into ______________ and ______________ property.

11. The term title is usually synonymous with ______________ of property.

12. Legal physical control over property is termed ______________.

13. The four basic sources of law in our legal system are ______________, ______________, ______________, and ______________.

14. Judicial use of case law is based on the doctrine of ______________.

15. In addition to law, basic forces shaping society are ______________, ______________, and ______________.

TRUE-FALSE CHOICES

1. _____ John Adams described our political system as "a government of laws and not men."
2. _____ The realist school of law gives great weight to the influence of religion in developing the law.
3. _____ The sociological school of law recognizes law as a scheme of social control.
4. _____ Uses of the word "law" are limitless.
5. _____ Civil law (such as the law of contracts) commands compliance.
6. _____ The number of lawsuits being filed today is declining.
7. _____ The size of the legal profession has doubled since 1970.
8. _____ The attorney-client privilege insures that communications between a lawyer and client are confidential.
9. _____ "Ambulance chasing" is an ethical legal practice.
10. _____ A lawyer serves in the capacities of counselor, advocate, and public servant.
11. _____ The same act may not be both a tort and crime.
12. _____ The common law is basically statutory in origin.
13. _____ Ethical values are affected by economic considerations.
14. _____ RICO gives the government the right to sue someone who has violated federal law.
15. _____ Over three-fourths of all RICO suits involve business frauds.

MULTIPLE CHOICE SELECTIONS

1. Select the incorrect statement:

   a. Crimes are wrongs in society that the state punishes.
   b. Felonies are punishable by imprisonment of one year or more.
   c. Misdemeanors are punishable by imprisonment of less than one year.
   d. White-collar crime is on the decrease.

2. Select the <u>incorrect</u> statement:

   a. A contract is a legally binding agreement between persons.
   b. Torts recognize that persons have a duty to live up to their contracts.
   c. Negligence includes assault and battery.
   d. A tort is a civil wrong.

3. Select the <u>incorrect</u> statement:

   a. Statutory law is based on the principle of stare decisis.
   b. Judge-made law is often called common law.
   c. Constitutions are our most basic and supreme law.
   d. In a sense, courts make law.

4. Select the most correct statement:

   a. Private law includes administrative and criminal law.
   b. Procedural law defines the legal relationship of people with other people.
   c. Civil cases are also those which are not criminal actions.
   d. A tort may not also be a crime.

5. Select the most correct statement:

   a. The ethics of society influence the law's content.
   b. The law influences the ethical expectations of society.
   c. Ethics may actually condemn that which the law allows.
   d. All of the above are correct.

DISCUSSION ANALYSIS

What are the basic sources of law in our society? Discuss which of these sources you consider to be the most important overall.

Chapter 2

The Powers and Functions of Courts

STUDY GUIDE AND OUTLINE

I. Introduction

A. Courts play a major role in the development of law. For example, they interpret legislation and apply it to specific situations.

B. Because there are so many court cases interpreting various laws, our common law system sometimes fails to provide certainty and predictability.

II. Judges and Justices

A. The judicial power is perhaps the most extensive power possessed by any branch of government. This power is exercised by trial court judges and reviewing court (appeals court) justices.

B. Trial court judges try cases. They have direct contact with litigation and litigants.

C. Justices hear appeals from the legal decisions made by trial courts. They give reasons for their decisions in written form, which become precedent and a part of our body of law. On review, justices are essentially concerned with issues of law. Issues of fact are resolved at the trial level.

D. Judges and justices have judicial immunity. This means that they have almost total personal immunity from legal actions against them based on their judicial acts, even when these acts are malicious or exceed authority.

III. The Jury

A. The Sixth and Seventh Amendments to the Constitution guarantee the right of trial by jury in both criminal and civil cases. In civil cases this right is preserved in lawsuits at common law when the amount in controversy exceeds $20.

B. There are two basic types of juries: the grand jury and petit jury.

C. A grand jury determines whether there is sufficient evidence of guilt to warrant indictment for criminal trials.

D. A petit jury determines the facts at a trial. Historically, this jury consisted of 12 persons. Today many state and federal courts provide for smaller juries in both criminal and civil cases.

E. In most states a petit jury's decision must be unanimous. However, in some states less than a unanimous verdict is constitutionally permissible for a 12-person jury.

F. "Mock" trials are being used increasingly by lawyers to help determine how real juries will respond to the presentation of evidence.

G. The jury system has been subject to much criticism.

H. Although many citizens attempt to avoid jury duty, there is a trend toward requiring jury duty of all citizens.

IV. Judicial Review

A. The doctrine of judicial review allows the courts to review laws passed by the legislature and actions taken by the executive branch and to declare them unconstitutional.

B. The Constitution does not expressly give the courts this power. Chief Justice Marshall announced the doctrine of judicial review in the famous case Marbury v. Madison.

C. An example of judicial review comes from the Watergate era when the Supreme Court ruled that it would be unconstitutional for President Nixon to refuse to hand over certain tape recordings to Congress. In another example the Court ruled that a legislative veto over acts of the executive branch of government was unconstitutional.

V. Attitudes Toward Judicial Review

A. As judges exercise the power of judicial review, they do so with varying attitudes and philosophies.

B. Judges who believe that judicial review should not be used except in unusual cases are said to believe in judicial restraint. Those who think that judicial review should be used whenever the needs of society justify its use believe in judicial activism. All judges believe in judicial restraint and all are activists to some extent. Often a judge may be an activist in one area of the law and a firm believer in judicial restraint in another.

C. Those who believe in judicial restraint think that constitutional issues are too important to be decided unless absolutely necessary and are to be avoided if there is another legal basis for a decision. They believe the proper use of their power demands that courts refrain from determining the constitutionality of an act of Congress unless it is absolutely required.

D. The philosophy of judicial restraint is sometimes called judicial abstention or strict construction. The former means that courts should abstain from deciding issues whenever possible, and doubts about the constitutionality of legislation should be resolved in favor of the statute. The latter means that the constitution should be interpreted in light of what the founding fathers intended.

E. Those who believe in judicial restraint feel that social, political, and economic change in society should result from the political process rather than from court action.

F. Throughout most of our history, judicial restraint has been the dominant philosophy, but all judges are to some degree activists. Activists believe that courts should use the Constitution to play a major role in correcting wrongs in our society. Activitists depend less than judicial restraintists on precedent. They believe that the Constitution is relative to the times in which it is being interpreted.

G. Activists have brought about substantial changes in the law, especially in such areas as civil rights, reapportionment of legislatures, and the criminal law.

VI. The Interpretation of Legislation

A. It is the responsibility of the courts to interpret the meaning of legislation and its frequently general language. Courts consider the legislative history (legislative debates, committee reports, etc.) to help them determine the meaning of legislation.

B. Rules of statutory interpretation also aid courts in determining the meaning of legislation. For example, tax laws and criminal laws are "strictly construed." This means that doubts about the applicability of a tax or criminal law will be resolved in favor of the taxpayer or criminal defendant. Statutes that grant remedies are "liberally construed."

C. There are very many other rules of statutory interpretation.

VII. Uniform Statutes

A. There are substantial differences in the laws of various states.

B. Uniformity in the law can be achieved by federal legislation or by enactment of the same law by various states.

1. The National Conference of Commissioners on Uniform State Laws proposes model uniform laws for state adoption.
2. The most significant uniform state law for business is the Uniform Commercial Code. It deals with the sale of goods, commercial paper such as checks, and security interests in personal property.

VIII. Case Law: Inherent Problems

A. Case law refers to the total collection of judicial opinions. These collected opinions make up a substantial portion of the volume in any law school library. State decisions are organized in state and regional reporters. There are also various reporters for the federal judiciary. Case law includes both common law and constitutional and legislative interpretations.

B. Judicial decisions (case law) create precedents, which courts apply and follow in subsequent decisions.

C. Case law, especially common law, is often difficult to apply with any degree of certainty.

1. Sheer volume of judicial decisions makes it difficult to locate the correct precedents.
2. Conflicting precedents are often easy to locate.
3. Each of the 50 states has its own body of case law.

D. The difference between precedent and mere dicta also complicates use of case law. Precedent arises from the holding a court makes on the precise legal issue, considering the exact facts of the case, which it confronts. Everything else the court says is mere dicta.

IX. The Weight to Be Given Precedent

A. The principle of stare decisis means that courts usually follow and apply prior precedents.

B. Stare decisis does not always mean, however, that prior precedents are followed. Courts sometimes overrule prior precedents, especially as courts become convinced that the prior precedents are wrong in light of changing social needs. Courts are most likely to follow precedents which involve interpretations of legislation. They are least likely to follow precedents involving constitutional law.

C. The amount of deference given to a prior precedent often depends on the conclusion a court wants to reach.

X. Selecting the Applicable Case Law

A. Each state has its own body of case law. The federal courts have their own body of procedural and substantive law on questions of federal and constitutional law. Federal courts also try cases based on diversity of citizenship, i.e., where the dispute involves state law but the plaintiff and defendant are citizens of different states. In these cases the federal courts apply their own procedural law, but apply the substantive law of the state in which the court is sitting.

B. Difficulties arise where disputes involve transactions with contact with more than one state. Questions as to which state's law applies are answered according to conflict of laws doctrines. Each state has a conflict of laws doctrine. One example of a common conflict of laws doctrine is that courts are to apply the law of the state where an accident occurred. Thus, if there were a car accident in Ohio, and the injured plaintiff sued the defendant in the defendant's home state of New York, the court in New York would apply the tort law of the state of Ohio.

XI. The Judicial Process

A. In any given case why do courts reach one conclusion rather than another? Some persons feel that logic is the basic tool of the judicial decision. Others contend that experience, personal opinions, and the attitude of the times are all important factors in judicial decision-making.

B. Benjamin Cardozo, a famous judge and justice, in his book The Nature of the Judicial Process, argued that judicial process is shaped by logic, history, custom, and utility. He observed a judge's decision is often "creative" and that law "is not found, but made."

COMPLETION EXERCISES

1. The power of courts to decide whether a law violates the Constitution is known as the power of ________________.

2. Judicial power is exercised by trial court ________________ and reviewing court (appeals court) ________________.

3. Issues of ________________ are resolved at the trial level. Reviewing courts are essentially concerned with issues of ________________.

4. The right to trial in cases of common law is constitutionally guaranteed if the amount in controversy exceeds ________________.

5. The two basic kinds of jury are the ________________ jury and ________________ jury.

6. The ________________ jury determines whether there is sufficient evidence of guilt to warrant indictment for criminal trials.

7. ________________ trials and ________________ trials are being used increasingly by lawyers to help determine how real juries will respond to the presentation of evidence.

8. The doctrine of ________________ allows courts to declare legislation unconstitutional.

9. Chief Justice ________________ announced the doctrine of judicial review in the famous case ________________.

10. In helping determine the meaning of legislation, courts frequently consider the legislative ________________.

11. Tax laws and criminal laws are strictly ________________.

12. _______________ refers to the total collection of judicial opinions.

13. Judicial decisions create _______________, which courts apply and follow in subsequent decisions.

14. Judicial comments that do not concern the holding of a case are called _______________.

15. The principle of _______________ means that courts usually follow and apply prior precedents.

TRUE-FALSE CHOICES

1. _____ The doctrine of judicial review is set forth expressly in the Constitution.
2. _____ Judicial review does not apply to actions of the executive branch.
3. _____ Tax and criminal laws are liberally construed.
4. _____ Precedent and dicta mean the same thing.
5. _____ The common law system of reliance on precedent is not very efficient.
6. _____ Courts have no power to change prior precedent.
7. _____ Courts are most likely to follow precedent in the area of constitutional law.
8. _____ Conflict of laws doctrines are used to settle disputes which involve the laws of different states.
9. _____ Tort conflict of laws doctrine usually says that courts shall apply the law of the state where an accident occurred.
10. _____ The laws of the various states differ substantially.
11. _____ Statutes that grant remedies are strictly construed.
12. _____ Each of the 50 states has its own body of case law.
13. _____ Federal courts try cases based on diversity of citizenship.
14. _____ Precedent arises from the holding a court makes on a precise legal issue.
15. _____ In diversity of citizenship cases federal courts apply the substantive law of the state in which the court is sitting.

MULTIPLE CHOICE SELECTIONS

1. Select the <u>incorrect</u> answer. Cardozo argued that the judicial process is shaped by:

   a. Logic.
   b. Power.
   c. History.
   d. Utility.

2. All of the following are examples of judicial review except:

   a. A ruling that it is unconstitutional for President Nixon to refuse to hand over certain tape recordings to Congress.
   b. A ruling that the Federal Trade Commission violated the First Amendment in its regulation of commercial speech.
   c. A ruling that the Occupational Safety and Health Act violates the Constitution by permitting a search of businesses without a warrant.
   d. All of the above are examples of judicial review.

3. Select the incorrect statement:

   a. The Constitution guarantees the right of trial by jury in certain types of criminal and civil cases.
   b. A grand jury determines whether an alleged criminal should stand trial.
   c. Today many state and federal courts provide for juries of fewer than 12 persons in both criminal and civil cases.
   d. Jurors are required to give reasons for the decision that they reach in a trial.

4. All of the following are inherent problems with the use of case law except:

   a. The sheer volume of judicial decisions.
   b. Conflicting precedents.
   c. The fact that there are 50 separate jurisdictions.
   d. All of the above are inherent problems.

5. Suppose that Congress has established a "legislative veto" over a federal regulatory agency. This vote allows Congress to override a rule of the agency without the President having the right to veto Congress' action or to sign it into law. If on behalf of the President, the Justice Department challenges the legislative veto concept in court, the court is likely to say that:

   a. The court has the power to decide the legislative veto's constitutionality.
   b. The separation of powers doctrine forbids the courts from deciding the veto's constitutionality.
   c. Anything the court could say in this case would be mere dicta.
   d. None of the above is correct.

Chapter 2

DISCUSSION ANALYSIS

Discuss the significance of the fact that our legal system recognizes both the principle of stare decisis and the power of the courts to overturn prior precedents. Relate your answer to the often heard statement that "the Constitution is relative to the times in which it is interpreted."

Chapter *3*

Court Systems

STUDY GUIDE AND OUTLINE

I. Introduction

A. Jurisdiction refers to a court's power over the parties to a lawsuit and over what the lawsuit is about (subject matter). Courts either have general or limited jurisdiction.

B. Courts of general jurisdiction may decide cases on most subject matters, but may have geographic limitations (e.g., a state court has jurisdiction only within the state).

C. Courts of limited jurisdiction are usually restricted as to the subject matter of the cases they decide (e.g., small claims courts lack jurisdiction over cases for more than a certain amount).

D. The case of Woodruff v. Georgia State University illustrates that even courts with general subject matter jurisdiction cannot decide every type of dispute. In this case the Georgia Supreme Court said that courts cannot review a teacher's academic assessment of a student's work. The student's professors had refused to recommend her to a Ph.D. program.

II. The State Court System: Governing Principles

Both state and federal courts are created and operated from three sources. Constitutions provide the general framework for the court system. Legislatures establish court jurisdiction and deal with such problems as tenure, selection, and duties of judges. Legislatures may also provide general rules of procedure to be used by courts. Finally, each court system sets forth its own rules of procedure within statutory limits.

III. Trial Courts

The basic trial court is frequently known as the circuit court. It may also be called the superior court, district court, or court of common pleas. In New York, it is called the supreme court. These trial courts have general jurisdiction, which means that they have power to hear any type of case.

IV. Reviewing Courts

A. Above the trial courts in most states are intermediate appellate courts and a court of final resort called the "Supreme Court of Appeals" or "Court of Appeals."

B. Courts of last resort in the state and federal systems (e.g., the Supreme Court) usually hear appeals in only the most important cases. Litigants usually have a right to appeal the legal decisions of the trial judge to an intermediate appellate court, but must petition the court of last resort and ask it to hear an appeal. The procedure is called "petition for leave to appeal" in some states and "petition for a writ of certiorari" in others.

V. Small-Claims Courts

Beneath the trial courts of general jurisdiction may be various specialized courts such as small-claims courts. These courts have low court costs and simplified procedures. Usually, lawyers need not represent the litigants. Small claims courts are subject to a dollar limitation on the amount of claims which may be made. These courts handle the majority of litigation between businesses and their customers. One continuing problem is that many successful litigants are unable to collect their judgments.

VI. The Federal Court System: Jurisdiction

A. Federal courts have limited jurisdiction. They have power over questions of federal law, the Constitution, matters in which the United States is a party, controversies between states, and diversity of citizenship cases (suits between citizens of different states).

B. Article III of the Constitution provides that judicial power be vested in the Supreme Court and such lower courts as Congress may create.

C. For diversity of citizenship purposes, a corporation is a citizen of its state of incorporation and also the place where it has its principal place of business.

VII. Diversity of Citizenship Cases

A. In diversity of citizenship cases, each plaintiff must meet the jurisdictional minimum amount, i.e., each plaintiff must claim at least $50,000 in damages.

B. Note that in a diversity of citizenship case each plaintiff must be diverse from each defendant, i.e., must live in a different state. In Navarro Savings Association v. Lee the Supreme Court ruled that the trustees of a business trust were the proper parties to consider for diversity purposes rather than the beneficiaries of the trust.

VIII. Federal Reviewing Courts

A. Following a trial, litigants are entitled to one appellate review as a matter of right. Usually this appeal is made to a court called the "court of appeals."

B. A losing party at a court of appeals can petition the Supreme Court (state or federal depending on whether the case is state or federal) for a writ of certiorari. Writs of certiorari are granted only in cases of substantial importance or when there is an obvious conflict between decisions of two or more courts of appeal. If certiorari is not granted, a party cannot have his or her case heard by the Supreme Court. In this event, a decision of the court of appeals is final.

IX. Transfer from the States to the Federal System

A. If a plaintiff files a lawsuit in a state court, and the case could have been brought into federal court, the defendant can have the case removed to the federal court. An example of this situation is when the case involves a plaintiff and a defendant from different states.

B. A party may appeal the decision of the highest state court to the U.S. Supreme Court when:

1. The case involves validity of a U.S. treaty or statute, and the decision is against its constitutionality.
2. The case involves a state statute against the charge that it violates the Constitution, and the decision is in favor of its validity.
3. Interpretation of federal law is involved. In this last instance, the appealing party must petition the Supreme Court for a writ of certiorari.

X. The Law in the Federal Courts

A. The federal courts apply both substantive and procedural law. The federal rules of procedure govern applicable procedural law. Where federal questions are involved, the federal courts apply federal substantive law.

B. In diversity of citizenship cases, the federal courts apply the substantive law of the state in which the federal court is sitting, including that state's conflicts of law doctrine if applicable. This result arises from the famous case of Erie R.R. v. Tompkins. Where there is no clear state law in such cases, the federal courts can invoke the doctrine of abstention and direct the litigants to try their case in the state court system.

C. Since federal courts use federal procedures and state substantive law in diversity cases, many decisions concern whether a given issue is one of substantive law or one of procedure. If the state rule law will affect the result of the case, the rule is always treated as substantive.

XI. Courts of Equity Contrasted with Courts of Law

A. Aristotle defined equity as the "correction of the law, where, by reason of its universality, it is deficient."

B. In our legal system equity has its origins in English law. Special courts called courts of chancery granted remedies such as specific performance of a contract where the legal (law court) remedy of damages was unfair (inequitable) to the plaintiff.

C. When dollar damages is an adequate remedy, a suit in equity will be dismissed. In Beckman v. Vassall-Dillworth Lincoln-Mercury the court dismissed an equitable lawsuit involving a dispute over a new car. The court ruled that a new car was not "unique" and that if the buyer had gotten one at another dealership at a higher price, the legal remedy of damages would have been adequate.

XII. Equitable Procedures

A. Courts of chancery (or equity) use maxims instead of rules of law. Some typical maxims of equity include:

1. "Equity will not suffer a right to exist without a remedy."
2. "He who comes into equity must do so with 'clean hands'."
3. "He who seeks equity must do equity."

B. In Tudor Engineering Co. v. Mouw the defendant was allowed the equitable remedy of redemption. The plaintiff, who had brought the defendant's $49,000 house for $385.65 at a judicial sale, had to allow the defendant to redeem it due to the inadequate purchase price and the fact that the defendant did not receive actual notice of the judicial sale.

C. Once courts of law and equity were separate. Today, they are joined. Still, however, there is the difference between legal and equitable remedies.

XIII. Contemporary Problems

A. The high cost of litigation (bringing lawsuits) has priced most minor disputes out of the court system.

B. Even for major cases court congestion and resulting delays in the court system are so great that it takes five or more years to get a case to trial.

C. Substantial delay also takes place in the trial and appeal of criminal cases.

D. Court congestion and delay have adverse consequences both for individuals who seek justice and for society.

XIV. **Delay: Some Solutions**

A. In many large cities the backlog of civil cases is so great that it takes five or more years to get a case to trial. Substantial delay also takes place in the trial and appeal of criminal cases. Court congestion and delay have adverse consequences both for individuals who seek justice and for society.

B. Changes to reduce court congestion and delay include:

1. Having six-person juries instead of twelve.
2. Requiring only majority verdicts instead of unanimous verdicts in trials.
3. Eliminating oral arguments on appeal whenever possible.
4. Implementing professional management techniques in the judicial system.
5. Eliminating jury trials in certain types of cases.

C. Recommendations for reducing delay and congestion in the federal court system include:

1. Raising the jurisdictional amount to $50,000.
2. Abolishing diversity of citizenship jurisdiction.

COMPLETION EXERCISES

1. If the remedy of damages is unfair to the plaintiff, an equity court may grant _______________ of the contract.

2. Courts of equity use _______________ instead of rules of law.

3. A party may appeal the decision of a state supreme court to the U.S. Supreme Court when the decision determines that a U.S. statute is _______________.

4. Federal courts have _______________ jurisdiction.

5. _______________ provides the general framework for the court system.

6. The procedure for requesting a review by the Supreme Court is called the _______________.

7. A continuing problem of the small claims court is that many successful litigants are unable to _______________.

8. _______________ of the Constitution provides that judicial power be vested in the Supreme Court and such lower courts as Congress may create.

9. In diversity of citizenship cases federal courts apply _______________ substantive law.

10. The jurisdictional amount in diversity of citizenship cases is _______________.

11. For diversity of citizenship purposes a corporation is a citizen of _______________ and of _______________.

12. In diversity of citizenship cases a federal court may invoke the doctrine of _______________ and force the litigants to try their case in the state court.

13. Courts having general jurisdiction have traditionally been divided into courts of _______________ and courts of _______________.

14. The "clean hands" principle is a maxim of _______________.

15. A poor person can obtain the best legal talent in a personal injury case because of the _______________ system.

TRUE-FALSE CHOICES

1. ______ One recommendation for streamlining the federal court system is to abolish diversity of citizenship jurisdiction.

2. ______ Today, issues of law and equity are determined in separate courts.

3. ______ The high costs of litigation have priced the settling of many disputes out of the court system.

4. ______ One recommendation for reducing federal court congestion is to eliminate diversity of citizenship jurisdiction.

5. ______ When there is no clear state law in diversity of citizenship cases, the federal courts must apply their own substantive law.

6. ______ Law and justice are synonymous.

7. ______ The general jurisdiction trial court is frequently known as the "circuit court."

8. ______ The small-claims court handles the majority of litigation between business and its customers.

9. ______ For there to be diversity of citizenship jurisdiction, every plaintiff must be from a different state than every defendant.

10. ______ Federal courts in diversity of citizenship cases do not apply a state's conflict of laws doctrine.

11. ______ A court of equity is the same thing as a court of chancery.

12. ______ Equity jurisdiction is used in cases where the remedy at law is inadequate.

13. ______ The backlog of civil cases is so great that it may take five or more years in many cities for a civil case to get to trial.

14. ______ He who seeks equity must do equity.

15. ______ Federal courts have general jurisdiction.

MULTIPLE CHOICE SELECTIONS

1. Select the most correct statement about the contingent fee system:

   a. Under the system the attorney is paid a fixed percentage of the total damages recovered in a case if he or she wins the lawsuit.
   b. The system operates to make available excellent attorneys to even very poor clients.
   c. Critics of the system point to the fact that attorneys often earn a lot for doing relatively little.
   d. All of the above are correct.

Chapter 3

2. Select the most correct statement:

   a. A losing party generally has the right to appeal to a state court of last resort.
   b. The judicial power is probably the most extensive power possessed by any branch of government.
   c. Appellate court judges usually render oral opinions regarding legal issues on appeal.
   d. Trial court judges are personally liable to injured parties when they render incorrect legal judgments.

3. All of the following help reduce court congestion and delay except:

   a. Arbitration.
   b. Reducing the number of jurors from twelve to six.
   c. The contingent fee system.
   d. Requiring less-than-unanimous jury verdicts.

4. John, a citizen of Georgia, is injured when he is struck negligently by a car driven by Mary, a citizen of Tennessee. Select the incorrect statement:

   a. If John files a lawsuit in state court, Mary cannot have the case removed to federal court.
   b. For a federal court to have jurisdiction, John must claim at least $50,000 in damages.
   c. If the accident happened in Georgia, and the case is tried in federal court in Tennessee, the federal court will likely end up applying the tort law of Georgia.
   d. A federal court in this case will apply its own procedural law.

5. A party may appeal or petition the decision of a state supreme court to the U.S. Supreme Court under all of the following circumstances except:

   a. When interpretation of federal law is involved.
   b. When interpretation of state law is involved and another state supreme court has interpreted a similar statute differently.
   c. When the case involves a state statute against the charge that it violates the Constitution, and the decision is in favor of its validity.
   d. When a federal law is declared unconstitutional.

DISCUSSION ANALYSIS

Discuss why court congestion and delay have adverse consequences for individuals and for society. List possible changes that will help reduce congestion and delay.

Chapter 4

Litigation

STUDY GUIDE AND OUTLINE

I. Introduction

Most disputes in our society are resolved by mutual agreement without resorting to litigation. Moreover, 90 percent of all lawsuits filed are settled without a court decision. The high cost of litigation, both financially and in lost time, is the major force in many settlements.

II. Pretrial: Parties to Litigation

A. In criminal cases a prosecutor (representing the people of the state) brings action against a named defendant. In civil cases the plaintiff describes the party who sues. There are some instances, especially in courts of equity, in which the parties are called petitioner and respondent. When a counterclaim is filed, the parties are described as counter-plaintiff and counter-defendant. When a trial court decision is appealed, the party appealing is referred to as appellant, and the other party is called appellee.

B. In most jurisdictions, the law allows all persons to join in one lawsuit as plaintiffs if the causes of action arise out of the same transaction and involve common questions of law or fact. Additionally, plaintiffs may join as defendants all persons who are necessary to a complete settlement of the questions involved.

III. Standing to Sue

A. The standing question is whether a litigant is entitled to have the court decide the dispute. This issue has two parts:

1. Does the court have jurisdiction?
2. If the jurisdiction is valid, should the court assume it in the exercise of its discretion?

B. The Constitution requires that a plaintiff must allege a case or controversy between himself and the defendant if the court is to have jurisdiction. Standing requires the plaintiff to allege such a personal stake in the outcome of the controversy to warrant invocation of the court's jurisdiction. Moreover, the court's jurisdiction can be invoked only when the plaintiff has suffered some threatened or actual injury resulting from the defendant's action.

C. In Havens Realty Corp. v. Coleman, the Supreme Court held that the plaintiff met Article III's injury-in-fact requirement. Plaintiff, a black tester, sued an apartment complex operator alleging racial discrimination in violation of the Fair Housing Act of 1968. Testers are individuals who pose as renters for the purpose of collecting evidence of unlawful racial steering practices. The court states that to have standing the plaintiff must allege an actual injury caused by the defendant's actions. In this case, the black tester met the injury-in-fact requirements by alleging injury to her statutory right to truthful housing information.

IV. Class Action Suits

A. A class action suit is one in which a person files suit on his or her own behalf and on behalf of all other persons who may have a similar claim, e.g., all consumers injured by a product manufactured by the defendant. Class action suits are popular because the combined interest of all the members makes litigation financially feasible, and large awards make it profitable for plaintiffs' lawyers.

B. At the federal level the Supreme Court has required that each member of a class action suit must meet the $10,000 jurisdictional amount, each member must receive actual notice of the pending suit, and plaintiffs bringing the class suit must pay all court costs. These requirements have greatly reduced the number of class actions in federal courts.

C. Notice to potential plaintiffs in state class action suits follows either an "opt out" or "opt in" procedure. Under the "opt in" procedure a potential plaintiff must return a form indicating a desire to be included in the class. The "opt out" procedure requires a potential plaintiff to return a form if he or she does not wish to be included automatically in the class. In Phillips Petroleum v. Shutts the U.S. Supreme Court held that the "opt out" procedure for class action suits was constitutional under the due process clause.

V. Jurisdiction of Courts

A. Jurisdiction refers to the power of a court to hear a case. To hear a case the court must have jurisdiction over the subject matter and the parties of the case. Subject matter jurisdiction exists if the case is of the type which the court is authorized to hear. For example, a probate court, which decides matters concerning estates, would lack power to hear a murder case.

B. Jurisdiction over the plaintiff comes from the plaintiff's filing suit. He or she voluntarily submits to the court's power. Jurisdiction over the defendant is usually obtained by the personal service of summons (or process). Sometimes it is obtained by the publication of notice and mailing of summons to the last known address.

C. Most states have long-arm statutes, which provide for the service of process beyond their boundaries. Such statutes are constitutional if they provide a defendant with due process of law. Due process requires that a non-resident defendant must have certain minimum contacts with the forum state (where the lawsuit was brought) so that the lawsuit does not offend "traditional notions of fair play and substantial justice."

D. In World-Wide Volkswagen Corp. v. Woodson, the Supreme Court reaffirmed the rule that a state court can exercise personal jurisdiction over a non-resident defendant only so long as there exist "minimum contacts" between the defendant and the forum state. In an Oklahoma state court, plaintiff sued a New York automobile dealer in a product liability action. The court found that the defendant's due process had been violated since there were no minimum contacts between the state of Oklahoma and the defendant. The defendant sold no cars nor engaged in any business whatsoever in Oklahoma. Therefore, personal jurisdiction cannot be based on one isolated event where a car sold in New York to a New York resident happened to be involved in an accident while passing through Oklahoma.

E. Some actions are in rem instead of in personam. This means that they relate to property rather than to persons. Suits involving title to real estate and property in divorces are examples. The defendants to an in rem suit can be notified by mail or newspaper publication. Due process does not require the same notice as does in personam jurisdiction.

F. The above discussion relates to civil suits. In criminal suits, the crime must have been committed within the state for the court to have jurisdiction. If the defendant is arrested in some other state, extradition is necessary. This is obtained by the governor of the state of arrest voluntarily turning the prisoner over to the governor of the requesting state.

VI. Venue

A. Venue refers to the place or court in which the lawsuit should be brought. While jurisdiction determines if a court has the power to hear a case, venue determines whether a court should hear the case when any one of several courts technically might have jurisdiction. Most venue statutes provide that suit must be brought in the county of residence of the defendant or in the county where the transaction occurred out of which the cause of action arose. Chartered corporations are residents of any county in which they have a registered office or are doing business. Partnerships are residents of any county in which a partner lives, in which there is an office, or in which the partnership does business. Also, most suits involving real estate must be brought in the county where the real estate is located.

B. Venue may be objected to by the defendant because of potential prejudice of either judge or probable jury. Another ground for change of venue is the doctrine of forum non conveniens, which means the place of trial is not convenient.

VII. Pleadings

A. Lawsuits begin by a plaintiff filing a complaint with the court clerk. The complaint contains allegations by the plaintiff and a statement of the relief sought.

B. The clerk issues a summons which is served on the defendant. The defendant must file an answer to deny or admit each allegation of the plaintiff's complaint. The answer may also contain counterclaims that the defendant has against the plaintiff.

VIII. Motions Before Trial

A. The defendant will make a motion to dismiss if the plaintiff's complaint does not state a proper legal basis for a lawsuit or fails to show proper jurisdiction or standing to sue.

B. In many cases the parties may be in complete agreement as to the facts, in which case the issues to be decided involve only questions of law. Then one of the parties may file a motion for summary judgment. In considering this motion, the court examines all papers on file, and if there are no factual questions, the court will decide the legal questions in favor of one or the other party.

IX. Discovery Procedures

Before trial the parties engage in the discovery process. Discovery ensures that each side is fully aware of all the facts prior to trial. Its purpose is to base the results of lawsuits on the merits of the controversy and not on the skill or cunning of counsel. Discovery procedures available to the parties include subpoena of documents, materials, and witnesses, deposition of witnesses (asking questions under oath), written interrogatories (written questions which must be answered), and compulsory physical exam.

X. Jury Selection

In addition to questions of law, most lawsuits involve questions of fact. Questions of fact are decided by the jury. In a typical lawsuit, the first order of business is to select a jury. The court clerk draws names randomly from lists of eligible citizens. Attorneys for each party then examine each juror as to his/her qualifications to hear the case. This is the process of voir dire examination. Potential jurors may be dismissed for cause or on the basis of a limited number of peremptory challenges.

XI. Opening Statements

After jury selection, the attorneys then make their opening statements. An opening statement is not evidence but only used to familiarize the jury with the essential facts in the case. After these statements are made, the plaintiff presents evidence.

XII. Introducing Evidence

A. Evidence is normally presented by examination of witnesses and production of documents. After the party calling the witness has completed direct examination, the other party may cross-examine the witness. After cross-examination, the party calling the witness once again may question the witness in a redirect examination. Finally, the opposing party is allowed a recross-examination of the witness. After the plaintiff finishes producing evidence in his/her case, it is the defendant's turn.

B. The court in Crawford Fitting Co. v. J.T. Gibbons, Inc. held that absent explicit statutory or contractual authorization for the "taxation" of the expenses of a litigant's witness as costs, federal courts are bound by the limitations set out in 28 U.S.C. §1821 and §1920. Although §1920 authorizes the court to "tax" witness fees as costs against the losing party, §1821 limits the witness fee to $30 per day, even for expert witnesses who are in fact paid much more.

C. After the party with the burden of proof has presented his or her evidence, the other party often makes a motion for a directed verdict. The judge will grant the motion if as a matter of law the party with the burden of proof has not met that burden.

D. The court in Safeway Stores, Inc. v. Willmon held that possible causes of a fall, as opposed to probable causes, do not constitute substantial evidence of negligence. The court granted a directed verdict in favor of the defendant.

XIII. Jury Instructions

When all the evidence is presented, the attorneys and the judge confer on the instructions to be given to the jury. The purpose of the jury is to determine the facts, and the court's function is to determine the law. The purpose of jury instructions is to bring these two together.

XIV. Deciding the Case

A. After the conference on jury instructions, the attorneys make closing arguments to the jury. The court then reads the jury instructions, and the jury retires to deliberate. The jury reaches a verdict and judgment is entered. Thereafter, the losing party has an absolute right to appeal within specified time limits.

B. The losing party often makes a motion for judgment notwithstanding the verdict. This motion is granted when the judge believes that as a matter of law the jury verdict is erroneous.

XV. Burden of Proof

A. The term burden of proof has two distinct meanings. It may describe the person with the burden of coming forward with evidence on a particular factual issue. The more common usage of the term is to identify the party with the burden of persuasion. The party with this burden must convince the jury on the factual issues involved or lose the lawsuit. The plaintiff or prosecutor usually bears this burden of proof.

B. The degree of proof required depends on the issue and the type of case. There are three levels of proof used in the law. For criminal cases, the burden of proof must be beyond a reasonable doubt. This means that before a defendant can be found guilty, the jury has no reasonable doubt about his or her guilt. In civil cases, the most frequent standard is the preponderance of the evidence standard. In terms of the scales of justice, it means that they must tilt more in favor of guilt than innocence in order for the plaintiff to win. Another standard used in civil cases is the clear and convincing proof standard. This requirement is used in certain situations where the law requires more than simple preponderance of the evidence, but less than proof beyond a reasonable doubt. The scales of justice must tilt heavily towards guilt for the plaintiff to prevail.

XVI. Rules of Evidence

A. In the conduct of a trial, the rules of evidence govern the admissibility of testimony and establish which facts may or may not be presented to the jury. One of the major rules of excluding evidence is called privileged communications. In addition to the Fifth Amendment privilege against self-incrimination, communications between an attorney and client are privileged.

B. The right to confront and cross-examine witnesses is also a fundamental right. This right provides the basis for the hearsay rule. Hearsay is an out-of-court statement which is being offered to prove the truth of the matter contained in the statement. The lack of cross-examination establishes that hearsay evidence should not be admitted. However, there are many exceptions to the rule. For example, the dying declaration of the victim of murder is an exception to the hearsay rule. There are many other exceptions, but each is based on the fact that cross-examination has either been had at a former time or is not required for a fair trial in the present case.

C. The parole evidence rule prevents proof of modification or change of a written document by use of oral evidence. The rule of relevancy requires that all evidence be relevant to the matter involved in the litigation.

D. In order to reduce the cost of litigation and speed up the search for truth, the federal courts have greatly expanded the admissibility of evidence.

XVII. Appellate Procedure

A. Courts of appellate review deal with the record of the proceedings in lower courts. The court of review studies the issues and testimony to determine whether errors of law were made by the lower court. Each party files a brief which contains the authorities on which the party relies and arguments for reversing or affirming the decision of the lower court. In addition to the brief, each party may explain orally to the court his/her position in the case. This also gives the justices an opportunity to question personally the attorneys about various issues of the case. After oral argument, an impression vote is taken and one justice is assigned to write the appellate court's opinion.

B. Courts of review are primarily concerned with questions of law. Findings of fact are not disturbed unless they are clearly erroneous.

C. One reason appellate courts give deference to the finding of facts at the trial is because the finding may depend heavily on a witness' demeanor and tone of voice. The "way" a witness gives evidence thus affects believability.

D. In Anderson v. City of Bessemer the U.S. Supreme Court states that an appellate court could not reverse a trial court's finding of sex discrimination merely because it disagreed with the trial court's finding.

XVIII. Enforcement of Judgments and Decrees

After a judgment becomes final, the losing party may still refuse to pay the amount of the judgment to the prevailing party. For example, the judgment debtor may not voluntarily pay damages due to the prevailing creditor. In such a case the judgment creditor may levy execution (legally seize) on the property of the debtor and have the proceeds of a public sale applied to the judgment. The creditor may also garnish the wages of the judgment debtor to satisfy the court's judgment. However, as in bankruptcy, all states allow a debtor to exempt certain assets from levy or garnishment.

XIX. Res Judicata

A. Once a decision of the court has become final it is said to be res judicata, literally meaning "the thing has been decided." Res judicata means that a cause of action finally determined by a competent court cannot ever again be litigated by the same parties. This prevents successive suits involving the same question between the same parties and brings disputes to a final conclusion.

B. The court in Cummings v. Dresher held that where a full opportunity has been afforded to a party to the prior action and he has failed to prove his freedom from liability or to establish liability on the part of another, there is no reason for retrying these issues.

COMPLETION EXERCISES

1. When a trial court decision is appealed, the party appealing is called a (an) ______________.
2. To meet the ______________ requirement, the plaintiff must have suffered some injury in fact.
3. Jurisdiction over ______________ is usually obtained by summons or by publication of notice.
4. Long-arm statutes are constitutional if they provide the defendant with ______________.
5. ______________ is the voluntary transfer of a prisoner from one state to another.
6. The doctrine of ______________ means that the place of trial is not convenient.
7. A ______________ is granted when no factual questions exist in a lawsuit, and the court alone decides the legal issues.
8. The purpose of ______________ is to take the surprise out of litigation.
9. ______________ is the process in which the attorneys examine the qualifications of prospective jurors.
10. The most frequent standard of proof used in civil cases is the ______________.
11. The lack of cross-examination provides the basis for the rule that ______________ evidence is inadmissible.
12. Courts of review are concerned primarily with questions of ______________.
13. The purpose of ______________ is to bring disputes to a final conclusion.
14. Communications between an attorney and client are ______________.
15. In a trial the purpose of the jury is to determine the ______________.

TRUE-FALSE CHOICES

1. _____ A plaintiff consents to the court's jurisdiction by the act of filing the lawsuit.
2. _____ At the federal level the number of class action suits has increased dramatically in recent years.
3. _____ A deposition is part of the discovery process.
4. _____ The judge instructs the jury on the legal principles governing a lawsuit.
5. _____ A losing party has an absolute right to appeal if it is filed in a timely manner.

6. ______ The burden of proof for criminal cases is higher than the standard used for civil cases.

7. ______ The parole evidence rule governs the type of evidence allowed in criminal trials.

8. ______ The federal rules of evidence are liberally construed to allow expanded admissibility of evidence.

9. ______ Appellate court decisions must be reached unanimously.

10. ______ Reviewing courts are concerned primarily with questions of fact.

11. ______ A judgment creditor can levy execution on the assets of a judgment debtor to satisfy an outstanding court judgment.

12. ______ The doctrine of res judicata prevents one party from suing another party when the two parties are in a privileged relationship.

13. ______ Res judicata means "the thing has been decided."

14. ______ The motion for a directed verdict is a pretrial motion.

15. ______ A motion for a summary judgment is granted when the parties have no legal issues in dispute.

MULTIPLE CHOICE SELECTIONS

1. X Corporation ships its widgets to independent distributors in all 50 states. Y, a Georgia resident, is injured when one of the widgets malfunctions. Y decides to sue the corporation. Select the most correct statement:

   a. Y cannot sue X Corporation in Georgia because the Georgia courts lack personal jurisdiction over X.
   b. Y cannot sue X Corporation in Georgia because Y lacks standing to sue.
   c. Y can sue X Corporation through Georgia's long-arm statute because X meets the minimum contacts test to establish jurisdiction.
   d. Y can sue X Corporation in Georgia, but only if X maintains its corporate headquarters in Georgia.

2. In a state court class action suit, plaintiff residents sue a nearby chemical plant for improper disposal of highly toxic wastes. Select the most correct answer:

   a. To meet the jurisdictional amount, each individual plaintiff must satisfy the $10,000 jurisdictional minimum.
   b. The residents have standing to sue since the defendant's action threatens immediate injury.
   c. The court lacks subject matter jurisdiction.
   d. The chemical plant has the initial burden of proof.

3. All of the following may occur in the typical civil lawsuit except:

   a. Examination by both attorneys of the same witness.
   b. A motion for a directed verdict.
   c. A successful challenge to a potential juror.
   d. Extradition of the defendant to the state where the lawsuit is being brought.

4. Sam and Kelly agree to submit all disputes that might arise out of a construction contract to arbitration proceedings. There is a disagreement about an installment payment and the two men submit their dispute to an arbitration panel. The arbitrators find for Sam, but Kelly disagrees with the decision. Select the correct statement:

   a. The only way Kelly can get court review of the decision is if there is proof of misconduct on the part of the arbitrators.
   b. Kelly cannot get court review of the decision because it is res judicata.
   c. Kelly can get court review of the decision if he can prove that the arbitrators were mistaken as to their analysis of the evidence.
   d. Kelly need not recognize the decision since arbitration is not legally binding.

5. Select the incorrect statement regarding the appeals process:

   a. Briefs submitted by each attorney to the appellate court describe the factual background of the lawsuit and give authorities to support respective arguments.
   b. As a general rule, courts of review do not disturb a trial court's findings of fact.
   c. A losing party has an absolute right to at least one appeal if it is filed within a statutory time period.
   d. Appellate courts frequently review new evidence that the plaintiff or defendant has uncovered.

Chapter 4

DISCUSSION ANALYSIS

The Zenith Transport Co. is incorporated in Delaware. Its headquarters are in Akron, Ohio. One of its trucks runs a stop sign in Los Angeles and injures the plaintiff, who wishes to sue Zenith Transport. What courts have personal jurisdiction over Zenith Transport? Explain.

Chapter 5

Arbitration

STUDY GUIDE AND OUTLINE

I. Introduction

A. There are several ways to resolve conflicts and disputes between parties, including formal litigation, submission to an administrative agency, arbitration, and mediation.

B. Arbitration is a nonjudicial means for submitting a controversy to a third person or persons for a binding decision, and may result from agreement of the parties or from legislation. It is especially important in international transactions and labor management relations.

C. Mediation describes a process in which a third party is brought into a controversy to help settle a dispute. A mediator cannot impose a solution upon the parties, but a mediator's viewpoint and suggestions are given significant weight.

II. Reasons for Arbitration

A. The fundamental premise upon which arbitration is founded is the goal of providing a relatively quick and inexpensive resolution of contractual disputes by avoiding extended court proceedings.

B. Arbitration is a private proceeding and there is no public record available to the press and others. This serves to preserve business relations and avoids litigation.

C. Arbitration is of special importance in labor relations where it is used to settle grievances that individual employees or the union have with the employer. Arbitration is required as part of the collective bargaining contract that the employer and the union agree to.

III. Arbitration Proceedings

A. Submission is the act of referring a matter to the arbitration process, and usually results from the agreement of the parties.

B. After a hearing is conducted, a decision known as an award is handed down. In most states, the arbitrator's award must be in writing. An opinion letter becomes a part of the award.

C. Parties who consent to arbitration have full control over the issues to be arbitrated and therefore are generally bound by the resulting award.

D. If no objections to the award are filed within a statutory period, the award becomes final. A court will enforce a final award just as it would a judgment of the court.

IV. The Submission

A. The issues submitted to arbitration may be questions of fact, questions of law, or mixed questions of fact and law.

B. Whether a particular dispute is arbitrable is a question for the court, unless by appropriate language the parties have agreed to arbitrate that question.

C. In AT&T Tech., Inc. v. Communications Workers, the Supreme Court held that a court must decide the issue of arbitrability. It is the court's duty to interpret an arbitration agreement and to determine whether the parties intended to arbitrate the issue of layoff grievances. Thus an employer's refusal to arbitrate layoffs and whether the issue of layoffs was properly arbitrable was an issue for the court to decide.

V. The Arbitrators

A. One reason to prefer arbitration over litigation is that the dispute can be submitted to an expert for decision in arbitration. This is especially important in labor-management relations.

B. Parties often choose labor arbitrators based on their knowledge of the "common law of the shop."

C. It is common to use either one arbitrator or a panel of three arbitrators. In Anderson v. Nichols, the court held that absent overt corruption or misconduct in the arbitration itself, no arbitrator appointed by a party may be challenged on the ground of his relationship to the party or that the arbitrator is biased toward the party. The court upheld a $105,000 award to a lessor of land for coal mining. The court did observe that an arbitrator's accepting a bribe or other corruption would be grounds for challenging the award.

VI. Court-Annexed Mandatory Arbitration

A. About one-third of the states have adopted mandatory arbitration as a means of reducing court congestion. These statutes cover only a few types of cases, e.g., cases involving money claims of less than $15,000.

B. The arbitrators in these situations have the power to determine the admissibility of evidence and to decide the law and facts of the case.

C. Any party who was present at the arbitration hearing, either in person or by counsel, may file a written notice of rejection of the award and request to proceed to trial; this single rejection is sufficient to enable the parties to proceed to trial on all issues of the case.

D. Many jurisdictions that require arbitration but permit rejection of the arbitration decision authorize fees and costs against parties who fail to improve their positions at trial after rejecting the arbitration decision.

The Federal Arbitration Act

VII. Impact on Federal Statutes

A. The Federal Arbitration Act covers any arbitration clause in a contract that involves interstate commerce. A court assumes arbitration was intended unless it can say with positive assurance that the arbitration clause was not intended to include the particular dispute.

B. The Supreme Court held in Shearson/American Express, Inc. v. McMahon that there was no basis for concluding that Congress intended to prevent enforcement of agreements to arbitrate RICO claims. Thus, the plaintiff customers could effectively vindicate their RICO claim in an arbitral forum against a stock brokerage agency.

VIII. Impact on State Laws

A. The federal policy favoring arbitration frequently conflicts with state laws favoring litigation as the means to resolve a dispute. The Commerce Clause and the Supremacy Clause of the United States Constitution are often used to set aside such state laws that deny arbitration.

B. In Southland Corp. v. Keating, the court held that California's Franchise Investment Law that undercut the enforceability of arbitration agreements in interstate commerce violated the Supremacy Clause of the Constitution and was therefore invalid.

C. The Supreme Court in Perry v. Thomas also invalidated a California law which provided that wage collection actions may be maintained without regard to the existence of any private agreement to arbitrate. The court stated that under the Supremacy Clause, the state statute must give way. The plaintiff had sued his employer alleging that his employer had failed to pay commissions on securities sales and the employer had petitioned the court to require arbitration as agreed to in the employment contract.

Judicial Review of Awards

IX. General Principles

A. Since the object of arbitration is to avoid the formalities, delay, and expenses of litigation in court, judicial review of an arbitrator's award is quite restricted and is more limited than appellate review of a trial court's decision.

B. The fact that the arbitrator made erroneous rulings during the hearing, or reached erroneous findings of fact from the evidence, is no ground for a court's setting aside the award, because the parties have agreed that he should be the judge of the facts. Error of law renders the award void only when it would require the parties to commit a crime.

C. Courts are sometimes called upon to set aside an award because it allegedly violates public policy. The Supreme Court in United Paperworkers Intern. Union v. Misco, Inc. held that an alleged public policy must be properly framed and the violation of such a policy must be clearly shown if an award is not to be enforced. A formulation of public policy based only on "general considerations of supposed public interests" is not the sort that permits a court to set aside an arbitration award. Thus the federal courts could not set aside an arbitrator's decision to reinstate an employee found smoking marijuana in the employer's parking lot on the basis that it was against some general public policy not to operate heavy machinery on drugs.

D. In order for an arbitrator to correct an "evident miscalculation of figures," there must be a miscalculation and it must be "evident."

X. Review Under Federal Law

A. For arbitrations covered by the Federal Arbitration Act, judicial review of an award is limited to the issues set forth in the applicable statute and to the scope of the submission.

B. Section 10 of the Federal Arbitration Act provides that an arbitration award may be vacated on four grounds; however, the decision of the arbitration board on all questions of law and fact is generally conclusive.

C. Where the award was procured by "undue means," there is a general requirement to show some type of bad faith in the procurement of the award.

D. An arbitrator exceeds his or her powers and authority when attempting to resolve an issue that is outside the scope of the arbitration agreement.

XI. Judicial Review - Statutory Arbitration

A. A higher than usual level of judicial review of an arbitration award is warranted when the arbitration is statutorily mandated rather than required by private agreement.

B. Compulsory arbitration may be constitutional if fair procedures are provided by the legislature and ultimate judicial review is available, especially when de novo judicial review is available to either party.

XII. Policy Trends and Ethical Considerations

A. A growing area for increased arbitration and mediation is consumer complaints, because most such complaints do not involve enough money to warrant litigation.

B. Many corporations have developed arbitration or mediation procedures to handle customer complaints in an effort to build consumer confidence and good will.

C. AUTOCAPS (Automobile Consumer Action Programs) are panels established by U.S. manufacturers of cars that handle consumer complaints involving sales and service. The panel's decision may be rejected by the consumer.

D. Connecticut and California have recently passed automobile "lemon laws" requiring a consumer to use any mediation or nonbinding arbitration procedures established by auto makers before going to court.

COMPLETION EXERCISES

1. The _______________ Act covers any arbitration clause in a contract that covers interstate commerce.

2. The federal policy favoring arbitration frequently conflicts with state laws favoring _______________.

3. Judicial review of an arbitrator's award is quite _______________.

4. Error of law renders an arbitrator's award void only when it would require the parties to commit a _______________.

5. Courts are sometimes called upon to set aside an award because it violates _______________.

6. An arbitrator exceeds his or her powers when attempting to resolve an issue that is _______________ of the arbitration agreement.

7. A higher than usual level of judicial review is warranted of an arbitration award when the arbitration is _______________.

8. Legislatively established compulsory arbitration is constitutional especially when _______________ judicial review is available to either party.

9. A growing area of arbitration is _______________ because they often do not involve enough money to warrant litigation.

10. Many companies have developed arbitration or mediation procedures to handle customer complaints in order to build consumer _______________ and _______________.

TRUE-FALSE CHOICES

1. ______ Under the Federal Arbitration Act a court usually assumes that an arbitration clause in a contract applies to a particular dispute.

2. ______ The Free Exercise Clause of the Constitution is often used to void state laws that deny arbitration.

3. ______ The object of arbitration is to avoid the formalities, delay, and expenses of litigation.

4. ______ An appellate court's review of a trial court's decision is more limited than its review of an arbitration award.

5. ______ An arbitrator's erroneous findings of fact are ground for a court's setting aside an arbitration award.

6. ______ In an arbitration agreement the parties agree that the arbitrator should be the judge of the facts.

7. ______ A formulation of public policy based only on general considerations of supposed public interests is not the sort that permits a court to set aside an arbitration award.

8. ______ Even an error of law made by an arbitrator does not usually render an award void.

9. ______ An arbitrator may correct an "evident miscalculation of figures."

10. ______ Under AUTOCAPS an arbitration panel's decision may be rejected by the consumer.

11. ______ In Connecticut and California a consumer must use any nonbinding arbitration procedures established by automakers before going to court.

12. ______ The Supreme Court has ruled that wage collection actions may be maintained without regard to the existence of any private agreement to arbitrate.

13. ______ The Supreme Court has ruled that RICO claims may not be settled in an arbitral forum.

14. ______ Arbitration may result from legislation or from contractual agreement of the parties.

15. ______ Mediation is binding on the parties to a dispute.

MULTIPLE CHOICE SELECTIONS

1. Select the most <u>correct</u> statement:

   a. Arbitration is a public proceeding.
   b. Submission usually results from private agreement.
   c. In most states the arbitrator's decision need not be in writing.
   d. Arbitration awards are generally unenforceable in court.

2. Select the most <u>correct</u> statement:

   a. Issues submitted to arbitration may involve facts but not law.
   b. Parties to arbitration may not select arbitrators who are generally biased in their favor.
   c. Whether a particular issue is arbitrable is a question for a court to decide.
   d. The "common law of the shop" was brought from England by the early colonists.

3. Select the most correct statement concerning when the federal policy favoring arbitration conflicts with state laws favoring litigation.

   a. State laws usually prevail.
   b. Federal policy prevails only in federal courts.
   c. State laws prevail in state courts.
   d. The Commerce Clause and Supremacy Clause are used to void the state laws.

4. A merchant and a supplier dispute the quality and quantity of a widget shipment. They submit this contractual dispute to an arbitrator. The arbitrator rules that since the merchant's business has not shown a profit for the last three years that the supplier must meet the merchant's demands. Select the most correct statement:

   a. If the award is appealed, it will likely be upheld by a court.
   b. If the award is appealed, it will be overturned only if it is not supported by substantial evidence.
   c. If the award is appealed, the court's review is limited to issues of fact.
   d. If the award is appealed, it will likely be overturned by a court.

5. Select the incorrect statement:

   a. Arbitration is especially important in international transactions and labor relations.
   b. Mediation is a nonbinding process.
   c. Arbitration is a matter of public record.
   d. Parties who consent to arbitration have full control over the issues to be arbitrated.

DISCUSSION ANALYSIS

Discuss why parties to a dispute may decide to arbitrate rather than to litigate. Explain an arbitration proceeding as part of your answer.

Chapter 6

The Constitution and Business

STUDY GUIDE AND OUTLINE

I. Organization

A. Under a constitutional system, the constitution of the governmental unit is its basic supreme law. All other laws, written or unwritten, must be consistent with it, or they are void.

B. The Preamble sets forth the general goals and purposes of the U.S. Constitution. Article I establishes the legislative branch and defines its functions, powers, and limitations. In a similar manner, Article II vests the executive power in the President. It also makes him/her the Commander-in-Chief. Article III creates the judicial branch of government. Article IV deals with relationships between the several states. Article V sets forth methods of amending the Constitution. There are <u>twenty-six amendments</u> to date. Finally, Article VI contains the <u>supremacy clause</u> which means federal laws and treaties are the supreme law of the land.

II. Separation of Powers

A. The doctrine of <u>separation of powers</u> arose out of the strong fear of our founding fathers that too much power might be concentrated in one branch of government.

B. The separation of powers doctrine has two aspects:

1. It describes how the executive, legislative, and judicial branches of government have separate functions to perform. Each branch limits the power and is limited by the power of the other two branches.
2. The second aspect of separation of power is <u>federalism</u>. This aspect recognizes the integrity between the federal and state levels of government. Each has separate and distinct functions to perform. While the federal government has supreme authority, the Tenth Amendment explicitly reserves certain powers to the states.

III. The Supremacy Clause

A. The <u>supremacy clause</u> makes federal law supreme over state law if the two are in conflict. To decide the validity of a state law, courts must interpret the federal and state laws to see if they are in conflict. A conflict exists if the state statute prevents the execution of the full purposes and objectives of Congress.

B. A federal law may preempt an area of law. If a federal law preempts an area, then any state law in that area is unconstitutional under the supremacy clause.

C. In Fidelity Federal Savings and Loan Ass'n. v. Reginald De La Cuesta the Supreme Court held that the rules and regulations of a federal administrative agency have the same preemptive effect of federal statutes.

IV. External Affairs

The Constitution grants the President power to make treaties with the advice and consent of the Senate. The United States is unique in that its treaties are part of the "Supreme Law of the Land." They have the internal force of the Constitution and of laws enacted by Congress. Moreover, federal laws are binding only if made pursuant to the Constitution, but Article II provides no such restriction on the effect of treaties.

V. The Contract Clause

A. The Constitution says that no state shall pass any law impairing the obligation of contracts. This provision does not apply to the federal government, which does in fact frequently pass laws that affect existing contracts.

B. In Allied Structural Steel Co. v. Spannaus the Supreme Court held that a Minnesota law substantially altered the contractual obligations of the plaintiff and was, therefore, unconstitutional. Plaintiff, a corporation with an office in Minnesota, had a qualified pension plan for its employees. Minnesota enacted a law which placed a large penalty on any corporation that terminated its pension plan or closed a Minnesota office and terminated its employees. The state assessed a $185,000 penalty. The Court stated that the contract clause is not to be construed literally but that five factors are important when analyzing a state law that impairs private contract rights:

1. The law must be enacted in an emergency situation.
2. The law must be broad to protect basic societal interests.
3. The relief must be properly tailored to meet those interests.
4. The conditions of the law must be reasonable.
5. The law must be limited to the duration of the emergency.

The court ruled that the Minnesota legislation did not meet these requirements. It imposed a totally unexpected liability on the plaintiff in a non-emergency situation. Therefore, the law was void under the contract clause.

VI. The Taxing Power

A. The taxing power is the power by which government raises revenue. The theory is that governments have the right to tax persons and property within their jurisdictions to defray the costs of necessary governmental functions. This power can be exercised only for public purposes.

B. The taxation power is exclusively exercised by the legislative branch of government.

C. The legislature uses the taxing power to accomplish many goals other than raising revenue. Taxation is a very important form of regulation. It is a major ingredient in government efforts to regulate the economy. Tax laws are also used to implement important social policies.

D. In South Dakota v. Dole, the Supreme Court held that even if Congress lacks the power to impose a national minimum drinking age directly, encouragement to state action is a valid use of the spending power. The Court upheld a federal statute that directed the Secretary of Transportation to withhold highway funds from states that failed to raise the drinking age to 21.

VII. The Import-Export Clause

The import-export clause prohibits states from taxing imports. It also prohibits both the federal and state governments from directly taxing exports.

VIII. States' Relation Article

A. Article IV is referred to as the states' relation article. Section 4 of the article guarantees every state a republican form of government and requires the federal government to protect the states from invasion.

B. Section 2 of Article IV contains the privileges and immunities clause. This clause places the citizens of each state on the same footing as citizens of other states concerning the advantages of citizenship. It keeps them from being aliens in other states.

C. In Supreme Court of N.H. v. Piper the U.S. Supreme Court ruled that a New Hampshire requirement limiting bar admission to state residents violated the privileges and immunities clause. The Court did note that discrimination against nonresidents is permitted when there is a substantial reason for the discrimination and the discrimination bears a "substantial relationship" to the state's objective.

D. Note that the non-discrimination required of the privileges and immunities clause applies to eliminate only those discriminations "bearing upon the vitality of the nation as a single entity."

E. Article IV also contains the full faith and credit clause. This means that final decisions or judgments rendered in any given state shall be enforced in other states as between the original parties. This is true, however, only if the court in the first state has jurisdiction to decide the issue.

IX. The Commerce Clause: Introduction

A. The power of the federal government to regulate business activity is found in the commerce clause of the Constitution. The broad grant of power to regulate is the power to prescribe the rules by which commerce is to be conducted.

B. The commerce clause states: "Congress shall have power to regulate commerce with foreign nations, and among the several states, and with the Indian Tribes." This is the single most important provision that gives Congress the right to regulate business.

C. The commerce clause has been interpreted as imposing limitations on the power of state government to regulate business under the state police power.

X. Foreign Commerce

A. The commerce clause grants the federal government the power to regulate exclusively all aspects of foreign commerce and trade. Exclusivity means that state and local governments may not regulate such commerce. State or local laws which interfere with federal regulation of foreign commerce are invalid as violations of the commerce and supremacy clauses.

B. States may not prohibit sale of imported goods any more than they can prohibit their import. The exclusive federal power over imported goods continues until the goods are mingled with the general property of the country.

XI. Interstate Commerce

A. The second part of the commerce clause is the power to regulate commerce "among the several states." Congressional legislation affecting business is constitutional if it aids in the effective regulation of interstate commerce.

B. Congressional power to regulate business also extends to those intrastate activities that substantially affect interstate commerce.

C. Today, economic legislation by Congress is presumed constitutional. An act will be declared invalid only if the court determined that Congress acted without a rational basis in adopting a particular regulatory scheme, or that there is no reasonable connection between the regulatory means and the asserted ends.

D. The court in Perez v. United States held that the activity of "loan sharking" substantially affects interstate and foreign commerce so that Congress could control even the local aspects of loan sharking.

E. The political process ultimately ensures that Congress will not unduly burden the states and their commerce.

XII. The Commerce Clause and the State Police Power

A. The Supreme Court has established three distinct subject areas involving governmental regulation of commerce. One subject area is exclusively federal. In addition to foreign commerce, this area concerns those internal matters where uniformity on a nationwide basis is essential. Any state regulation of such areas is absolutely void.

B. The second area involves activities that are exclusively local. This area embraces intrastate activities that do not have a substantial effect on interstate commerce. Today, it is almost impossible to find a truly exclusively local subject matter that does not affect interstate commerce.

C. The third subject area concerns when joint federal-state regulation may be permissible. This subject matter can be divided into three subjects:

1. If Congress has preempted the area by express language or by comprehensive regulation, any state or local law pertaining to the same subject matter is unconstitutional under the supremacy clause. The net effect is to make such areas exclusively federal.
2. Possible joint regulation occurs when the federal regulation of a subject matter is not comprehensive enough to preempt the field. Here state regulation is permitted, but when state law is inconsistent or irreconcilably conflicts with the federal law, it is unconstitutional.
3. Possible joint regulation also exists when there is no federal law at all. When there is no federal regulation of a subject, state regulation of interstate commerce is permissible. Such state regulation must neither discriminate against interstate commerce in favor of intrastate commerce nor place an undue burden on interstate commerce.
4. Kassell v. Consolidated Freightways Corp. illustrates how the Supreme Court balances the goal of the state legislations against the burden imposed on interstate commerce. Consolidated Freightways challenged an Iowa statute that prohibited the use of 65-foot double trailers on Iowa highways. The state defended the law as a reasonable safety measure. The Court stated that trial courts are required to balance the state's safety interest against the federal interest in free interstate commerce. Despite the "special deference" usually accorded to state safety regulations, the record here failed to show that 65-foot doubles were less safe that 55-foot single trailers. Since the statute substantially burdened interstate commerce by prohibiting these trailers without legitimate state purpose, it was an undue burden on interstate commerce.

XIII. The Commerce Clause and Taxation

A. Taxes imposed by state and local governments are subject to the limitations imposed by the commerce clause. However, since taxation distributes the cost of government among those who receive its benefits, interstate commerce is not exempt from state and local taxes. The purpose of the commerce clause is to ensure that interstate commerce only pays its fair share.

B. Constitutional issues involving taxation of interstate commerce include:

1. Whether there is proper apportionment of taxes between different states taxing the same business activity.
2. Whether there is a minimum connection (nexus) between the tax and the activity taxed.
3. Whether a tax discriminates against interstate commerce or unduly burdens it.
4. Whether the tax is fairly related to services provided by the state.

C. In D.H. Holmes Co. Ltd. v. McNamara the U.S. Supreme Court held that there was a sufficient nexus between the owner of 13 department stores in Louisiana and the state to uphold Louisiana's imposition of a use tax on the owner as not violative of the Constitution.

COMPLETION EXERCISES

1. The doctrine of _______________ arose out of the fear of our founding fathers that too much power might be concentrated in one branch of government.
2. _______________ makes federal law superior over state law if the two are in conflict.
3. The theory supporting _______________ is that the government has a right to compel persons to defray the costs of necessary governmental functions.
4. The _______________ clause prohibits states from taxing imports.
5. The _______________ clause enhances the equality of treatment for all citizens by inhibiting state discrimination against nonresidents.
6. The _______________ clause means that final decisions rendered in any state shall be enforced as between the original parties in other states.
7. A federal economic statute will be held invalid only if the court determines that Congress acted without a _______________ basis in adopting a particular regulatory scheme.
8. The regulation of foreign commerce is within the _______________ jurisdiction of the federal government.
9. _______________ are a popular way in which states attempt to give their own citizens preferential treatment over nonresidents.
10. The _______________ is the basic and supreme law of the land in the United States.
11. The doctrine of _______________ recognizes the interplay between the federal level and state level of government.
12. The _______________ is given power to make treaties, with the advice and consent of the _______________.
13. The Constitution states that no state shall pass any law impairing the obligations of _______________.
14. The _______________ power is exercised exclusively by the legislative branch of the government.
15. No state can constitutionally place an undue burden on _______________.

TRUE-FALSE CHOICES

1. _____ Federalism describes how each branch of the federal government limits the power and is limited by the power of the other two branches.

2. ______ Although the federal government has specified authority in which it is supreme, the Tenth Amendment reserves all other powers to the states.

3. ______ The preemption doctrine applies only to statutes passed by Congress.

4. ______ States may discriminate constitutionally in favor of intrastate commerce.

5. ______ There are situations in which a state constitutionally may pass a law that impairs the obligations of existing contracts.

6. ______ The single most important provision that gives Congress the right to regulate business is the power to tax.

7. ______ The federal government has the exclusive power to regulate foreign trade and commerce.

8. ______ Under the commerce clause, Congress cannot regulate purely local activities that do not have a substantial effect on interstate commerce.

9. ______ A state law is not in violation of the commerce clause if it furthers a legitimate public interest and does not place any burden on interstate commerce.

10. ______ States and municipalities cannot tax businesses that engage in interstate commerce because the federal government has exclusive jurisdiction in that area.

11. ______ Treaties have the internal force of the Constitution and are part of the supreme law of the land.

12. ______ If a federal law preempts a subject area, any state law in that area is unconstitutional under the supremacy clause.

13. ______ Economic legislation passed by Congress is presumed constitutional.

14. ______ As long as the federal government has not acted, the states may legislate in an area where nationwide uniformity is necessary.

15. ______ The import-export clause prohibits Congress from taxing imports.

MULTIPLE CHOICE SELECTIONS

1. Which of the following is <u>not</u> a part of the four-prong test used by the Supreme Court to analyze a state tax and its effect on interstate commerce?

   a. The activity must have a nexus with the taxing state.
   b. The tax must be fairly apportioned.
   c. The tax must not place a burden on interstate trade.
   d. The tax must not discriminate against interstate commerce.

2. All of the following are important factors when considering the validity of a state law that impairs existing contract rights <u>except</u>:

   a. The law is in response to an emergency situation.
   b. The relief is properly tailored to meet broad societal interests.
   c. The conditions of the law are reasonable.
   d. The subject area involved is subject to joint federal-state regulation.

3. A comprehensive federal statute requires that sellers of liquor comply with various licensing and taxing provisions. A subsequent state law prohibits the sale of all liquors on Sunday in the state. Select the most correct answer:

   a. The state law is unconstitutional since the federal government has clearly preempted the subject area of liquor sales.
   b. The state law is unconstitutional on its face since it violates the supremacy clause.
   c. The state law is constitutional if both it and the federal law can be complied with and it does not impose an undue burden on interstate commerce.
   d. The federal law is invalid since the sale of liquor is inherently an intrastate activity that does not affect interstate commerce.

4. A state requires that all applicants who wish to take the admissions test to become a licensed physician be a state resident for at least one year prior to testing. Select the most correct answer:

   a. The residency requirement is probably unconstitutional since less discriminatory alternatives are available.
   b. The statute is a valid exercise of state police power.
   c. The privileges and immunities clause is inapplicable since no federal statute is at issue here.
   d. The residency requirement violates the commerce clause since it inhibits interstate travel.

5. A state levies a tax on all imported foreign automobiles. The purpose of the tax is to increase the cost of foreign cars so as to make American-made vehicles more attractive. The auto industry is in a severe depression with thousands of unemployed workers. Select the most correct answer:

   a. Since there is no federal statute in conflict with the tax, the law is constitutional.
   b. The tax is unconstitutional since only the federal government has the power to tax imports under the import-export clause.
   c. The tax is constitutional since it does not unduly inhibit the free flow of imported goods among the states.
   d. The tax is unconstitutional under the privileges and immunities clause.

DISCUSSION ANALYSIS

A federal law requires that all operators of large vessels on navigable waters be certified captains. The law states that all power to regulate captains of merchant ships is reserved by Congress. A San Francisco ordinance requires that ships using the bay and docks pay a port tax. The purpose of the tax is to defray the expenses of the port authority. However, vessels registered under California title are specifically exempt from the ordinance.

Is the local ordinance constitutional under the supremacy clause? Under the commerce clause? Under the privileges and immunities clause?

Chapter 7

The Bill of Rights and Business

STUDY GUIDE AND OUTLINE

I. Introduction

A. The first ten amendments to the Constitution, called the Bill of Rights, are the foundation of the personal liberties enjoyed by individuals in our society. However, very important aspects of these freedoms relate to business activity.

B. Keep in mind that constitutional rights are not absolutes. They are limited depending upon the nature of the competing public policy in a given case. Moreover, constitutional rights vary from time-to-time. The Supreme Court constantly re-applies and re-examines constitutional principles.

II. The First Amendment: Freedom of Religion

A. The First Amendment grants us rights of (1) freedom of religion, (2) freedom of speech, (3) freedom of press, (4) freedom of assembly, and (5) freedom to petition the government for a redress of grievances.

B. Freedom of religion is based upon two clauses. The First Amendment bans any law "respecting an establishment of religion" (the establishment clause), or "prohibiting the free exercise thereof" (the free exercise clause). Most business-related freedom of religion cases involve the free exercise clause.

C. In Hobbie v. Unemployment Appeals Com'n of Florida the U.S. Supreme Court ruled that the state's refusal to grant unemployment compensation to a discharged employee violated the free exercise clause. The employee was discharged when she joined the Seventh-Day Adventist Church and refused to work at the employer's jewelry store on her Sabbath.

III. Freedom of the Press

A. Freedom of the press authorizes a private business to provide organized scrutiny of government. Yet this freedom is not absolute. The press is not free to print anything it wants without liability. Rather, freedom of press is construed typically to prohibit prior restraints on publication.

B. The press frequently asserts greater rights for its members than those possessed by nonmedia citizens. For example, the press often asserts the existence of privileged communications between informants and members of the press. However, the courts have held that no privileged communication exists. Even where a state "shield" law protects press sources, the right of the press must be balanced with the rights of others.

C. A major area of litigation involving freedom of the press is defamation. The tort of libel is used to compensate individuals for harm to character inflicted by defamatory printed falsehoods. Since the threat of a libel suit could have a chilling effect on freedom of the press, the law has a higher standard for imposing liability when printed matter concerns a public issue. In such cases, if a person involved is a public official or public figure, the plaintiff must prove actual malice in order to recover damages. Actual malice includes knowledge of falsity or circumstances showing a reckless disregard for whether the statements were true or not. The plaintiff can question the journalist as to his or her state of mind in order to prove actual malice. If a plaintiff is not a public figure or official, there is liability for libelous statements without proof of malice.

IV. Freedom of Speech

A. Freedom of speech, sometimes called freedom of expression, covers both verbal and written communications. It also covers conduct considered symbolic speech. Freedom of speech exists to protect the ideas of the minority. It means freedom to express unpopular ideas.

B. Freedom of speech protects the listener as well as the speaker. It protects corporations as well as individuals. However, freedom of speech does not protect obscene expression. Pornography is not entitled to First Amendment protection. The difficult issue in obscenity cases is defining obscenity and determining whether or not particular items are obscene. Today, the decision of whether something is obscene is determined by the standards of the community involved.

C. While freedom of speech does not protect obscenity, it does prevent most prior restraint, i.e., most attempts to censor publication of speech in advance.

D. Freedom of speech protects corporations as well as individuals. In Consol. Edison v. Public Service Com'n the U.S. Supreme Court declared unconstitutional an order of the Public Service Commission of New York. The Commission had prohibited utility companies from using inserts in customers' bills to discuss political matters.

V. Commercial Speech

A. Historically, commercial speech was not protected by the First Amendment. However, as illustrated in Va. St. Bd. of Pharm. v. Va. Cit. Cons. Council, the Supreme Court began in the 1970's to recognize that free commercial speech was essential to the public's right to know. The Virginia State Board of Pharmacy prohibited pharmacists from advertising the retail prices of prescription drugs. Plaintiff consumers sought an injunction against enforcement of the rule. The Supreme Court held that commercial advertising is not disqualified from First Amendment protection merely because the speaker's interest is purely economic. The particular consumer, and society in general, has a vital interest in the free flow of commercial information. Since this type of advertising was not false nor misleading, it could not be constitutionally prohibited.

B. Commercial speech is not protected constitutionally to the same extent as noncommercial speech. Commercial speech is protected only if it concerns a lawful activity and is not misleading or false. A restriction on commercial speech is valid if it seeks to implement a substantial governmental interest, directly advances that interest, and reaches no farther than necessary to accomplish the objective.

VI. Other First Amendment Freedoms

A. First Amendment freedoms also include the right to assemble and associate. The right of association is more than the right to attend a meeting. It includes the right to express a philosophy by group membership. It also includes the right not to join a group.

B. The purpose of the guarantee of freedom of association is to prevent guilt by association. It also ensures privacy in one's association. Protection also extends to forms of association that are not political, such as the social, legal, and economic benefits of group membership. Association is a form of expression of opinion. The right to assemble extends to all persons irrespective of their race or unpopular ideology.

VII. The Fourth Amendment

A. The Fourth Amendment protects individuals and corporations from unreasonable searches and seizures. Its primary purpose is to protect persons from unwarranted intrusions into their individual privacy. In recent years, courts have narrowed Fourth Amendment protections. For example, police officers may search someone being arrested and his/her surroundings for weapons. Moreover, the right to search for evidence extends to the premises of persons not suspected of criminal conduct.

B. The U.S. Supreme Court has held that searches of businesses may require a search warrant under many circumstances. However, in New York v. Burger the Supreme Court ruled that the fourth amendment does not require a warrant for a search of a "closely regulated" industry (in this case a junk yard) because a business owner's expectation of privacy is reduced when the business is so regulated.

VIII. The Fifth Amendment

A. The Fifth Amendment contains five basic constitutional liberties. It:

1. Requires indictment by a grand jury for capital offense or infamous crime.
2. Prohibits double jeopardy.
3. Requires just compensation in eminent domain proceedings.
4. Contains a due process clause.
5. Protects against compulsory self-incrimination.

B. A grand jury must decide whether there is sufficient evidence of guilt to justify a trial. A grand jury is typically made up of twenty-three persons, and it takes a majority vote to indict a defendant. (It takes less proof than it does to convict an accused defendant.)

IX. Eminent Domain

A. Protection against double jeopardy means that a person cannot be tried twice for the same offense. This protection applies to corporations as well as individuals. Eminent domain is used by the government to acquire real property for public purposes. The Fifth Amendment requires just compensation for even a temporary public taking of private property.

B. The Fifth Amendment protects life, liberty, and property from deprivation by the federal government without due process of law. The Fourteenth Amendment has an identical clause which applies to the states. Due process basically requires "fundamental fairness."

C. In Nollan v. California Coastal Com'n, the Supreme Court held that the Commission could not use its land permit process as a way of securing an easement across plaintiff's land without paying for the easement. Such an easement would be a taking and required just compensation.

X. Self-Incrimination

A. Protection against compulsory self-incrimination is not absolute. It does not apply to corporations. All that is protected is extortion of information from the accused himself/herself.

B. In 1988 in the case of Braswell v. U.S., the Supreme Court held that the custodian of corporate records could not resist a subpoena for such records on the ground that the act of production would incriminate him in violation of the Fifth Amendment.

XI. The Sixth Amendment

A. The Sixth Amendment provides multiple protections in criminal cases. Its protections give one the right to:

1. Obtain a speedy and public trial.
2. Have a trial by jury.
3. Be informed of the charge against him or her.
4. Confront one's accuser.
5. Subpoena witnesses in one's favor.
6. Have the assistance of an attorney.

B. Juries are drawn from a fair cross-section of the community. Juries are not required to be composed of twelve persons nor to render unanimous verdicts. However, if a jury is less than twelve, the verdict must be unanimous.

C. The right to counsel once existed only at trial. Now courts recognize that the right exists even before the indictment. The right exists whenever an investigation focuses upon an accused and a jail sentence is possible punishment.

XII. The Seventh Amendment

The Seventh Amendment guarantees the right to trial by jury in suits at common law where the amount in controversy exceeds $20. There is <u>no</u> constitutional right to jury trial:

1. In suits in equity.
2. In cases against the government.
3. When causes of action did not exist at common law but have been created by legislation.

XIII. The Fourteenth Amendment: Introduction

A. The Fourteenth Amendment states that all persons born or naturalized in the United States are both American citizens and citizens of the state in which they reside. It also contains the privileges and immunities clause, the due process clause, and the equal protection clause.

B. The due process clause has played a unique role in constitutional development. This role has been to make most of the provisions of the Bill of Rights applicable to the states. In 1925, the Supreme Court began incorporating various portions of the first eight amendments into the Fourteenth Amendment due process clause in order to apply them to all states.

C. Not all jurists agree with the "incorporation theory," but today only a few provisions of the Bill of Rights, such as grand jury indictment, a jury trial in civil cases, and excessive bail, are not yet picked-up by the due process clause.

XIV. Due Process of Law

A. The term <u>due process of law</u> cannot be defined narrowly. It describes fundamental fairness and decency. It means that government may not act in a manner that is arbitrary, capricious, or unreasonable. The due process clause applies only to <u>government</u> action, <u>not</u> arbitrary behavior of private individuals or corporations.

B. The due process clause consists of two distinct protections: procedural due process and substantive due process. <u>Substantive due process</u> issues arise when property or other rights are directly affected by governmental action. <u>Procedural due process</u> cases are concerned with whether proper notice has been given and a proper hearing has been conducted.

C. The court in Peralta v. Heights Medical Center, Inc. held that where a person has been deprived of property in a manner contrary to the most basic tenets of due process, there is not available as a defense that in this particular case due process of law would have led to the same result because the person did not have a good case on the merits. In other words, each person must be given due process of law regardless of the particular merits of the claim.

D. Today there is in effect a double standard in the application of the due process clause. Economic legislation is presumed to be constitutional, and few due process challenges succeed against this legislation. But legislation which tends to restrict fundamental rights, such as freedom of speech, press, and religion, is suspect and subject to closer judicial scrutiny. Thus courts are the guardians of fundamental liberty, but do not administer our economic system.

XV. Equal Protection

A. Almost no law treats all persons equally. Laws inherently draw lines and treat people differently. The equal protection clause says that no law imposed by the state should classify people differently without a satisfactory reason making such treatment fair.

B. The courts use two distinct tests in applying the equal protection clause. When the minimum rationality test is used, the challenged law and its classifications are typically found constitutional. However, if the strict scrutiny test is used, the classifications are usually found to be in violation of the equal protection clause.

C. The strict scrutiny approach is used if the classification involves either a suspect class, or a fundamental constitution right.

1. A suspect class is one subjected to such a history of purposeful unequal treatment as to require extraordinary protection from the majority rule. For example, classifications directed at race, national origin, or alienage are suspect. These classifications are subject to strict judicial scrutiny and are in effect unconstitutional unless the state can prove that they are based upon some compelling state interest.
2. The second group of cases in which strict scrutiny is applied are those which involve classifications directed at fundamental rights. Among such rights are the right to vote, the right to privacy, and the right to travel.

D. Other classifications imposed by the state (e.g., a mandatory retirement age) are measured by the minimum rationality approach. Under this approach a classification is constitutional if it has a rational connection to some permissible state goal. Such classifications are presumed constitutional because courts recognize that the drawing of lines creating distinctions can hardly be avoided in the writing of legislation.

E. Some cases actually fall between the two previously discussed approaches. These cases use a quasi-strict scrutiny test because the classifications are only partially suspect or the rights involved are not quite fundamental. Such classifications are unconstitutional unless they are substantially related to an important government objective. Cases involving classifications based on sex or legitimacy typically are subject to this modified strict scrutiny approach.

COMPLETION EXERCISES

1. The ______________ bans any law which supports or maintains a particular religion.

2. Freedom of ______________ constitutionally authorizes a private business to provide organized scrutiny of the government.

3. ______________ are used sometimes to censor speech in advance of publication.

4. Commercial speech is protected by the First Amendment only if it concerns a lawful activity and is not _______________ or _______________.

5. The _______________ protects individuals from unreasonable searches and seizures.

6. _______________ is used by the government to acquire private property for public purposes.

7. The _______________ requires a grand jury indictment for a capital offense or infamous crime.

8. The _______________ tells the accused that they have the right to remain silent and the right to a court-appointed attorney if they cannot afford one.

9. The Seventh Amendment guarantees the right to a _______________ in suits at common law where the amount in controversy exceeds $20.

10. A _______________ clause is found in both the Fifth and Fourteenth Amendment.

11. _______________ concerns whether proper notice has been given and a proper hearing has been conducted before the government can deprive a person of life, liberty, or property.

12. The _______________ says that no law should treat people differently without a satisfactory reason making such treatment fair and equitable.

13. Under the strict scrutiny test, a classification is unconstitutional unless the classification is necessary to a _______________ state interest.

14. Classifications based on sex or legitimacy are subject to a _______________.

15. The Fifth Amendment's prohibition against _______________ means that a person cannot be tried more than once for the same offense by the same governmental body.

TRUE-FALSE CHOICES

1. _____ The Bill of Rights are absolute liberties which can never be infringed upon by the government.

2. _____ There is no constitutional right of privileged communications between members of the press and their sources of information.

3. _____ If plaintiff is a public figure, there is liability for libelous statements only if made with actual malice.

4. _____ Obscene materials are not entitled to First Amendment protections.

5. _____ Prior restraints on speech are unconstitutional per se.

6. _____ Like pornography, commercial speech has no First Amendment protection.

7. _____ The right to petition the government for a redress of grievances is given only to American citizens.

8. _____ The right to counsel exists whenever an investigation focuses upon an accused and a jail sentence is possible punishment.

9. _____ The Fifth and Sixth Amendments provide most of the fundamental constitutional protections for defendants to criminal cases.

10. _____ There is no right to jury trial in suits in equity.

11. _____ The Fifth Amendment protects life, liberty, and property from deprivation by the states without due process of law.

12. _____ Economic legislation is rarely declared unconstitutional as violating the due process clause.

13. _____ Under the minimum rationality standard, it is enough to show that if a law has a disproportionate impact on a racial minority, it violates the equal protection clause.

14. _____ The strict scrutiny approach is used if classifications are based upon either a suspect class or a fundamental right.

15. _____ The Fifth Amendment protection against compulsory self-incrimination does not apply to corporations.

MULTIPLE CHOICE SELECTIONS

1. President Carter enacted the draft registration law which requires all males to register with the Selective Service by their eighteenth birthday. The purpose of the law is not to draft men, but to acquire a pool of available names of potential draftees so that the conscription process is speeded up in time of war. Plaintiff is an eighteen year old male who claims that the law is discriminatory since females are not required to register. Select the most correct answer:

   a. The law is invalid under the due process clause because it deprives plaintiff of his fundamental right of liberty without an opportunity to be heard.
   b. The law is valid under the equal protection clause because it is economic legislation which satisfies the minimum rationality approach.
   c. The law is valid under the equal protection clause because this gender-based classification satisfies the quasi-strict scrutiny test.
   d. This law is invalid under equal protection analysis since draft registration is not a compelling state goal.

2. Ben is the illegitimate child of Fred. Fred died without a will, leaving neither spouse nor any children other than Ben. State law provides that an illegitimate child may not inherit his father's property. In challenging the validity of the state statute, Ben's strongest argument would be that:

   a. There is no substantial relationship between the denial of inheritance by illegitimate children and the state's interest of discouraging illicit sex. Therefore, the law violates equal protection.
   b. He was deprived of property without due process because his fundamental right to inherit has been inhibited without a compelling state need.
   c. The law violates the privileges and immunities clause of the Fourteenth Amendment.
   d. The law violates the Fifth Amendment because Ben's property is taken by the state without just compensation.

3. Stortz is a member of the Nazi Socialist Party. He believes that all racial minorities should attend segregated schools. Standing on a street corner dressed in full Nazi uniform, Stortz attempts loudly to persuade passersby to join the Nazi Party. Stortz is arrested for breach of the peace. Select the most correct statement:

   a. Freedom of expression protects both verbal and symbolic speech. Stortz has a constitutional right to express his views even if they are unpopular and deplorable.
   b. The arrest violates Stortz's right of association. He has the constitutional right to join any group that he desires.
   c. The arrest is valid since it can be reasonably expected that Stortz's speech would incite a fight and a breach of peace.
   d. The arrest is valid since the Nazi Party holds views which are anti-American.

4. The government has banned television advertisements of cigarettes. If the tobacco companies claim that the ban violates the First Amendment, what is the government's best argument in favor of the regulation?

   a. This is a valid restriction on commercial speech because cigarette TV ads are per se misleading.
   b. This is a valid restriction on commercial speech since the state has a substantial interest in the public's health, and the ban does not prohibit other forms of advertisements besides TV.
   c. This is a valid restriction because the First Amendment does not protect purely economic commercial speech.
   d. None of the above is correct.

5. Police arrest defendant for reckless driving and driving without a license. Both offenses are misdemeanors punishable only by fines of up to $500. Defendant is convicted for both offenses and now claims Sixth Amendment violations because he was given neither a Miranda Warning nor provided with a court-appointed attorney. Defendant's Sixth Amendment right to counsel:

   a. Was not violated because court-appointed attorneys are only available for indigent defendants.
   b. Was not violated because he effectively waived the right by not requesting an attorney.
   c. Was not violated because neither offense was a possible jail sentence.
   d. Was violated because the right to counsel attaches immediately after arrest.

Chapter 7

DISCUSSION ANALYSIS

The city of Ashmore has three adult theaters. The city requires that before showing any adult films to the public, the theaters must first submit the films to a city licensing board for approval. If the movies are not declared obscene, the theaters can legally show them. If the movies are declared obscene, the theater has the right to a judicial appeal. The city states that the purpose of the licensing procedure is to protect the safety and morals of the community from the hazards of pornography. Does this procedure violate the theaters' First Amendment right of free speech?

Chapter
8

Administrative Law

STUDY GUIDE AND OUTLINE

I. Introduction

A. As society has grown complex, the problems of society have grown more complex. Society has turned to the administrative process for solutions to many of these problems.

B. The day-to-day legal impact on business of rules and regulations adopted by administrative agencies probably exceeds the impact of the other branches of government.

C. While this chapter focuses on federal agencies, there are also state and local administrative agencies.

II. Reasons for the Use of Administrative Agencies

A. It is impossible for the legislature to legislate in sufficient detail to cover all aspects of a problem.

B. Courts cannot handle all disputes and controversies that arise.

C. Many problems need to be referred to experts for solution and management.

D. Some agencies exist to protect the public from harm.

E. Some agencies exist to provide services.

III. Functions

A. Administrative agency functions include

1. Prosecuting
2. Advising
3. Supervising
4. Adjudicating
5. Investigating

B. It is a federal crime to make intentionally a false statement in any matter within the jurisdiction of a federal agency. In United States v. Yermian the defendant supplied false statements to his employer in connection with a Defense Department security questionnaire. The Supreme Court ruled that it was unnecessary for the prosecution to prove that the defendant knew he was under the jurisdiction of a federal agency.

C. Many agencies exercise quasi-legislative power by issuing rules and regulations that have the force of law.

D. Agencies also exercise quasi-judicial authority by having their own administrative law courts to decide complaints brought against violators of administrative law.

E. Many complaints brought by agencies are settled through consent orders, which state that the charged party (called respondent) agrees not to engage in the business activities which were the subject of the complaint, but does not admit it has been guilty of a violation of the law. Once accepted, a consent order has the same legal force as a final cease and desist order issued by an administrative law court.

IV. Organization

A. Administrative agencies usually have a chairperson and four other members. These individuals control the agency by majority vote. They are appointed by the President and confirmed by the Senate for specified lengths of office. Usually no more than three of the members may belong to the same political party.

B. Many agencies have a general counsel. This person is the chief law officer and legal advisor.

C. Many agencies also have administrative law judges. They hear agency cases alleging law violations.

D. In Cuyahoga Valley Railway Company v. United Transportation Union, the Supreme Court held that it was the Secretary of Labor, and not an administrative agency, who has authority to determine if a citation should be issued to an employer for unsafe working conditions. The Commission's function is to act as a neutral arbiter.

V. Influencing Agency Decisions

A. Statutes require that agencies give public notice of proposed rules and hold public hearings on them.

B. The Hobbs Act grants judicial review in the federal Court of Appeals from all final orders of federal administrative agencies.

C. Although agencies are not elected, they sometimes respond dramatically to public opinion.

VI. Judicial Review of Agency Decisions: Introduction

A. The executive branch is a check on administrative action in that it normally appoints the top officials of an agency and makes budget recommendations to the legislature for that agency.

B. The legislature controls administrative activity by granting agencies their power, and legislating changes to agencies, and setting agency budgets. There is also a present trend for Congress to retain power to exercise a legislative veto over agency rules.

C. Courts act as a check on administrative bodies through the power of judicial review and interpretation of statutes under which agencies operate.

VII. Judicial Review of Agency Rulemaking

A. Agencies adopt rules and regulations as part of their quasi-legislative function. They decide controversies in performance of the quasi-judicial function. Parties who are unhappy with the rules or decisions of an administrative agency may challenge the agency in court, or seek to influence public opinion and political decision-makers. Lawsuits against agency personnel are also a possibility.

B. There are two basic issues in litigation challenging the validity of a rule made by an administrative agency:

1. Is the delegation of authority to the administrative agency valid?
2. Has the agency exceeded its legislatively granted authority?

C. The Supreme Court has ruled that power granted to an agency by Congress must be both definite and limited. If not, the delegation of power is unconstitutional. However, the Court has upheld delegation of authority to make rules in very broad language, such as the authority to make rules as required by the "public interest, convenience and necessity."

D. In the Board of Governors v. Dimension Fin. Corp., the Supreme Court held that since the meaning of an enactment had previously been determined, the Federal Reserve Board could not redefine the meaning of such enactment.

VIII. Review of Adjudications: Procedural Aspects

A. Judicial review of agency adjudications is quite limited. For example, courts reviewing administrative interpretations of law often defer to an agency's own interpretation of the statute governing the agency.

B. Administrative agencies frequently develop their own rules of procedure, unless their governing statutes specify particular procedures. In reviewing administrative determinations, courts are alert in seeing that parties are given a fair procedure, i.e., a due process.

C. An important issue as to whether a party can obtain judicial review of an administrative determination is whether the party is "an aggrieved party," i.e., whether the party has standing to sue.

IX. Exhaustion of Remedies

A. Before a party can obtain judicial review of agency determinations, the party must usually comply with the doctrine of exhaustion of remedies. This doctrine states that before courts review administrative actions, a complaining party must exhaust all administrative remedies and procedures available within the administrative agency.

B. Exhaustion of remedies is sometimes not required where constitutional rights are abridged or irreparable injury is threatened by agency action.

C. A doctrine similar to exhaustion of remedies is known as primary jurisdiction and applies where a claim is originally cognizable in the courts.

X. Review of an Agency's Determination of Facts

A. When reviewing the finding of facts made by an administrative agency, a court considers them to be correct as long as they are supported by substantial evidence in the record. Thus, the findings of an agency are not set aside by the courts unless they are clearly unsubstantiated by the record of the agency's proceedings.

B. In reviewing agency determinations, courts do not reweigh the evidence, do not make independent determinations of fact, and do not substitute their view of the evidence for that of the agency.

C. In Baltimore Gas & Electric v. Natural Resources Defense Council the NRDC challenged certain environmental rules of the Nuclear Regulatory Commission as failing to comply with the National Environmental Policy Act. The Supreme Court stated that it was not the task of the court to determine what decision it would have reached had it been the Commission. The court's only task is to determine whether the Commission considered the relevant factors and applied a rational connection between the facts found and the choice made. The Supreme Court held that the Commission had.

XI. Damage Suits

A. Government officials generally have immunity from damage suits for conduct that is within the scope of their duties and responsibilities, irrespective of their motives for the conduct. However, if a government official does an unconstitutional act, or one that is clearly beyond his or her legal authority, there is no immunity from lawsuit.

B. Immunity is granted to public officials for two reasons:

1. It would be unjust in the absence of bad faith to subject a public official to liability for exercising administrative discretion even if that discretion is poorly exercised.
2. The threat of liability would deter public officials in the performance of their duties.

C. Public prosecutors, administrative judges, and hearing examiners have absolute immunity when carrying out their duties because of the importance of their function and the need to prevent harassment of them.

D. The federal law waiving tort liability is known as the Federal Tort Claims Act. The "discretionary function" exception to liability exists for employees of the government when the alleged tort involved an element of judgment or choice.

XII. Equal Access to Justice

A. The Equal Access to Justice Act requires the federal government to pay the legal costs of those who sue the federal government and win. Certain eligibility limitations apply.

B. The government agency isn't required to pay these legal costs if it can show that its original decision was substantially justified.

XIII. Common Criticisms

A. Independent regulatory agencies and the administrative process are probably subject to more criticism than any other part of government.

B. Because of their size, agencies have often been charged with being inefficient and ineffective. Not only are there so many rules and regulations that it frequently is impossible to know them all, the rules and regulations of various agencies sometimes conflict with each other.

C. The Peter Principle - that many persons are promoted to their level of incompetency - clearly applies to many bureaucrats.

D. It has been charged that too often agencies favor the industries being regulated rather than the public. One reason for this is the so-called "revolving door" -- regulators are often persons with high executive positions in the industries they regulate. Also, agency employees frequently go into high-paying jobs in the industries they have been regulating.

XIV. Cost of Regulation

A. The total direct and indirect cost of business regulation probably exceeds 100 billion dollars per year. The financial burden of complying with many regulations is high because it requires new equipment, additional personnel, or paperwork.

B. Under many existing regulatory acts, there is no cost-benefit analysis required when new rules and regulations are proposed. In American Textile Manufacturers Institute, Inc. v. Donovan the Supreme Court considered the legality of a "cotton dust standard" issued by the Occupational

Safety and Health Administration. Petitioners, representing the interest of the cotton industry, contended that the Occupational, Safety, and Health Act requires OSHA to demonstrate that its standards reflect a reasonable relationship between the costs and benefits associated with the standards. The Act required that OSHA protect employees from health hazards "to the extent feasible." Considering the legislative history of the Act, the Supreme Court ruled that the term feasible did not mean that there had to be a reasonable relationship between costs and benefits. The Court stated that Congress anticipated that costs might actually exceed benefits in eliminating workplace health hazards.

C. Agencies under the President's authority (these do not include independent regulatory agencies) must, by executive order, apply cost-benefit analysis to "significant" new regulations unless legislation otherwise prohibits it.

COMPLETION EXERCISES

1. To solve many problems presented by the complexities of modern society, the government has turned to the ________________.

2. Reasons for the use of the administrative process include ________________, ________________, and ________________.

3. The power of administrative agencies to issue rules and regulations is called the ________________ power.

4. In Steadman v. SEC, the Supreme Court ruled that in reviewing evidence the SEC should use the ________________ standard of proof.

5. The consent order has the same legal force and effect of a final ________________ order.

6. The quasi-judicial functions of agencies are performed by ________________.

7. The FTC is divided into the bureaus of ________________ , ________________ , and ________________.

8. The two basic issues in litigation challenging the validity of a rule made by an administrative agency are ________________ and ________________.

9. In general, courts refuse to review agency actions until a complaining party has ________________ available to him or her before the administrative agency.

10. Government officials faced with damage suits usually assert the defense of ________________.

11. ________________ laws require that agencies planning to issue rules or regulations, give public notice of such plans, and hold public hearings before rules or regulations are adopted.

12. ________________ laws limit the power of agency heads to fire federal employees.

13. The legislation which discourages former government employees from taking unfair advantage of their government service is the ________________.

14. The total direct and indirect cost of business regulation exceeds ________________ dollars per year.

15. In American Textile Manufacturers Institute v. Donovan, the Supreme Court ruled that OSHA was not required to engage in ________________ analysis in issuing a standard limiting occupational exposure to cotton dust.

Chapter 8

TRUE-FALSE CHOICES

1. ______ Administrative agencies are found only at the federal level.

2. ______ One reason for the development of administrative agencies is that courts have difficulty in handling all disputes and controversies that arise.

3. ______ Administrative agencies not only regulate business they also provide services to the public.

4. ______ Quasi-judicial proceedings usually begin with the filing of a cease and desist order.

5. ______ Many agency complaints are settled through issuance of a consent order.

6. ______ The members (or commissioners) of a federal administrative agency are appointed by Congress.

7. ______ Congress could abolish an independent regulatory agency if it chose to do so.

8. ______ Delegations of quasi-legislative authority to administrative agencies must be both definite and limited.

9. ______ In FCC v. Midwest Video the Supreme Court upheld the FCC's power to issue rules regulating cable television systems.

10. ______ In reviewing agency action, courts can make independent determinations of fact.

11. ______ Administrative judges and public prosecutors have limited immunity from liability for actions taken in the course of their duties.

12. ______ Regulators have often been executives in the industries they regulate.

13. ______ Federal law prevents all business contact between a former agency official and his or her agency for five years.

14. ______ All federal laws require cost-benefit analysis when new rules and regulations are proposed.

15. ______ The regulatory agencies have sometimes been referred to as a "fourth branch" of government.

MULTIPLE CHOICE SELECTIONS

1. All of the following are functions of administrative agencies except:

   a. Prosecuting alleged violators.
   b. Adjudicating alleged violations of law.
   c. Deciding the constitutionality of the actions of alleged violators.
   d. Advising business persons on the legality of their contemplated actions.

2. The Acme Corporation seeks to have the federal courts review the fact-finding of the FTC, which has found it in violation of the FTC Act. Select the most correct statement:

   a. The reviewing court will reweigh the FTC's evidence.
   b. The reviewing court will hear new evidence which the Acme Corporation wishes to introduce.
   c. The reviewing court will substitute its view of the evidence for that of the FTC.
   d. None of the above is correct.

3. All of the following are common criticisms of administrative agencies except:

   a. Agency officials usually lack discretion to implement action.
   b. Administrative agencies are inefficient.
   c. At top levels of employment, the compensation is probably too low to attract the very best employees.
   d. Voters cannot easily express their dissatisfaction with an agency rule or position.

4. Select the incorrect statement:

   a. A frequently voiced criticism of many agencies is that there is unnecessary delay in rendering decisions and providing service.
   b. Paperwork is a major cost of complying with regulation of business.
   c. The "revolving door" sometimes gives regulated industries excessive influence on the agencies which are supposed to regulate them.
   d. Cost-benefit analysis is free from ethical criticism.

5. Select the most correct statement:

   a. In Dixon v. Love, the Supreme Court ruled that agencies need not observe due process.
   b. In FCC v. Midwest Video Corp., the Supreme Court ruled that the FCC had no power over cable TV systems.
   c. In Dunlop v. Bachowski, the Supreme Court ruled that the Secretary of Labor had violated federal law.
   d. None of the above is correct.

Chapter 8

DISCUSSION ANALYSIS

Discuss reasons for growth of the administrative process in this century. Your answer should include possible reasons for mounting criticism in recent years of administrative agencies.

Chapter 9

Contract Law and Private Enterprise

STUDY GUIDE AND OUTLINE

I. Contract Law and Its Place in Private Enterprise

A. A contract is a legally enforceable promise. Note that it need not usually be a formal, written document.

B. The law of contracts promotes certainty that agreements will be kept and permits reliance on promises. It encourages the flow of commerce.

II. Sources of Contract Law

A. Most of the contract law in this chapter is common law.

B. In specific areas of businesses, contract law is sometimes controlled by statute or regulation. For example, contracts of insurance are so controlled.

III. Classification of Contracts

A. An executory contract is one that the contracting parties have not yet performed. An executed contract is one that the parties have performed.

B. An express contract is one which arises following actual discussion of the terms of the agreement. An implied contract arises from the conduct or action of the parties, rather than by words. For example, seeking professional services at a doctor's office implies contractual agreement to pay for the services.

C. A unilateral contract involves a present act given in return for a promise of future performance. A loan of money in return for a promise to repay at interest illustrates the unilateral contract. In a bilateral contract each party makes a promise to perform for the other.

D. A void contract is one that lacks an essential contractual element. An illegal gambling contract lacks the element of legality.

E. A voidable contract binds one of the parties to the agreement but gives the other party the option of withdrawing from it. For example, contracts based on fraud or misrepresentation are voidable. Also contracts induced by duress (force) or undue influence are voidable.

F. When one party is unjustly enriched at the expense of another, the law may imply duty on the first party to pay the second, even though there is no contract between the parties. The doctrine which requires this result is quasi-contract.

IV. Remedies for Breach of Contract

A. A party who does not live up to the obligation of contractual performance is said to breach the contract.

B. Remedies for breach of contract include negotiated settlement, arbitration, various damage awards, specific performance, and rescission.

C. The most common remedy for breach of contract is the negotiated settlement. The parties voluntarily reach an agreement to resolve the breach of contract because trial litigation is very expensive and time-consuming.

D. The victim of a contract breach must take reasonable steps to mitigate damages, i.e., to reduce them.

V. Offer to Contract

A. A contract begins when an offeror makes an offer to an offeree. An offer contains a specific promise and a specific demand.

B. There may sometimes be confusion over what is and what is not an offer. In Pioneer Realty and Land Company v. Mortgage Plus some home buyers had applied for mortgages. When buyers applied for the mortgages, they were told that the interest was 11 1/2 percent. While the applications were being processed, the percentage rate was raised, and the defendant refused to honor the 11 1/2 percent rate. The buyers sued. The court held that the defendant did not show a willingness to be legally bound at 11 1/2 percent. The 11 1/2 percent quotation was not a legal offer. It simply informed the potential borrowers of the current rate.

C. Contractual terms must be definite and specific, except that under the Uniform Commercial Code (UCC) contracts for sale of goods can leave open nonquantity terms to be decided at a future date.

D. An offer can terminate for several reasons:

1. By provision in the offer.
2. By lapse of a reasonable period of time if the offer fails to specify a time.
3. By rejection of the offer.
4. By the offer being revoked (withdrawn).
5. By destruction of the contractual subject matter.
6. By the offeror's death or insanity.
7. By the contractual performance becoming illegal.

VI. Acceptance of Offer

A. An offer to enter into a bilateral contract is accepted by the offeree's making the required promise. A unilateral contract is accepted by performing a requested act, not by making a promise.

B. The acceptance usually binds the parties when the offeree dispatches it. Since the offeree frequently mails the acceptance, the acceptance becomes binding when it is deposited with the postal service.

C. Common law required that the acceptance must "mirror" the offer, that is, must match it exactly. The UCC, however, has changed this rule regarding merchants contracting for the sale of goods. An acceptance between merchants may create a binding contract even though it proposes new or different terms.

D. An offeree's failure to reject an offer does not imply acceptance unless a prior course of dealing between the parties indicates that silence is acceptance, or conduct of the buyer and seller of goods indicates that silence may be acceptance.

VII. Voluntary Consent to Contracts

A. To be enforceable, a contract must be made voluntarily. The previously discussed doctrines of fraud, misrepresentation, duress and undue influence show that a contract is voidable when both parties do not reach it through a voluntary, knowing consent.

B. When both parties to a contract are mistaken about a material fact involving a contract, either party to the contract may void and rescind it due to mutual mistake.

C. A unilateral mistake arises when only one of the parties to a contract is wrong about a material fact. In this event the mistaken party cannot legally withdraw from it under most circumstances. In Libby, McNeil & Libby v. United Steelworkers the Libby company had agreed to give the union pension benefits that duplicated benefits granted the union by another company. When Libby sued to have the court declare that Libby did not owe certain early retirement benefits to employees, the court ruled that Libby's mistake about the nature of the union's arrangement with the other company was unilateral. Libby's mistake did not excuse it from having to pay the benefits.

VIII. Consideration in the Contract

A. Courts will not enforce contractual promises unless they are supported by consideration. Consideration is the assuming of a legal obligation or a surrendering of a legal right. Consideration must be bargained for.

B. An agreement not to sue can be legal consideration. When an amount owed under a contract is disputed and the parties both surrender the right to have a court determine exactly what amount is owed, such an agreement and the payment of the agreed upon amount is called an accord and satisfaction..

C. A party to an agreement does not give consideration by promising to do something that he or she is already required to do.

D. The UCC states that parties to a sale of goods contract may make modifications to it without both parties giving new consideration. The rules of consideration also do not apply to a firm offer, which exists when a merchant offering goods promises in writing that the offer will not be revoked for a period that does not exceed three months.

E. Consideration is also not required when the doctrine of promissory estoppel is applied. This doctrine arises when an offeree justifiably has relied on the offeror's promise to his or her injury when the promise has been revoked before the offeree can accept it. Esquire Radio & Electronics, Inc. v. Montgomery Ward & Co. illustrates the application of promissory estoppel. Esquire stockpiled spare inventory for certain electronic products carried by Ward. On several occasions Esquire expressed concern about the size of its inventory, and Ward assured Esquire that it would eventually buy the parts. When Ward terminated its relationship with Esquire and refused to buy the remaining inventory of parts, Esquire sued. Although the court stated that there was no contract between Ward and Esquire, it ruled that promissory estoppel forced Ward to pay for the remaining inventory.

F. When it is not clear whether there is consideration to support a promise, a court will often examine the transaction as a whole.

Chapter 9

IX. Capacity of Parties to Contract

A. Capacity refers to a person's ability to be bound by a contract.

B. In most states minors can usually not be bound to contractual promises unless they involve necessaries of life such as food, clothing, shelter, medical care, and, in some states, education.

C. An intoxicated or mentally incompetent person lacks the capacity to contract if he or she is incapable of understanding the nature and purpose of the contract.

X. Illegal Contracts

A. Illegality makes a contract void. Courts will generally take no action on a void contract, and they will leave the parties to the contract where they have put themselves. In Mason v. Hosta the court held that the plaintiff could get no damages for breach of an illegal contract. The contract provided that a doctor would pay various hospital administrators each time an administrator could convince a patient to use the doctor's services.

B. There are certain exceptions to the general rule that courts will take no action on an illegal contract.

XI. When Contracts Should Be in Writing

A. The law requiring that certain contracts be evidenced in writing is the statute of frauds. Evidence of writing is required for the following contracts:

1. Contracts for the sale of an interest in land.
2. Collateral contracts promising to pay the debt of another person.
3. Contracts that cannot be performed in one year.
4. Sale of goods contracts for $500 or more.

B. A collateral promise to pay another's debt refers to a promise to pay only if the other person does not pay. In Garland Co., Inc. v. Roofco Co. the president of Roofco personally promised that he would pay a debt owed by Roofco to Garland. The court ruled that this was a primary rather than a collateral promise. It did not have to be in writing to be enforceable.

C. Some states specify that other business-related contracts must be in writing.

D. In some states the statute of fraud requires that the actual contract between the parties must be in writing. However, most states merely require that the contract be evidenced by writing and be signed by the party to be held to the agreement (the defendant).

E. Each provision of the statute of frauds permits exceptions under certain circumstances.

XII. The Parol Evidence Rule

A. The parol evidence rule states that parties to a complete and final written contract cannot introduce oral evidence in court that changes the intended meaning of the written terms.

B. An exception to the rule allows evidence of oral agreement that merely explains the meaning of written terms, without changing the terms. Also, oral evidence can be given if necessary to prevent fraud.

XIII. Interpretation of Contracts

A. Courts have created a number of rules to assist in interpreting contracts.

B. Common words are given their usual meaning. However, if the word has a particular trade usage, courts will give it that meaning. Some words have special legal meanings and, of course, courts give those words their special meanings.

C. Certain rules of priority apply to contracts according to the way the terms are written. For example, typewritten terms control printed terms and handwritten terms control typewritten terms if these various terms conflict with one another.

D. Courts interpret ambiguous or vague contractual terms against the party who drafted them. For example, in State Farm Mutual Automobile Ins. Co. v. Queen an insurance policy provided that only the first person named on the policy was to be insured for liability when driving a vehicle owned by someone else. The policy listed the people insured as follows: "Queen, Gary A. and Rhonda R." The court interpreted that Rhonda Queen was insured while driving someone else's car since the last name of both parties insured was "Queen."

XIV. Assignment of Contracts

A. An assignment is a transfer (generally a sale) of rights under a contract.

B. With certain exceptions, the person who receives an assignment (assignee) is subject to any defense that the person who made the assignment (assignor) is subject to. Otherwise, the assignee can usually enforce the contract.

C. It is vital that the person receiving an assignment notify immediately the person obligated to perform under the contract. Otherwise, the person who owes the performance may perform it to the person who made the assignment.

D. Certain types of contracts cannot be assigned. For example, a party to a contract cannot assign performance of duties when performance depends on the character, skill or training of that party.

XV. Contracts Benefiting a Third Party

A. The performance of a contract may benefit persons who are not parties to the contract. Such persons are called third-party beneficiaries. However, such persons cannot sue under the contract unless it was intended that they be benefited.

B. In Bridgman v. Curry the plaintiffs, Bridgman, had sold their farm to John and Edna Curry. The Currys were obligated to make annual payments to the plaintiffs. Later, the Currys assigned part of the farm to the four defendants, who promised "to be bound by the terms of the Bridgman contract." The Iowa Supreme Court ruled that the plaintiffs were intended third party beneficiaries of the contract the four defendants had with the plaintiff.

C. When performance under a contract is meant as a gift to a third party, that person is a donee beneficiary. An incidental beneficiary is a third party that unintentionally benefits from a contract; that person has no rights under the contract.

XVI. Performance of Contracts

A. At the time that the parties reach agreement under a contract, the duty of performance becomes binding. Failure to perform breaches the contract.

B. If something must take place in the future before a party has a duty to perform, it is called a condition precedent. A condition subsequent excuses contractual performance if some future event takes place. Under concurrent conditions each party's contractual performance is triggered by the other party's offering performance.

C. Courts generally recognize three levels of contract performance:

1. Complete performance recognizes that a contracting party has fulfilled every duty required by the contract.
2. Substantial performance occurs when the contracting party has honestly attempted to perform but has fallen short. One who substantially performs is entitled to the price promised by the other less that party's damages.
3. Material breach is a level of performance below what is reasonably acceptable. A party who has materially breached a contract cannot sue the other party for performance and is liable for damages arising from the breach.

XVII. Discharge of Contracts

A. A party to a contract is discharged when the party is released from all further obligation of performance.

B. A party is discharged under a contract when his or her performance becomes impossible to perform. Mere increased difficulty, however, does not constitute impossibility of performance. A related standard is the commercial impracticability standard that applies under the UCC to sale of goods contracts.

C. Many other things discharge a party to a contract.

XVIII. Trends in Contract Law

A. As commercial transactions have grown more complex, courts and legislatures have created more exceptions to the traditional requirements of contract formation. For instance, the UCC provides that contracts can be modified without new consideration being given.

B. With ever greater frequency, parties use arbitration, mediation, and negotiation when business problems arise under contracts. They avoid litigation when possible.

C. One recent development affecting business and consumer contracts is enactment of "plain English" statutes that require certain consumer contracts be written in a clearly understandable way.

D. Another trend is that more than half of the country's biggest corporations have employment contracts with top management.

XIX. Contractual Ethics

A. Recent scandals involving bidding for federal government contracts have raised substantial issues of contractual ethics.

B. Traditional rules of contract law cannot always be used to predict what courts will do when one party acts in bad faith or violates the expectations that another party brings to a business arrangement.

C. Eventually, ethical values may provide the basis for legal rules: the growing use of promissory estoppel and implied contract doctrine shows the willingness of courts to make binding business arrangements that in the past would have been unenforceable without an express contract.

COMPLETION EXERCISES

1. The _______________ rule states that parties to a written contract cannot introduce oral evidence in court to change the intended meaning of the written terms.
2. In contractual interpretation, typewritten contractual terms are controlled by _______________ terms.
3. Persons who benefit from a contract, yet who are not parties to the contract, are called _______________ beneficiaries.
4. If something must occur in the future before a party has a duty to perform a contract, it is called a _______________.
5. A _______________ excuses contractual performance if some future event takes place.
6. _______________ performance recognizes that a contracting party has fulfilled every duty required by the contract.
7. A _______________ is a level of performance below what is reasonably acceptable in a contract.
8. A contract that has not yet been performed is called a _______________ contract.
9. The act of loaning money in return for a promise to repay at interest illustrates the _______________ contract.
10. A _______________ contract lacks an essential contractual element.
11. A _______________ contract binds one of the parties to the agreement but gives the other party the option of withdrawing from it.
12. When one party is unjustly enriched at the expense of another, the law may imply duty on the part of the first party to pay the second under the doctrine of _______________.
13. A party who does not live up to the obligation of contractual performance is said to _______________ the contract.
14. The contractual agreement begins with an _______________, which contains a specific promise and a specific demand.
15. A _______________ mistake arises when one of the parties to a contract is wrong about a material fact.
16. Where there is a disputed contractual debt and each party surrenders the right to have a court determine exactly what amount is owed, the agreement and payment that follows is called an _______________.

TRUE-FALSE CHOICES

1. ______ A contract is a legally enforceable promise.
2. ______ An implied contract arises from the conduct or actions of the parties.
3. ______ Both fraud and duress make a contract voidable.
4. ______ In a contract based on duress or undue influence neither party to the agreement can take legal action under it.
5. ______ Under the UCC all terms of a contract must be definite and specific.

6. ______ The parties' prior course of dealing may overcome the general assumption that silence is not acceptance.

7. ______ Neither party can enforce a contract based upon mutual mistake.

8. ______ Under the UCC, the rules of consideration apply to a firm offer.

9. ______ Even minors can be held legally liable for necessaries of life.

10. ______ The doctrine of promissory estoppel is an important exception to the rule requiring consideration.

11. ______ In general, a plaintiff can get damages for breach of an illegal contract.

12. ______ In interpreting contracts, a word that is a legal term is given the common meaning of the word.

13. ______ A person receiving assignment of contractual rights is subject to all the defenses that the person transferring the rights is subject to.

14. ______ A third-party beneficiary can sue to enforce a contract even if the contract was not intended to benefit that person.

15. ______ A party to a contract can assign performance of duties that depend on the character, skill, or training of the assigning party.

MULTIPLE CHOICE SELECTIONS

1. The most common remedy for breach of contract is the:

   a. Damage award.
   b. Specific performance of the contract.
   c. Rescission of the contract.
   d. Negotiated settlement.

2. All of the following will terminate an offer to contract except:

   a. The offeror's death.
   b. The offeror's marriage.
   c. Rejection of the offer.
   d. Lapse of a reasonable period of time.

3. On May 1, Realty Associates receives a mailed offer from Mart Development, offering to buy a 100-acre piece of land for $500,000. On May 2, Realty mails back its acceptance of the offer. On May 3, Realty receives a phone call from the president of Mart that revokes the offer. Select the most <u>correct</u> statement:

   a. The statute of frauds does not apply to this situation.
   b. If the acceptance is not received by Mart until May 4, its revocation on May 3 is effective.
   c. A binding contract resulted on May 2.
   d. None of the above is correct.

4. Select the <u>incorrect</u> statement about consideration:

   a. Consideration must be bargained for.
   b. A party to an agreement gives consideration by promising to do something that he or she is already obligated to do.
   c. An agreement not to sue may be consideration to support a promise.
   d. A firm offer exists when a merchant offering goods promises in writing that the offer will not be revoked for a period that does not exceed three months.

5. The statute of frauds applies to all the following contracts except:

   a. Collateral contracts to pay the debt of another person.
   b. Contracts that cannot be performed within one year.
   c. A sale of goods for $500 or more.
   d. All of the above must be evidenced in writing.

Chapter 9

DISCUSSION ANALYSIS

Discuss the importance of contract law to private enterprise.

Chapter 10

Torts in the Business Environment

STUDY GUIDE AND OUTLINE

I. The Development of Tort Law

A. Legally, a tort is a civil wrong other than a breach of contract. Most torts involve injury to persons or property.

B. Prior to 1800 much of the law of personal or property injury was founded in the doctrine of trespass. Defendants were strictly liable for damages caused by any unpermitted direct contact to the defendant's property or person.

C. As life changed during the Machine Age of the 1800's, so did the law. The doctrine of negligence emerged, imposing liability only where the defendant was at fault and had failed to act as a "reasonable man." In an effort to protect the infant industries of the late 1800's, many judges placed tort losses on injured plaintiffs whose own behavior had contributed to their injuries. This was accomplished through various judge-created defenses, such as contributory negligence and assumption of risk, which barred recovery when plaintiffs contributed to their injuries or assumed job-related risks.

D. Beginning in the 20th century, economic conditions caused the pendulum to swing back toward strict liability. Industries no longer needed the liability protection required in the 1800's. In this century many negligence defenses have been eased or abolished. Legislatures have passed worker's compensation statutes, and strict product liability laws have been adopted. The effect has been to distribute accident losses away from injured victims and place them on defendants, who are often businesses able to spread losses through insurance or higher prices.

E. Today, torts are generally divided into three categories:

1. Intentional torts involve deliberate actions which injure others.
2. Negligence arises from failure to use reasonable care which causes injury.
3. Strict liability imposes legal responsibility for injuries under certain circumstances even though defendants neither intentionally nor negligently cause the harm.

Intentional Torts

The main similarity in the following torts is intent. The legal definition of intent includes achieving not only desired results but also results which are substantially likely to flow from some action.

II. Assault and Battery

A. An assault is the placing of another in immediate apprehension for his or her physical safety. "Apprehension" has a broader definition than "fear." It includes the expectation of an imminent injury.

B. Battery is an illegal, unpermitted touching of another. Many times a battery follows an assault.

III. Intentional Infliction of Mental Distress

A. This judge-made tort is a "battery" to the emotions. The plaintiff must prove that the defendant's outrageous behavior causes not only mental distress but also physical symptoms, such as headaches or sleeplessness.

B. In Ford v. Revlon, Inc. the Arizona Supreme Court ruled that an employer's failure to investigate promptly the employee's complaint about a supervisor's sexual harassment met the test for intentional infliction of mental distress.

IV. Invasion of Privacy

A. This is a relatively new tort that comprises three principal invasions of personal interest:

1. Liability is imposed on a defendant who appropriates the plaintiff's name or likeness for his or her own use without the plaintiff's consent. For instance, advertisers are liable to individuals when pictures of them are used without authorization to promote products.
2. The defendant's intrusion upon the plaintiff's physical solitude is a second invasion of privacy. Illegal searches, eavesdropping, and wiretapping can provide the basis for this invasion of privacy tort.
3. The defendant's public disclosure of highly objectionable private information about the plaintiff also gives rise to an invasion of privacy. The news media can, under the First Amendment, disclose even objectionable truthful statements about public figures, but a much stricter standard is required when reporting about private individuals.

V. False Imprisonment and Malicious Prosecution

A. False Imprisonment is the intentional, unjustified confinement of a non-consenting person. Suspected shoplifters often charge merchants with false imprisonment when merchants use unreasonable force or lack justifiable grounds for detaining shoppers.

B. Malicious prosecution is the tort of having someone arrested criminally without proper grounds.

VI. Trespass

A. Trespass is entering another's land without consent or remaining there after being asked to leave. The civil remedy is usually injunctive relief, but monetary damages may also be awarded. As with many intentional wrong-doings, trespass is often also a statutory crime.

VII. Conversion

A. Conversion is the wrongful and unlawful exercise of dominion and control over the personal property of another. The deprivation must constitute a serious invasion of the owner's property rights. Stealing property, failing to return properly acquired property, or delivering property to the wrong party are all conversions, and the converter is absolutely liable for any damage done to the property.

VIII. **Defamation**

A. Defamation is the publication of false statements about another which holds up that individual's character or reputation to contempt or ridicule. "Publication" means the falsehood must be communicated to third parties. Oral defamation is slander while written defamation or defamation published over television or radio is termed libel.

B. Under the First Amendment the news media are not liable for defamatory falsehoods about public officials unless plaintiffs can prove that the untruths were published with evil intent (malice). In Dun & Bradstreet v. Greenmoss Builders, Inc. the Supreme Court ruled that the Constitution did not require a plaintiff to show "actual malice" in order to prove defamation against a nonmedia defendant whose speech did not involve an issue of public concern. The case arose over a false credit report.

C. Truth is an absolute defense to a claim of defamation. Privileged communications, such as statements made by legislators, judges, and attorneys, are in most circumstances also a defense to defamation.

D. Nearly one third of all defamation suits are currently brought by employees against present and former employers.

IX. **Business Torts**

A. Business torts is a vague label that embraces several different kinds of torts which involve interference with business relations.

B. "Injurious falsehood" or "trade disparagement" is a common business tort. Somewhat like defamation, it consists of the publication of falsehoods which disparages the plaintiff's ownership of his property. It differs from defamation, however, in that it usually applies to the plaintiff's business rather than reputation or character.

C. Intentional interference with contractual relations is another type of business tort. Inducing employees to breach employment contracts is an example of this tort. However, in Welch v. Bancorp Management Advisors, Inc., an Oregon court ruled that it was not a tort for an investment advisor to urge an investment trust to breach its loan agreement with the plaintiff. The court said the relationship between the advisor and the trust was "privileged."

D. Wrongfully obtaining a rival competitor's trade secret is a tort. A trade secret must be confidential information, and a former employee has the duty to protect such secrets from future rival employees or face possible tort liability.

X. **Trademarks and False Advertising: The Lanham Act**

A. Trademark law covers trademarks, service marks, certification marks, and collective marks. A trademark is any mark, work, picture, or design which attaches to goods to indicate their source.

B. The Lanham Act of 1946 provides the principal protection for trademarks. The act recognizes that property rights extend beyond ownership of actual goods to the intangible goodwill which trademarks represent. The Lanham Act requires that a trademark be registered on the Principal Register and be in current use on goods and services in interstate commerce.

C. Any person who infringes on another's registered trademark in connection with the sale or advertising of goods and services, is in violation of the Lanham Act and subject to damages and injunction. Willful infringement may result in treble damages.

D. The competitive tort of false advertising is prohibited by Section 43(a) of the Lanham Act. Any false description or representation of one's goods or services which may damage a competitor gives rise to an action for civil damages. Note that this section applies only to falsehoods made about the defendant's own goods or services, not the plaintiff's goods or services, which would constitute the common law tort of disparagement.

XI. Patents and Copyrights

A. Patents give inventors a seventeen-year legal monopoly over the use and licensing of new processes, products, and machines. To be patentable, an invention must be nonobvious, novel and useful. Only when a newly discovered fact is reduced to a specific application through a new machine or process may it be patented.

B. Federal patent law provides remedies of injunction and damages against anyone who infringes on the patent. Having a patent properly registered with the Patent Office only creates a presumption of validity. Courts find that over half of litigated patents are either invalid or unenforceable.

C. Copyright law protects authors rather than inventors. An author is one who creates works of a literary, dramatic, musical, graphic, audio, or visual nature and the Copyright Act of 1976 automatically protects these works from the moment the author creates them. The copyright runs for the author's lifetime plus fifty additional years.

D. Where the author has observed the proper formalities (filed the work with the Copyright Office and placed a copyright symbol to the work), the author may recover actual or statutory damages, attorney fees, and lost profits for copyright infringement.

E. The law permits a fair use of copyrighted work for teaching, research, and reporting, but it forbids its reproduction for profit without the author's permission. In Sony Corp. of America v. Universal City Studios the U.S. Supreme Court held that noncommercial home use of videotape recorders to record copyrighted television programs was a "fair use."

XII. Constitutional Torts

A. Section 1983 of the Civil Rights Act of 1871 creates tort liability for any public official or employee who injures a person by depriving him or her of constitutionally guaranteed rights. It also applies to city governments who support constitutional abuses by "custom, practice, or policy."

Negligence

The second major field of tort liability involves behavior that causes an unreasonably great risk of causing injury. This field of tort is called negligence. A complaint for negligence must show duty, breach of duty by unreasonable behavior, causation, and injury.

XIII. Duty of Care

A. Duty is a critical element of the tort of negligence. There are primarily two different types of care:

1. One owes a duty generally to any foreseeable person who might suffer injury from one's unreasonable behavior. Most courts impose negligence liability only if the defendant's active conduct is unreasonable. There is usually no liability for unreasonable non-conduct, such as the failure to warn about imminent danger or failure to rescue an endangered person. There is no liability because there exists no general duty to refrain from unreasonable non-conduct.
2. However, if there exists a special relationship between the parties, then there is a duty to refrain from unreasonable non-conduct as well as unreasonable conduct. Such relationships as doctor/patient, innkeeper/guest, common carrier/passenger, and landlord/tenant all require a duty to take specific steps to warn about or protect others from danger.

B. The judicial trend indicates a steady broadening of the duty element of negligence. Several courts have imposed negligence liability for non-conduct (e.g., failure to warn) even when the defendant was not in a special relationship with the plaintiff.

XIV. Unreasonable Behavior

A. In the United States more lawsuits allege negligence than any other single cause of action. At the core of negligence law is the unreasonable behavior which breaches the duty of care that the defendant owes the plaintiff.

B. Judge Learned Hand defined this unreasonable behavior as being determined by "the likelihood that the defendant's conduct will injure others, taken with the seriousness of the injury if it happens, and balanced against the interest which he must sacrifice to avoid that risk."

C. Res ipsa loquitur, meaning "the thing speaks for itself," is a negligence doctrine that aids the plaintiff in cases where there is a strong suspicion that the defendant has acted unreasonably, but the plaintiff has difficulty in proving what exactly happened. When the thing causing harm was in the sole control of the defendant and when injury normally wouldn't have occurred without negligence, res ipsa loquitur shifts the burden of proof from plaintiff to defendant. Instead of the plaintiff having to prove the defendant negligent, the defendant has to prove use of ordinary and reasonable care.

XV. Causation: Cause in Fact

A. Even if the plaintiff can show that the defendant's conduct was unreasonable, there is no liability unless the plaintiff can also establish that the unreasonable conduct caused the plaintiff's injury. There are two kinds of cause: cause in fact and proximate cause.

B. Cause in fact is the term that courts use to mean that the plaintiff must prove the defendant actually caused the injury. This is an issue of fact left almost entirely to the jury's discretion as long as the evidence reveals that a defendant's alleged negligence could have been a substantial, material factor in bringing about an injury.

C. When two or more persons are guilty of negligence, but only one of them actually causes the injury (and the plaintiff cannot tell which one), then the burden of proof as to cause in fact is placed on the defendants. Each defendant must prove that his/her conduct was not the cause of the injury. If the defendant cannot prove this, the joint tortfeasor rule requires that each defendant is jointly and severally liable for the entire judgment.

D. In Sindell v. Abbott Laboratories, the California Supreme Court adopted what it called the "market share theory." When the plaintiff could not identify which defendant in fact manufactured the drug which injured her, the court held all defendants liable according to the percentage of the market they had at the time the plaintiff's mother took the drug.

E. In Abel v. Eli Lilly and Co. the Michigan Supreme Court ruled that the joint tortfeasor rule applied to help an injured plaintiff sue all manufacturers of the drug DES even though no one manufacturer could be identified as the supplier of a particular prescription.

XVI. Causation: Proximate Cause

A. To establish liability, a plaintiff must prove proximate cause as well as cause in fact. The doctrine of proximate cause states that those engaged in unreasonable activity are legally liable only for the foreseeable risks which they cause. Foreseeability means that the plaintiff must be one whom the defendant could reasonably expect to be injured by a negligent act.

B. Example: The defendant ran a red light and hit a car. The loud crash startled the plaintiff, who was walking up some stairs a block away. The plaintiff fell, injuring himself, and now sues the defendant. Even though the defendant in fact caused the injury, a court would likely dismiss the plaintiff's complaint because the injury was not proximately (foreseeably) caused by the negligence.

C. The trend today is for courts to allow juries to decide issues of proximate cause. In general, this has resulted in greater liability for defendants and reflects current concern about distributive justice.

XVII. Defenses of Negligence

A. Contributory negligence or contributory fault aims at the plaintiff's failure to use reasonable care on his/her own behalf. As originally applied, the contributory negligence defense absolutely barred recovery if the plaintiff's fault contributed to the injury in any degree, however slight. In recognition of the harshness of this "all or nothing" approach, the majority of jurisdictions today apply the doctrine of comparative negligence, which compares the plaintiff's fault with the defendant's and reduces the damage award proportionally to the plaintiff's fault.

1. In Insurance Co. of North America v. Pasakarnis the Florida Supreme Court ruled that comparative negligence applied when the plaintiff's automobile accident injuries were caused in part by failure to wear an available seat belt.

B. Voluntary assumption of the risk defense arises from the plaintiff's knowing and willing undertaking of an activity made dangerous by the negligence of another, e.g., a baseball spectator assumes the risk of being hit by a foul ball. Unlike the comparative fault used in the contributory negligence defense, a voluntary assumption of the risk usually totally bars the plaintiff from any recovery for the defendant's negligence.

Strict Liability in Tort

Strict liability in tort is a catchall phrase. It applies to torts that impose liability when the injury-causing behavior is neither negligent nor intentional.

XVIII. Respondeat Superior

A. An employer is strictly liable for an employee's torts that arise in the "scope of employment." This doctrine is called respondeat superior ("let the master reply").

B. Respondeat superior liability exists because the employer has set the employee in motion and is responsible for the employee's acts.

C. The primary defense an employer has to the strict liability of respondeat superior is that the employee was outside the scope of employment (frolic and detour).

XIX. Other Strict Liability Torts

A. In most states courts impose strict liability for ultrahazardous activities such as transporting and using explosives and poisons.

B. The majority of states impose strict liability upon tavern owners for injuries to third parties caused by their intoxicated patrons ("dram shop acts").

C. Common carriers, transportation companies licensed by the public, have strict liability in most instances for damage to goods being transported by them.

D. Strict tort liability for defective products and workers' compensation also apply a type of strict liability. These doctrines are discussed in separate chapters.

XX. Damages

A. The size of damage awards is largely one that juries determine, and jury sympathy toward badly injured plaintiffs plays an important part in the award process.

B. Most damages awarded in tort cases compensate the plaintiff for injuries suffered. To make the plaintiff whole again, at least financially, is the purpose of compensatory damages. These damages include:

1. Past and future medical expenses.
2. Past and future economic losses.
3. Past and future suffering.

C. Punitive or exemplary damages are also available if the plaintiff can prove that the defendant's misconduct was intentional or that it constituted "gross" or "willful and wanton" negligence. Punitive damages are criminal in nature in that they punish those who commit aggravated torts and act to deter future wrongdoing.

D. Note that instead of punishing guilty management for wrongdoings, punitive damages against corporations end up punishing innocent shareholders by reducing their dividends and possibly punishing the consuming public by higher prices for products.

E. As litigation expenses have climbed, plaintiffs and defendants have sought ways to contain costs.

F. One of the most significant cost containment trends is the rapid growth of the structured settlement of awards in personal injury cases. Structured settlements, which provide periodic payments of an award over a term of years, protect plaintiffs who may not possess the necessary experience to handle large sums of money. There are also tax advantages to structured settlements that do not exist with a lump sum award. Structured settlements also benefit defendants and their insurers in that these awards often can be negotiated at lower total costs than the payment of lump sums.

G. Many tort reforms have been proposed at both the state and federal levels.

COMPLETION EXERCISES

1. _______________ imposes legal responsibility for injuries even though the liable party neither intentionally nor negligently causes the harm.

2. _______________ is an illegal, unpermitted touching of another.

3. _______________ is an absolute defense to a claim of defamation.

4. _______________ is a special type of aggravated negligence which shows an extreme disregard for others.

5. _______________ is a negligence doctrine that means "the thing speaks for itself."

6. The "Summers Rule" requires that each tortfeasor is _______________ liable for the entire judgment.

7. _______________ compares the difference between the plaintiff's fault and the defendant's fault and reduces the recovery proportionally.

8. _______________ damages are criminal in nature in that they punish those who commit aggravated torts.

9. _______________ states that if injury occurs because of the negligence of another employee, the negligent employee rather than the employer is liable.

10. _______________ provides the principal statutory protection for trademarks.

11. _______________ usually provide for periodic payments of awards over a term of years rather than in lump sums.

12. Prior to 1800 much of the law of personal property injury was based on the law of ______________.

13. ______________ is the intentional, unjustified confinement of a non-consenting person.

14. If there exists a ______________ between the parties, then there is a duty to refrain from unreasonable non-conduct as well as unreasonable conduct.

15. ______________ is the term used by judges to mean that the plaintiff must prove that the defendant actually caused the injury.

TRUE-FALSE CHOICES

1. _____ The trend toward shifting injury losses off plaintiffs and onto defendants who can best spread the losses shows a concern with "distributive justice."

2. _____ The crucial element of proximate causation is foreseeability.

3. _____ In the U.S. more lawsuits allege negligence than any other single cause of action.

4. _____ Patent protection runs for the inventor's lifetime plus 50 years.

5. _____ Registration of a patent in the Patent Office only creates a presumption of validity.

6. _____ The competitive tort of trade disparagement is prohibited by Section 43(a) of the Lanham Act.

7. _____ Structured settlements mainly favor defendants and offer little or no benefit to injured plaintiffs.

8. _____ Most states have adopted the doctrine of comparative negligence.

9. _____ Truth is an absolute defense to a claim of defamation.

10. _____ Conversion is the wrongful and unlawful exercise of dominion and control over the personal property of another.

11. _____ "Legal cause" is another name for "cause in fact."

12. _____ "Injurious falsehood" is the publication of false statements about another which holds up that individual's character or reputation to contempt or ridicule.

13. _____ More lawsuits allege negligence than any other single cause of action.

14. _____ Workers' compensation statutes have abolished contributory negligence, assumption of risk, and fellow servant defenses in workers' compensation cases.

15. _____ The purpose of compensatory damages is to deter future wrongdoing.

MULTIPLE CHOICE SELECTIONS

1. John is a paying passenger on Barto's Bus Lines. The bus driver knows that another passenger plans to assault John because of his unpopular political views. The driver fails to warn John, and he is injured by the other passenger. Select the most correct answer:

   a. Barto's Bus Lines and the driver would not be liable to John because they did not in fact cause his injuries.
   b. Barto's Bus Lines and the driver are liable since they have a special relationship to John.
   c. Since John knew his political views were unpopular, he voluntarily assumed the risk of injury when he rode in a bus full of people.
   d. Barto's Bus Lines and the driver are not liable since the injury to John was not reasonably foreseeable.

2. All of the following are intentional torts except:

   a. Respondeat superior.
   b. Conversion.
   c. Injurious falsehood.
   d. Trespass.

3. Which of the following statements is false when applied to the negligence doctrine of res ipsa loquitur?

   a. The burden of proof is shifted to the defendant to disprove his or her negligence.
   b. The injury must be one that does not normally occur but for the defendant's negligence.
   c. The defendant must have had exclusive control of the thing that caused the injury.
   d. There must exist a "special relationship" between plaintiff and defendant.

4. Peter Pedant hands out copyrighted materials to his class of 200 college students. He has no permission from the copyright holders. Select the most correct statement:

   a. The handouts violate the copyright laws.
   b. Handouts of collected newspaper clippings to students would not likely violate copyright laws.
   c. Copyright protection is limited to an author's lifetime.
   d. Copyright protection is limited to printed material.

5. All of the following favor plaintiff recovery except:

   a. Joint tortfeasor rule.
   b. Comparative negligence.
   c. Contributory negligence.
   d. Strict liability.

Chapter 10

DISCUSSION ANALYSIS

Discuss trends in torts that favor plaintiffs. In your discussion explain the role the court system has played in these tort trends.

Chapter 11

Products and Service Liability

STUDY GUIDE AND OUTLINE

I. Historical Development of Products Liability

A. Prior to 1800 there were few manufactured products.

1. Tort law of personal and property injury was based on the doctrine of trespass.
2. The trespass doctrine was a strict liability one, i.e., the fact that the defendant was not at fault was irrelevant.

B. In the 1800's products liability law began to change.

1. Negligence law emerged. Product sellers were liable only if they were negligent, i.e., if they failed to use "reasonable care" in selling their wares.
2. The "privity" doctrine further limited sellers' liability. Sellers were liable only to those who had actually bought an injury-causing product from them. This insulated manufacturers from liability unless product users purchased products directly from the manufacturers. Retailers were usually not liable even if they were in privity with an injured party, since they were not negligent.
3. The 1800's were truly a time of caveat emptor, "let the buyer beware."

C. In the 20th century product liability law began to move back toward strict liability.

1. The states gradually abolished the privity doctrine as applied in negligence law.
2. In food, drink, and drug cases courts began to impose the type of strict liability based on an implied warranty which sellers supposedly made to those who might be affected by these products. In the late 1950's the implied warranty doctrine was expanded to cover all types of products.
3. Also in the 1960's courts began to impose strict liability in tort. The first case to impose such liability was the famous Greenman v. Yuba Power Products. In that case the California Supreme Court ruled that a products liability case should not depend upon the complexities of warranty law. The plaintiff could establish strict liability in tort by showing that he was injured while using a defective product in an intended matter. The court stated that a major purpose of strict liability in tort was to force sellers to spread the risk of loss from injuries in the price of the products.

II. Basic Theories of Liability: Introduction

A. Sellers are subject to products liability only when they have breached some legal duty which is owed to an injured party. Such duties may arise:

1. Because of the conduct of the seller.
2. Because of the quality of the product.
3. Because of promises or representations the seller has made.

B. Sellers of products are not insurers. They are not absolutely responsible for all injuries which may occur from the use of their products. There must first exist some duty and a breach of that duty before liability arises.

III. Duty Based Upon Conduct of the Seller: Negligence

A. Sellers are held liable in products liability law for negligence when they breach their duty to use "ordinary and reasonable" care toward someone and that breach of duty "proximately" causes an "injury."

B. Retailers are usually not negligent when they sell defective prepackaged products. It is not legally "reasonable" to expect that a retailer will open every packaged product sold to search for possible injury causing defects.

C. In products liability cases which apply res ipsa loquitur, the plaintiff must show that the product defect occurred while the product was within a defendant's sole control.

D. The doctrine of "proximate cause" holds that even where a defendant injures a plaintiff by unreasonable conduct, the defendant is liable only for injuries that are "foreseeable." It is not foreseeable, e.g., that by running a stop sign and causing a traffic accident a defendant should also cause an elderly man to slip and fall on icy stairs a block from the scene of the accident.

E. In Germann v. Smithe the defendant Smithe sold the plaintiff's employer an hydraulic press with a detachable safety bar. The Minnesota Supreme Court ruled that the employer's removal of the safety bar during servicing was foreseeable and that the defendant owed the plaintiff a duty to warn about the operation of the press without the safety bar.

F. As a products liability theory, negligence is not as important as it once was. Strict liability theories have taken over but negligence concepts are still in widespread use in cases involving defectively designed products. Moreover, juries awards are more likely to be higher for the plaintiffs when the defendant acted unreasonably as contrasted to being held merely strictly liable.

IV. Duty Based Upon Quality of the Product

A. In negligence the seller's duty is to use reasonable care. In strict products liability the duty of the seller is to avoid selling defective products. The emphasis in strict liability is upon the quality of product rather than the conduct of the seller.

B. Strict liability in tort applies in all but a few states. The usual form of this doctrine creates liability for those in the business of selling a product who sell it in a "defective condition unreasonably dangerous to the user or consumer or to his property." A seller may be liable even if he has exercised all possible care. All sellers in the distribution chain, from manufacturer to retailer, can be held liable.

C. Another theory of strict products liability arises from the implied warranty of merchantability.

1. This warranty is implied by law under the Uniform Commercial Code (UCC) into every contract for the sale of goods by one who is in the business of selling goods (i.e., a merchant).
2. Under this warranty it is the seller's duty to supply a product which is "fit for the ordinary purposes for which such goods are used."
3. The implied warranty of merchantability may be disclaimed by the seller under certain conditions.

4. An injured party relying upon this warranty must give notice of the defect to the seller within a "reasonable" time following the injury.
5. This warranty applies only to the sale of goods, but has been recently expanded to cover buyers of new houses that have major construction defects. This theory is called the "implied warranty of habitability."

D. In Hanson v. Funk Seeds International the plaintiff's seed corn failed to grow properly. The court found "unconscionable" a disclaimer in the contract of sale for the seed corn that limited the plaintiff-buyer's remedy for breach to a return of the purchase price. The doctrine of unconscionability is similar to the doctrine of contractual illegality studied in Chapter 9.

V. Duty Based Upon Promises or Representations

A. Sellers place upon themselves an absolute duty of performance for any statements made about products when such statements are a part of the bargain made with the buyers.

B. Under the UCC sellers create an express warranty for any promises about a product. The words "warranty" or "guarantee" do not have to be used in order for the express warranty to arise. A simple statement such as "all moving parts are made of steel" is sufficient to create such a warranty. If the product is not as described or it does not perform as promised, the seller is liable. Special federal law covered in Chapter 13 applies to the making of written warranties to consumers.

C. Also under the UCC if a purchaser relies upon the seller's skill and judgment to select a product to serve a particular mentioned purpose, the seller is liable if the product fails that purpose. This warranty is called the implied warranty of fitness for a particular purpose.

D. The Second Restatement of Torts places tort liability on anyone who misrepresents to the public a material fact about the quality of a product through advertising or labeling.

The Plaintiff's Case

The plaintiff bears the burden of proving his or her case. Whatever the legal theory, there are certain standard elements which a plaintiff must usually prove in a products liability lawsuit. These elements include (1) that the product was defective, (2) that the defect occurred in the hands of the defendant, (3) that the defect caused harm, and (4) that the defect made the product unreasonably dangerous.

VI. Product Defect

A. Except in cases which involve a seller's absolute duty of performance, such as express warranty, it is necessary for the plaintiff to establish that the product causing injury is defective.

B. There are two main types of product defects.

1. Production defects exist where products do not meet the manufacturer's own internal production standards.
2. In a design defect the product acts just as the manufacturer intended it should. A plaintiff alleging a design defect contends that the product's design is not as safe as it should be. In these types of cases the expectations of the user and of society are important.

VII. Defect in the Hands of the Defendant

In order to win a products liability suit, the plaintiff must prove that the product was defective when it was sold by each defendant. Considering a long distribution chain from manufacturer through retailer, one must recognize that it is sometimes very difficult to prove that the defect existed while in the control of each defendant who has been sued. The plaintiff usually consults expert witnesses.

VIII. The Defect Must Have Caused the Harm

To win a products liability lawsuit, the plaintiff must show that a particular defect caused the injury. In dealing with complex products which may have been destroyed in an accident, it is frequently difficult to determine what precise defect caused the harm.

IX. Defect Must Make the Product Unreasonably Dangerous

A. Many products are dangerous. Knives cut, matches burn. This does not mean that sellers of such products are liable when knives wound or when matches start fires. Sellers are liable only when their products are "unreasonably dangerous." Whether or not a product is unreasonably dangerous is a question which most often arises in design defect cases.

B. Proper warnings which accompany a potentially dangerous product can go far toward reducing the possibility that a court might find the product unreasonably dangerous.

C. The court in Karns v. Emerson Electric Co. held that a manufacturer cannot defend on the basis that perfect compliance with its instructions would have prevented the accident when the warnings given are "unclear or inadequate to apprise the consumer of the inherent or latent danger."

X. The Defendant's Case: Parties

A. In products liability lawsuits, plaintiffs usually sue several different parties who may have responsibility for the manufacture, distribution, and sale of the defective product. Different products liability theories may apply to these various parties.

B. Courts in most jurisdictions presently impose strict liability on commercial lessors of defective products.

C. Negligence theory may be applied in every products liability case where the defendant has failed to use ordinary care and has proximately injured the plaintiff. Retailers are usually not negligent in selling pre-packaged products.

D. Courts have applied strict liability in tort and implied warranty of merchantability to all commercial sellers in the distribution chain. This includes retailers, wholesalers, manufacturers, raw material suppliers, manufacturers of component parts, and assemblers of parts. Increasingly, lessors of products and franchisors are being held subject to liability under these legal theories.

XI. Defendant's Defenses

A. The defense of contributory negligence can be raised in a negligence case. To prove this affirmative defense the defendant must show that the plaintiff's failure to use reasonable care contributed to the injury. When contributory negligence is proved, approximately 40 states require the judge to instruct the jury to reduce the amount of any recovery granted the plaintiff by the percentage the jury thinks the plaintiff's conduct contributed to the injury.

B. Most states do not recognize contributory negligence as a bar to recovery under strict products liability theories. There seems to be a trend, however, toward allowing the plaintiff's fault, including assumption of risk and misuse, to be used to offset any damages which might be granted.

C. Where a plaintiff has voluntarily assumed the risk of a defective product, the defendant may raise this as an affirmative defense.

D. Another defense is the state-of-the-art defense. This theory absolves manufacturers of liability for failure to warn of a danger that was undiscovered at the time of product marketing and that was undiscoverable given the state of scientific knowledge at that time. Not all states recognize this defense.

E. The defendant may also avoid the liability showing that the plaintiff deliberately misused the product. Some courts, however, have been reluctant to forbid the plaintiff's recovery where the misuse is foreseeable by the manufacturer.

XII. Industrial Accidents Involving Products

A. Products liability accidents involving employees at work account for almost half of the insurance payout for bodily injury claims.

B. In many states the employer who has paid workers' compensation to an employee because of a product-related injury has the right to recover the entire amount from the manufacturer or seller if there is a product liability claim which can be made. This right is known as a right of "subrogation."

C. Products liability suits arising from on-the-job injuries are of special concern to manufacturers because:

1. The injury-causing equipment has frequently been altered or modified by the employer, and after the accident it is difficult to determine what changes were made in the equipment.
2. In many states the doctrine of subrogation permits an employer to have a full recovery against the manufacturer for workers' compensation payments made by the employer, even if the injury was due to the employer's negligence as well as due to a defective product.

XIII. Indemnification

A. The principle of indemnification permits any seller who is required to pay an injured plaintiff to obtain a full recovery from the party who sold the defective product to the seller. Thus, a retailer who is held liable in a products liability suit can obtain indemnification from the manufacturer, providing that the defect can be traced back to the manufacturer.

B. Where more than one defendant is guilty in a products liability suit and either defendant pays the entire amount of an adverse judgment, that defendant can seek contribution from the other defendant. The exact formula for contribution varies from state to state.

XIV. Product Liability Trends

A. The number of product liability lawsuits has increased rapidly in the past 20 years.

B. Legal developments and growing public awareness have contributed to this increase.

C. A major problem of the products liability system is litigation costs.

D. The Magnuson-Moss Act provides that in breach of warranty cases a losing defendant shall pay the plaintiff's attorney fees and costs. This act has been responsible for increased product liability litigation involving relatively small damages.

XV. Legislative Revision of Products Liability

A. Presently, many manufacturers and insurers are lobbying Congress to pass federal products liability law. This law is seen as bringing uniformity and certainty to products liability.

B. Approximately half the states have enacted legislation reforming the common law development of products liability.

XVI. Management Planning for Products Liability

A. Until recently few companies formally evaluated the dangers of product liability and then followed procedures to lessen them.

B. Today, however, many companies are taking steps to reduce potential products liability:

1. Products safety officers report to top management.
2. Pre-production testing is carried out.
3. Product design is compared with the state of the art.
4. Support documents (such as buyer instructions, labeling, warranties, and advertising) are carefully reviewed by the legal department before a product is released into the marketplace.
5. The company makes plans for possible product recall and monitors buyer experience with the product.

XVII. Service Liability: Overview

A. Another component of the liability explosion in the business and professional communities is service liability. Providers of services frequently become defendants when the services they render cause personal or property injuries.

B. Strict liability theory has not yet reached cases that involve purely the sale of services.

C. Sale of services lawsuits are tried currently under negligence concepts of ordinary and reasonable care.

D. Professional negligence is termed malpractice. The duty to avoid negligence which is placed upon professionals is the duty to act as a reasonable professional.

E. Standards of professional practice set or followed by professional groups are persuasive with courts in determining the presence or absence of liability, though they are by no means conclusive.

XVIII. Malpractice and the Accounting Profession

A. Accountants must exercise that degree of care and competence reasonably expected of members of their profession. Failure to exercise such care amounts to malpractice and liability is based on breach of contract or in tort for negligence.

B. Accounting malpractice toward a client can arise when accountants present a negligently prepared financial statement to a client, and the client relies on it and is injured. Malpractice can also occur during an audit when accountants fail to pursue evidence that a client's employee is defrauding the client.

C. A major issue is when third parties who rely on financial statements negligently prepared for an accountant's client can sue the accountant.

1. Most states impose liability in such instances when the accountant "knows specifically" that a certain third party will rely on a client's financial statement.
2. Some states go further and extend liability when the accountant "specifically foresees" that a limited class of third parties will rely on the financial statement.
3. As Sibdee-Dosco, Inc. v. Cherry, Bekaert & Holland shows, liability for accountants' negligent misrepresentation extends not only to those with whom the accountant is in privity or near privity, but also to those persons or classes of persons, whom he knows will rely on his/her opinion, or whom he knows his client intends to have rely on his/her opinion.

D. Liability for fraud is usually imposed on an accountant with regard to any third party who relies on misstatements in a financial statement where the accountant knows the information is false or is reckless as to its correctness.

COMPLETION EXERCISES

1. _______________ is a contract doctrine once applied in products liability tort cases which limited liability of sellers to those specific persons with whom they had a contract.

2. _______________ is the doctrine of "let the buyer beware."

3. The failure to act as a "reasonable man" which proximately causes injury to another is known as _______________.

4. The doctrine that anyone engaged in the business of selling a product who sells it in a "defective condition unreasonably dangerous to the user or consumer or to his property" is liable for injuries caused by the defective product is known as _______________.

5. _______________ is a guarantee by the seller that the product sold is "fit for the ordinary purposes for which such goods are used."

6. _______________ is a type of liability which makes a seller an insurer. Such liability may be found where the seller has breached an _______________.

7. A doctrine which gets the plaintiff to the jury on the issue of breach of duty in a negligence case where the product was within the sole control of the defendant when it became defective and when the defect would not normally have occurred in the absence of negligence is _______________.

8. In product liability cases the defendant is liable only for injuries that are "foreseeable" under the doctrine of _______________.

9. The defense that a manufacturer was not aware of a product design defect because the danger was scientifically unknown at the time of manufacture is known as the _______________ defense.

10. _______________ is a defense based on plaintiff's conduct where the plaintiff knowingly and voluntarily encounters a known product danger.

11. The condition in a product which causes it to fail to meet the standards of safety which society expects is called the _______________.

12. The principle of _______________ permits any seller who must pay an injured plaintiff full recovery from the party from whom the seller purchased the defective product.

13. The right of an employer who has paid workers' compensation to an employee injured by a defective piece of equipment to stand in the place of the employee for purposes of exercising a products liability claim is the right of _______________.

14. A limit on the time period during which products liability suits may be brought because of a defective, injury-causing product is created by _______________.

15. The duty to avoid negligence that is placed upon professionals is the duty to act as a _______________.

TRUE-FALSE CHOICES

1. _____ An express warranty places an absolute duty of performance on a seller.

2. _____ Most states impose malpractice liability against accountants in favor of all foreseeably injured third parties.

3. _____ Some courts have imposed products liability even when injured plaintiffs have misused products.

4. ______ Prior to 1800 much of the tort law of personal and property injury was based on the doctrine of trespass.

5. ______ The development of privity doctrine enhanced the ability of the plaintiff to recover from sellers in products liability cases.

6. ______ It is legally "reasonable" to expect that a retailer will open every can of peas to discover whether or not there is a nail in them.

7. ______ Section 402A of the Second Restatement of Torts specifically extends strict tort liability to "bystanders."

8. ______ Most states allow injured parties to recover "economic" damages under strict tort liability.

9. ______ The implied warranty of merchantability guarantees that goods sold are properly packaged.

10. ______ "Seller disclaims all warranties" is sufficient language to exclude the implied warranty of merchantability from a sale.

11. ______ The meeting of government standards for product design ensures that a seller will not be held liable in a court for defectively designing the product.

12. ______ A "merchant" is any person who sells a product for use or consumption.

13. ______ The seller of a used product is not held liable under products liability theories when the product is defective and injures a buyer.

14. ______ The state-of-the-art defense is available in all jurisdictions since it is a provision of federal products liability law.

15. ______ An accountant may not be held liable for malpractice if he/she was observing "generally accepted accounting principles."

MULTIPLE CHOICE SELECTIONS

1. All of the following were products liability developments of the late 1970's except:

   a. Insurance premium rates grew rapidly.
   b. The number of products liability suits filed declined slightly.
   c. The average damage award received by plaintiffs grew dramatically.
   d. Product managers became concerned about releasing new products onto the market.

2. John Consumer uses a frying pan to hammer a nail into the wall. Under the force of the blows, the handle snaps off, and the heavy pan drops on John's foot, permanently injuring it. John is unlikely to be able to recover against the manufacturer of the pan in a products liability suit because of:

   a. Assumption of risk.
   b. Subrogation.
   c. Misuse.
   d. Caveat venditor.

3. The highest duty placed on a seller of a product may be found in the doctrine of:

   a. Negligence.
   b. Strict tort liability.
   c. Implied warranty of merchantability.
   d. Express warranty.

4. A defective soft drink bottle explodes in a grocery store and puts out the eye of the shopper who has just picked it up. The store manager was also injured by the same explosion when the loud noise caused him to slip from a chair on which he was standing to replace a light bulb on the other side of the store. Select the correct statement:

   a. The shopper is unlikely to be able to recover against anyone since he had not actually purchased the product.
   b. The implied warranty of merchantability will probably enable the injured store manager to recover for his injury.
   c. The shopper assumed the risk by picking up the bottle.
   d. The store manager will likely be barred from recovery due to the proximate causation doctrine.

5. "These shirts are permanently pressed." This statement made by a manufacturer's sales representative to a retailer who subsequently purchases a gross of the shirts creates:

   a. An express warranty.
   b. An implied warranty of merchantability.
   c. An implied warranty of fitness for a particular purpose.
   d. No warranty.

Chapter 11

DISCUSSION ANALYSIS

The Johnson Company sells 100 power lawnmowers to All-City Wholesalers, which resells twenty of the mowers to Harold's Hardware. Harold's sells one of the mowers to Mr. Doe. While using the mower one day, Mr. Doe's gardener is injured when a defective blade-bolt breaks and the blade flies off and slashes his leg. The blade ricochets off a telephone pole and badly cuts the arm of Mrs. Smith, a nearby pedestrian.

Considering these facts in light of products liability law, carefully analyze the rights and liabilities of each party mentioned.

Chapter 12

Selecting the Form of Business Organization

STUDY GUIDE AND OUTLINE

I. Introduction

A. The question of selecting the best-suited organization for a business' purpose is of vital importance when it encounters a substantial change, such as rapid growth.

B. The selection process balances advantages against disadvantages in order to identify the organizational form deemed most suitable to the business.

II. Alternatives of Organizational Form

A. Business is conducted under a variety of legal forms, including the:

1. Sole proprietorship, which is a business owned by one person. Its income is taxed to the individual owner. All debts incurred are those of the proprietor.
2. Partnership, which is a business operated by two or more persons for profit. If some of the partners have limited liability, a limited partnership, as contrasted with a general partnership, is created.
3. Corporation, which is a business owned by stockholders. There are specialized forms of corporations, such as the professional corporation, which is an organization for such services as law and medicine. An S corporation is a closely held corporation that is taxed like a partnership.

B. Before a business is created, there must be significant consideration given to selection of the appropriate form of organization. Factors such as legal capacity, creation, taxation, liability, operation, and continuity are important considerations in this decision-making process.

III. General Factors: Advantages and Disadvantages of Partnerships

A. Advantages of partnerships include:

1. Easy, low-cost formation.
2. No taxes as an entity.
3. Equal voice in management for every partner, unless agrees otherwise.
4. Multistate operation without getting a license in each state.
5. Less government regulation as a general rule.

B. Disadvantages of partnership include:

1. Practical limits on the number of persons who can be partners.
2. Dissolution of the partnership everytime a partner dies or withdraws from it.
3. Unlimited personal liability for each partner.
4. Taxation of partnership profits to each partner, whether or not the profits are distributed to the partners.
5. Inability of limited partners to participate in partnership management.

IV. General Factors: Advantages and Disadvantages of Corporations

A. Advantages of corporations include:

1. Ease of bringing together many investors.
2. Possibility of having corporate control in those with a minority of the total investment.
3. Ease of having ownership in unequal shares.
4. Liability limited to investment.
5. Perpetual corporate existence.
6. Owners may also be employees entitled to benefits.

B. Disadvantages of corporations include:

1. Expense of forming and maintaining a corporation.
2. Corporate fees and special taxes.
3. Double taxation of corporate incomes (first to corporation, then to the shareholder).
4. Requirement that a corporation be licensed in each state where it does business.
5. Greater government regulation.
6. Requirement that an attorney represent the corporation in any litigation. In Land Management v. Department of Environmental Protection a Maine court ruled that a corporation could appear in court only if represented by an attorney. To allow otherwise would mean that an agent of the corporation who was not an attorney would be representing a client in court.

V. Legal Capacity

A. Legal capacity refers to the capacity of a business organization to:

1. Sue and be sued in its own name.
2. Own and dispose of property.
3. Enter into contracts in its own name.

B. A corporation has full legal capacity. Modern statutes also permit a partnership to sue and be sued and to buy and sell property in its own name.

VI. Creating Partnerships

A. A partnership is created by an agreement of two or more parties to carry on a business for profit. If the agreement is in writing, it is usually known as Articles of Copartnership.

B. A partnership may also arise by implication from the parties' conduct. The sharing of net profits of a business enterprise by two persons raises a presumption of partnership between them. A partnership may also exist when a partner by conduct leads third persons to believe a partnership exists, and the third person acts in reliance on this conduct (partnership by estoppel).

C. Lupien v. Malsbenden illustrates that conduct may create a partnership though the parties do not call themselves partners. In this case the plaintiff Lupien contracted with Craig to build him a Bradley car. In checking upon his car, however, Lupien usually dealt with Malsbenden. Malsbenden loaned him a car and advised him on paying for the Bradley. After Craig disappeared, Malsbenden had physical control of the premises. When the Bradley was not forthcoming Lupien sued Malsbenden. The court ruled that Malsbenden was a partner of Craig even though Malsbenden claimed that he had only financed Craig's business.

D. In selecting a partnership name, the partnership may not imply that it is a corporation. Also, if the name is other than the name of the partners, it must be registered under the assumed name statute.

VII. Creating Corporations

A. A corporation is created by the state's issuing a charter upon the application of individuals known as incorporators. Corporations are more costly to form than partnerships. There are also annual costs in continuing the corporation such as franchise taxes, the cost of shareholders' meetings, and legal fees. Unlike partnerships, corporations must retain an attorney for representation in any litigation.

B. The corporate charter contains the proposed name of the corporation. It must not be the same as, or deceptively similar to, any other corporation authorized to do business in that state. The name is a part of goodwill and, as such, it is legally protected.

C. Incorporators apply for a corporate charter by filing Articles of Incorporation with the state. In addition to a proposed name, these articles contain information about the:

1. Corporation's period of duration.
2. Purpose for which the corporation was formed.
3. Class, value, and number of shares of stock.
4. Names and addresses of the board of directors.
5. Corporate agent for receiving legal papers.

VIII. Creating Limited Partnerships

A. A limited partnership is a hybrid between a general partnership and a corporation. It has at least one general partner with unlimited liability and one or more limited partners whose liability is limited to the extent of their investments. Like a general partnership, it is created by agreement. But, like a corporation, a certificate similar to a charter must be recorded in a public office to give public notice as to the details of the organization.

B. The certificate must be recorded in every county where the partnership does business. The certificate must be updated as the limited partnership changes. Failure to comply with these requirements gives the limited partners the unlimited liability of general partners.

C. The court in Reilly v. Randers Management, Inc. held that when the number of partners is increased, it is not a change in the method of allocation of the profits and losses, but rather, is simply a change in the number of people to whom the profits and losses will be allocated.

IX. Continuity of Organizations

A. A corporate charter may grant a corporation perpetual existence if the incorporators request it. Most do.

B. A partnership dissolves whenever a partner dies, withdraws, or is added.

C. Dissolution does not necessarily mean that the business must end. If the partners arrange a buy and sell agreement in their articles of copartnership, they can value the partnership and use insurance or some other arrangement to buy out the dissolving partner's interest in the business.

D. Buy and sell agreements can also be used in corporations owned by only a few investors ("closely held" corporations). In Renberg v. Zarrow an Oklahoma court ruled valid a corporate buy and sell agreement allowing surviving shareholders the right to purchase the shares of any deceased shareholder.

X. Control in Partnerships

A. Unless there is an agreement to the contrary, each partner in a general partnership has an equal voice in the firm's affairs and has an equal right to possess partnership property. In a limited partnership, the general partners with unlimited liability have legal control.

B. Each general partner can bind the partnership for acts within the scope of the partnership business. What is and is not within the scope of business is highly technical. Some of these technical rules are covered in the next chapter.

XI. Control of Large Corporations

A. Corporations are controlled legally by their board of directors who are elected by shareholders. In very large corporations, management often dominates boards by soliciting voting proxies from shareholders at corporate expense.

B. Corporations are sometimes controlled by persons who have contributed less than a majority of the investment funding. One way to get this type of minority control is for both voting and nonvoting stock to be issued. As long as a majority of the voting stock is controlled, a person can control the corporation even when he or she has paid in a minority of the total investment.

XII. Control of Closely Held Corporations

A. In a closely held corporation, the owners of the minority interest are usually subject to the wishes of the majority. This control presents opportunities for abuse. The majority owners can appoint themselves as highly paid employees and never declare a dividend.

B. Minority interest owners in a closely held corporation should always insist on buy and sell agreements so they can sell their stock when they want to get rid of it.

C. If the majority shareholders act illegally in controlling the corporation, the minority may sue to collect damages or enjoin them through a derivative action on behalf of the corporation.

XIII. Liability Factors: Partnerships

A. General partners have joint and several liability. Each is potentially liable for all partnership debts.

B. The liability of limited partners is limited to their investment. A limited partner can lose limited liability if she:

1. Allows use of her surname in the partnership name, or
2. Participates in management of the business.

C. In Trans-Am Builders, Inc. v. Woods Mill, Ltd., a Georgia court ruled that a limited partner did not become liable as a general partner merely upon advising the general partner and visiting the partnership business.

XIV. Liability Factors: Corporations

A. Traditionally, investors in a corporation have limited liability. But this is an oversimplification. Although an investor of a large publicly held corporation usually will incur no risk greater than the investment, the shareholders of a small, closely held corporation will be required by creditors to guarantee personally most corporate debts.

B. Shareholders are also personally liable for corporate debts when a court "pierces the corporate veil." Piercing the corporate veil occurs when:

1. The corporation is used to defraud or otherwise to avoid obligations, e.g., a duty not to compete.
2. The corporation is used to evade a statute.
3. One corporation is organized and controlled in a manner that makes it the mere alter ego of another corporation.

C. In Castleberry v. Branscum, the court held that constructive fraud (the standard for disregarding the corporate fiction on the basis of a sham to perpetrate fraud) had occurred and the defendants were individually liable.

XV. Taxation Factors: Partnerships

A. A partnership is not a taxable entity, but this does not mean that the profits are free of income tax. A partnership files an information return which allocates to each individual partner a proportionate share of profits or losses. Partners then pay individual income tax on allocated profits and use losses to offset personal income gained from non-partnership sources.

B. The use of limited partnerships in the 1980s has dramatically increased. When thousands of limited partners are involved master limited partnerships have been formed.

XVI. Taxation Factors: Corporations

A. A corporation pays income tax on its earnings. Currently, the tax rate runs from fifteen to thirty-four percent.

B. In addition to the direct tax, corporate income is taxed again to shareholders when distributed as dividends. The rate of this second tax depends on the personal tax rate of the shareholder receiving the dividend.

C. In addition to double taxation, a tax disadvantage of the corporate form is that operating losses cannot be used to offset individual shareholder income from other sources.

XVII. Avoiding Double Taxation

A. There are certain techniques for partially avoiding the double taxation on corporate income, such as:

1. Deduction of reasonable salaries paid to corporate officials as a business expense. In a closely held corporation in which most shareholders are employees, this technique avoids double taxation of a substantial amount of income. The IRS disallows deduction for excessive compensation and treats such payments as dividends.
2. The use of interest-bearing loans from shareholders in which the interest is a deductible business expense. Just as in the case of salaries, the IRS does not allow all interest deductions. If the corporation is found to be undercapitalized, interest payments are treated as dividends and disallowed as deductions.
3. The subchapter S corporation. The IRS allows closely held business corporations to be treated as partnerships for income tax purposes, and to avoid corporate income tax. Subchapter S corporations cannot have over 35 shareholders, each of whom must elect to be taxed as a partner. This method of organization has distinct advantages for a corporation operating at a loss because the loss is immediately deductible on the returns of the individual shareholders.

Chapter 12

COMPLETION EXERCISES

1. A ______________ corporation is a closely held corporation that is taxed like a partnership.

2. ______________ is where a partner by his conduct leads third persons to believe a partnership exists, and the third person acts in reliance on this conduct.

3. ______________ is the phrase used when the corporate entity is disregarded.

4. ______________ partners do not participate in management of the partnership.

5. The purpose of the ______________ tax is to compel companies to distribute any profit to shareholders that is not needed to conduct normal business operations.

6. A partnership is easily created since all that is required is a ______________.

7. ______________ is a business owned by one person and its income is taxed to the individual.

8. Limited partners generally have ______________ liability.

9. Modern statutes permit a partnership to sue and be sued and to buy and sell property ______________.

10. A written partnership agreement is usually referred to as ______________.

11. If a partnership name is other than the name of the partners it must be registered under the ______________.

12. A corporation is created by the state's issuing a ______________.

13. If a corporation is not to be denied access to the courts, it must be ______________ in every state where it does business.

14. If a partner dies or withdraws from a partnership, or if a new partner is admitted, the partnership is ______________.

15. A corporation owned by only a few investors is called a ______________.

TRUE-FALSE CHOICES

1. ______ A general partnership can be established only after approval by the state.

2. ______ Since partnerships are distinct entities, they must retain an attorney in any litigation.

3. ______ A proposed corporate name must not be the same as, or deceptively similar to, that of any other legitimate corporation in the state.

4. ______ A partnership is not a taxable entity and therefore must not file any return with the Internal Revenue Service.

5. ______ One way to avoid the double taxation of corporate income is to deduct reasonable salaries paid to officers as a business expense.

6. ______ Interest bearing loans from stockholders to their corporations can help reduce the impact of double taxation.

7. ______ All salaries paid to corporate employees are deductible as reasonable business expenses.

8. ______ As a practical matter, the management of large publicly held corporations often control their boards of directors.

9. ______ Buy and sell agreements are an essential part of the creation of partnerships and small corporations.

10. ______ Partners may use partnership losses to offset personal income gained from nonpartnership sources.

11. ______ Double taxation of corporate income is largely unavoidable.

12. ______ In the Subchapter S form corporate profits are subject to double taxation.

13. ______ A limited partnership with thousands of limited partners is called a "master limited partnership."

14. ______ In the 1980s the use of limited partnerships declined.

15. ______ If majority shareholders act illegally in controlling the corporation, the minority may sue to collect damages or to enjoin them through a derivative action.

MULTIPLE CHOICE SELECTIONS

1. Mr. Jones and Mr. Smith want to start a business but do not know what form of organization would best serve their purposes. They each have minor children and wish to give the business income to them. Jones and Smith also forecast losses in the business for the first four years, but each has enough outside income to keep the business operating until it can turn a profit. Select the best form of business organization to meet their needs:

   a. General Partnership - Each partner would be taxed individually so the early business losses can immediately be used to offset the partners' other income.
   b. Corporation - Each party can make his children stockholders and funnel income to taxpayers in a lower tax bracket.
   c. Subchapter S Corporation - Has the advantages of both a. and b.
   d. Sole Proprietorship - Let either Mr. Jones or Mr. Smith actually own the business and pay the other a high salary, thereby creating a large deductible business expense.

2. Which of the following is not a characteristic of a limited partnership?

   a. The limited partners have liability limited to their investment.
   b. The limited partners do not participate in the day-to-day affairs of the partnership.
   c. There must be one or more general partners in a limited partnership.
   d. To be created a limited partnership needs only an agreement between the parties.

3. Select the incorrect statement. Legal capacity refers to the capacity of a business organization to:

   a. Pay out profits to its investors.
   b. Sue and be sued in its own name.
   c. Own and dispose of property.
   d. Enter into contracts in its own name.

4. Select the incorrect statement. Advantages of corporations include:

   a. Ease of bringing together many investors.
   b. Perpetual existence.
   c. Multistate operation without getting a license in each state.
   d. Possibility of having control in those with a minority of the total investment.

5. Mr. Holmes is chairman of the board and majority stockholder of a closely held corporation. He wishes to expand the company's facilities and needs to sell additional stock to raise the required capital. Which of the following would raise the required capital without risk that Mr. Holmes would lose control of the corporation?

   a. Issue and sale of non-voting preferred stock.
   b. Issue and sale of voting common stock.
   c. Sale of stock options to employees.
   d. None of the above is correct.

DISCUSSION ANALYSIS

John and Mary wish to set up a business to manufacture exercise equipment. Start-up costs are estimated to be $200,000. John plans to contribute $50,000 and is willing to help promote the business, but wishes not to participate in the day-to-day running of the business since he holds another job. Mary has no money to contribute, but she intends to help promote the business and to participate in the management of the business. The business will likely lose money for the first three years of its existence. Discuss what kind of business organization might best suit this new enterprise.

Chapter *13*

Liability of Business Organizations and Managers

STUDY GUIDE AND OUTLINE

I. Terminology

A. The term agency applies to those situations where one person acts on behalf of another. A principal is the person or organization controlling the activities of an agent who acts on behalf of the principal.

B. Principals and agents owe to one another the duty of loyalty and honesty. This is called the fiduciary relationship.

C. In general, a third party who has signed a contract with an agent wants the principal bound to the contract. Likewise, when a third party is injured by an employee, that third party usually wishes to recover from the employer because the employer has a "deep pocket." Liability is imposed in these situations only when the agent is acting "within the scope of authority" or the employee is acting "within the scope of employment."

II. Actual Authority

A. An agent may bind the principal contractually if the agent has actual authority. Actual authority can rise from two sources:

1. A principal can give express authority to an agent in written or oral form.
2. Actual authority may also be implied from the conduct of the parties from customary practices or from a particular situation. Implied authority is necessary for an agent to carry out the express authority granted.

III. Apparent Authority

A. Apparent (or ostensible) authority arises when the principal has led third parties to believe that the agent has authority even though none has been granted. When apparent authority exists, the principal is bound to the third party as if the agent were acting within actual authority.

B. Apparent authority may also increase the actual authority of an agent. Note that the agent cannot create his or her own apparent authority. It must be based on the principal's words or conduct.

C. The typical situation of apparent authority is when the actual authority is terminated, but notice is not given to third parties of the termination.

IV. Ratification

A. In general, a principal is not liable for the unauthorized acts of an agent. However, the principal may ratify the unauthorized acts of an agent.

B. For a valid ratification to occur, the principal must

1. Have capacity to do what the agent has done.
2. Be known to the third party.
3. Have full knowledge of the facts.

C. The court in Perkins v. Philbrick held that for ratification of an agent's actions to occur, it is necessary that all material facts be known by the principal.

V. Introduction to Agency and Contract Liability

A. Generally, a known agent has no personal liability to third parties on contracts authorized by the principal. However, an agent who exceeds authority granted is personally liable on contracts.

B. Also, an agent who fails to disclose the principal's identity or the agency relationship is personally liable. Partial disclosure occurs when the third party knows a principal exists but does not know the principal's actual identity.

VI. Liability of Principals

A. The principal is obligated to hold the agent free from liability if the agency acted within the scope of the actual authority granted. The principal thus has an obligation to indemnify the agent.

B. When the principal is disclosed, that principal becomes contractually bound to the third party if the agent acted with actual or apparent authority or if the principal has ratified an agent's unauthorized actions.

VII. Liability of Agents to Principals

A. The fiduciary duty of loyalty requires that agents avoid conflicts of interest. For example, agents cannot enter into contracts on behalf of the principal with themselves as the other party unless the principal gives permission after full disclosure of all facts. The principal may void such contracts and recover any profit made by the agent in violation of the duty of loyalty.

B. Many violations of the duty of loyalty often involve improper use of confidential information. In J&K Computer Systems, Inc. v. Parrish an employer sued a former employee and his corporation to obtain damages and to enjoin them from using or disclosing the plaintiff's confidential computer programs. The court held that although the former employee could use general knowledge or experience obtained from working for the plaintiff, he could not misuse trade secrets belonging to the plaintiff. The defendants were enjoined and ordered to pay $7,500.

VIII. Liability of Third Parties

A. A third party is bound to a disclosed principal on contracts negotiated by an agent who had actual or apparent authority or if an agent's acts were ratified.

B. Generally, a third party does not become personally liable to the agent because the principal is substituted for the agent; however, there are several exceptions.

IX. Agency and Tort Liability - Basic Concepts

In addition to the contract liability issues arising out of an agency, questions of liability for injuries to a third party's person or property also may be present.

X. Respondeat Superior

A. In Sanford v. Kobley Bros. Const. Corp. the court ruled that an employee is always liable for his or her own torts, even if the employer is also liable. The court found that an employee who authorized a negligent construction of a house was jointly and severally liable along with the employer.

B. The doctrine that an employer is liable for the torts of an employee if the employee acts within the scope of his or her employment is called respondeat superior. This doctrine serves the public policy by placing liability on a party who is most capable of paying for the damage done.

Liability of Organizations

XI. Introduction

When the principal (master) is a business, that organization also may have liability due to its employees' acts.

XII. Liability Based on the Criminal Law: Business Organizations

A. Although corporate organizations cannot be imprisoned, they can be fined for crimes committed by their agents.

B. A number of other chapters cover various statutes that impose criminal liability on business organizations.

XIII. Civil Liability

A. In addition to criminal penalties, business organizations may become liable to pay money damages.

B. The complicity rule seeks to determine the blameworthiness of the organization for the injury. The court in Mercury Motor Express v. Smith held that since the plaintiff alleged no fault on the part of the employer and relied entirely on the master-servant relationship, the employer was not vicariously liable for punitive damages.

C. Palmateer v. International Harvester Co. teaches that the foundation of the tort of retaliatory discharge lies in the protection of public policy, and there is a clear public policy favoring investigation and prosecution of criminal offenses.

XIV. Special Aspects of Managerial Liability: Partners

A. The general laws of agency apply to partnerships. Each partner is an agent of the organization and both a principal and an agent with respect to all fellow partners.

B. Each partner is potentially liable for the torts and contracts of every other partner. However, any partner who has liability due to another partner's tort can seek contribution from the partner at fault.

XV. Managerial Liability: Officers and Directors

A. The liability of corporate officers and directors most frequently arises because of violation of the fiduciary duty of loyalty owed to the corporation.

B. Directors and officers of a corporation are liable to the corporation for failure to exercise due care in their duties. Directors of a corporation are not liable for honest mistakes as long as they are using their best business judgment in decision making.

XVI. **Corporate Officers and Directors - Contracts and Torts**

A. The officers and directors of a corporation may become personally liable for breach of a contract or for committing a tort.

B. The court in Mississippi Printing v. Maris, West & Baker held that when a corporate officer directly participates in or authorizes the commission of a tort, even on behalf of the corporation, he may be held personally liable.

C. Based on the general legal principles of agency, the officers and directors of a corporation may become personally liable for breach of a contract or for a tort.

D. Note that an officer or director of a corporation is liable for a tort that he or she commits, sanctions, or approves.

XVII. **Liability Based on Criminal Law: Corporate Executives**

A. Corporate executives can be liable for criminal acts of employees under certain circumstances.

B. In United States v. Park the CEO of a large national food chain was held criminally liable under the Food, Drug, and Cosmetic Act. The Supreme Court ruled that he could be found guilty by virtue of the fact that his position and power allowed him to prevent the exposure of food shipments to rodents, although he claimed that one of his "dependable subordinates" was responsible for handling the situation.

XVIII. **Ethical Considerations**

A. True loyalty to a corporation should involve seeing that the corporation operates within the law.

B. Many corporate codes of ethics require that employees operate within the law.

COMPLETION EXERCISES

1. A _______________ is the person or organization who controls the activities of an agent.

2. Actual authority may take two basic forms. It can be _______________ or _______________.

3. Apparent authority is sometimes called _______________ authority.

4. A principal can become liable for the unauthorized acts of an agent that are beyond express or apparent authority if he or she _______________ the unauthorized acts.

5. An agent can become liable on a contract made with a third party on behalf of his or her principal upon failing to _______________ the principal's identity to the third party.

6. An employer is not liable for the torts of an _______________ contractor.

7. For ratification of an agent's actions to occur, the principal must know all _______________ facts.

8. When an agent is acting within the scope of agency and incurs personal liability, the principal must _______________ the agent.

9. Whether a person is an employee or an independent contractor is determined by the degree of _______________ the employing party exercises.

10. In recent years, courts increasingly have imposed liability upon businesses even though they have not violated a statute, upon the basis of _______________.

11. _______________ authority is that which is given orally or in writing to the agent by the principal.

12. A principal's liability for the torts of an agent is created by the doctrine of _______________.

13. The _______________ rule seeks to determine an organization's civil liability for punitive damages.

14. The _______________ prohibits corporate directors from acting with a conflict of interest.

15. Employers are liable only for employee torts committed while the employees are acting _______________.

TRUE-FALSE CHOICES

1. _____ For a ratification to be valid the principal must have full knowledge of all the facts associated with the agent's actions.

2. _____ The principal must hold the agent free from liability if the agent has acted within the scope of the actual authority granted.

3. _____ Respondeat superior requires that agents avoid conflicts of interest.

4. _____ In general, agents are personally liable to third parties for contracts that they enter on behalf of their principals.

5. _____ Generally, a third party does not become personally liable to the agent with whom he signs a contract.

6. _____ An employee who commits a tort within the scope of his employment is not personally liable for the damages he or she causes.

7. _____ Respondeat superior is based on a "deep pocket" theory of liability.

8. _____ Although corporations cannot be imprisoned, they can be fined criminally.

9. _____ The general laws of agency apply to partnerships.

10. _____ An agent who fails to disclose the principal's identity is personally liable on contracts.

11. _____ General partners are liable for all transactions entered into by other partners in the scope of the partnership business.

12. _____ The doctrine of respondeat superior makes businesses liable for the torts of their independent contractors.

13. _____ Directors owe no fiduciary duties to their corporations.

14. _____ A CEO of a large corporation can be convicted of an employee's crime even when the CEO has no direct connection with its commission.

15. _____ In general, a principal is not liable for the unauthorized acts of an agent.

MULTIPLE CHOICE SELECTIONS

1. Select the incorrect statement regarding the liability of principals:

   a. The principal is obligated to hold the agent free from liability if the agent has acted within the scope of the actual authority granted.
   b. When the principal is disclosed, he or she becomes contractually bound to the third party upon ratifying an agent's unauthorized actions.
   c. When an undisclosed principal's identity becomes known, a third party can hold the principal liable on a contract entered into with the principal's agent.
   d. All of the above are correct statements.

2. Select the incorrect statement about the liability of agents:

   a. An agent may be liable to the principal for breach of the fiduciary duty.
   b. Violations of fiduciary duty often involve improper use of confidential information.
   c. An agent may not exceed actual authority and still contractually bind a disclosed principal to the third party.
   d. When a principal is bound because of the apparent authority of the agent, the principal may recover from the agent for any performance the principal owes to the third party.

3. Select the incorrect general statement about agency and tort liability:

   a. An employee committing a tort is liable for the damage done.
   b. An employer is liable for the torts of employees who were acting within the scope of employment.
   c. An employer who hires an independent contractor usually is not liable for the torts of that independent contractor.
   d. All of the above statements are correct.

4. Kelly is a part-time employee of Mr. Pots. Kelly's duties include odd jobs such as running errands for Mr. Pots. While driving on an errand in a company truck, Kelly negligently injures a third party. Select the most correct answer:

   a. Kelly is personally liable, but Mr. Pots is not since he was not driving.
   b. Kelly is liable and so is Mr. Pots under the doctrine of respondeat superior.
   c. Kelly is liable, but Mr. Pots is not since the business is a sole proprietorship.
   d. Kelly is not liable, but Mr. Pots is since the accident occurred while Kelly was driving a company vehicle.

5. Mr. X is a buying agent for Mr. Y. Mr. X enters into a contract to purchase goods from a third party, but fails to notify the third party that he is an agent of Mr. Y's. Select the most correct answer:

   a. If Mr. X executed the contract according to his actual authority, only Mr. Y can be held liable on the contract.
   b. Mr. X cannot act as an agent without disclosing the identity of his principal.
   c. The third party can sue Mr. X personally if there is a breach of the contract.
   d. Mr. X has ostensible authority to enter into the contract.

Chapter 13

DISCUSSION ANALYSIS

Ms. Orange is acting as the agent for a large chemical company that is seeking to buy land for a new plant site. She is instructed by her principal not to disclose her agency relationship. She enters into contracts with a number of land owners in her own name. When the local newspaper reports that a large chemical company is buying up land in the area, the sellers realize that Ms. Orange was really representing the chemical company. Can they void their contracts with Ms. Orange? Is Ms. Orange liable on the contracts? Is the chemical company liable on the contracts? Explain.

Chapter 14

International Transactions

STUDY GUIDE AND OUTLINE

I. Introduction

A. International business activities generate more than one-third of the U.S. gross national product.

B. Internationally, not only may the law of one country differ from the law of another, but fundamental variations may exist in the basic structure of the legal systems.

C. The relevant international legal environment does not consist of a body of uniform principles. It contains:

1. U.S. domestic law.
2. The laws of other countries.
3. Multilateral and regional agreements or treaties.
4. Customary international law.

D. This chapter discusses selected important issues for firms engaging in international business transactions. They include:

1. Methods of conducting international business,
2. Risks involved in international trade,
3. The legal institutions and agreements affecting international business,
4. Domestic laws having international trade consequences.

E. Choosing a method of doing business in other countries requires the consideration of many factors. They include marketing and finance factors as well as international law ones.

Methods of Conducting International Business

II. Foreign Sales

A. An irrevocable letter of credit is commonly used in international transactions to insure that a buyer will pay for goods ordered. The letter of credit comes from an issuing bank in the buyer's country. It goes to a confirming bank located in the United States. The letter of credit guarantees that the purchase price of the goods will be paid when the seller presents evidence (bill of lading) to the confirming bank that the goods have been shipped. The confirming bank then forwards the bill of lading to the issuing bank that enables the buyer to take possession of the goods when they arrive.

B. Both U.S. laws and the laws of other countries may prohibit the sale of certain types of goods to foreign countries.

III. Licenses or Franchises

A. Licensing concerns the transfer of intangible property rights, such as patents, copyrights, trademarks, or manufacturing processes, in exchange for the payment of royalties in the foreign country.

B. Licensing is often used as a transitional technique for firms expanding international operations, since the risks are considerably less than with direct foreign investment.

IV. Direct Foreign Investment

A. Most countries will permit a foreign firm to conduct domestic business only if an individual or firm of the host country is designated as its legal representative. The usual practice then is for the foreign firm to create a subsidiary in the host country.

B. The form of subsidiary most closely resembling a U.S. corporation is known as a societe anonyme (S.A.) or, in German-speaking countries, an Aktiengesellschaft (A.G.).

C. In many instances, the only legally or politically possible means a firm has to invest in a foreign country is to engage in a joint venture with an entity from the host country.

V. Expropriation and Nationalization

A. If a domestic firm locates assets in a foreign country, these assets may be expropriated. Expropriation is the seizure of foreign-owned property by a government. In the United States, expropriation is called power of eminent domain.

B. Expropriation (sometimes called nationalization) of domestic firms by foreign governments, when accompanied by unsatisfactory offers of compensation, has led domestic companies to file suit in U.S. courts to seek more satisfactory compensation. Two related doctrines pose serious obstacles for recovery in such situations:

VI. Sovereign Immunity and the Act of State Doctrine

A. The act-of-state doctrine provides that "the courts of one country will not sit in judgment on the acts of the government of another." The Foreign Assistance Act of 1964 directs that the act-of-state doctrine shall not be applied in the U.S. in cases when property is confiscated in violation of international law, unless the president advises that application of the doctrine is necessary. Federal courts, however, have not received this provision enthusiastically. The party moving for application of the doctrine has the burden of proving that the doctrine is appropriate. The court in Republic of the Phillipines v. Ferdinand E. Marcos held that the burden of proving that the alleged criminal acts were acts of state was not successfully met.

B. The sovereign immunity doctrine provides that a foreign sovereign is free from lawsuit in the United States. In 1976, Congress enacted the Foreign Sovereign Immunities Act that rejects immunity for commercial acts carried on in the United States which have direct effects in this country. The court in Transamerican Steamship v. Somali Democratic Republic held that the defendant did not sustain the burden of proving that its activities were not commercial in nature. Therefore, the SDR was subject to suit in the United States.

VII. Export Controls

A. The United States controls the export of strategic goods and technology abroad to Soviet bloc nations and countries engaged in or supporting international terrorism. The United States' export control system currently is regulated by the Departments of State and Commerce, pursuant to authority provided under the Export Administration Act and the Arms Export Control Act.

B. The court in Dresser Industries v. Baldridge upheld Commerce Department regulations, issued under the Export Administration Act, forbidding export to the Soviet Union of U.S.-origin commodities and technical data as well as non-U.S.-origin products owned by U.S. companies.

C. The Coordinating Committee for Multilateral Export Controls (COCOM) is an organization created by the major Western nations to limit on a multilateral basis the flow of strategic exports to the Soviet Union, China, and other Eastern European countries.

D. The Omnibus Trade and Competitiveness Act of 1988 imposes comprehensive penalties for present and future COCOM violators.

VIII. International Economic Boycotts

A. The Arab boycott of Israel assumes three basic forms: primary [refusal by Arab nations to trade with Israel or its nationals]; secondary [refusal by Arab states to trade with third parties which contribute to Israel's economic and military strength]; and tertiary [forbidding utilization of materials, equipment, or services of an ostracized business by a non-blacklisted firm].

B. The United States has adopted antiboycott laws aimed at prohibiting a U.S. company or person from participating in an international boycott without approval of the U.S. government.

C. In Briggs & Stratton Corp. v. Baldridge, the federal court held that firms cannot use the first amendment protection of free speech to escape the provisions of a U.S. law which requires disclosure of any requests to participate in a boycott or to furnish information about customers.

IX. Foreign Corrupt Practices Act (FCPA)

A. In 1977, following disclosures of payments by domestic firms to officials of foreign governments, Congress enacted the Foreign Corrupt Practices Act.

B. The Act has two accounting provisions:

1. Financial records and accounts must be kept "which, in reasonable detail, accurately and fairly reflect the transaction and disposition of assets" of a firm.
2. Firms must "devise and maintain a system of internal accounting controls sufficient to provide reasonable assurances" that transactions are being carried out with management's authorization.

C. As a result of intensive lobbying by the American business community, Congress amended the FCPA in 1988 in an effort to eliminate ambiguity and uncertainty over what constitutes improper conduct. The amendments establish clearer standards for firms to follow in overseas operations. Criminal penalties have been increased to a maximum of $2 million for companies violating the FCPA.

X. Antitrust Laws

A. Antitrust laws represent the legal embodiment of our nation's commitment to free markets and the competitive process.

B. In November 1988, the Department of Justice issued new Antitrust Enforcement Guidelines for International Operations to provide international businesses with general guidance as to how the government analyzes certain commonly occurring international issues affecting its enforcement decisions.

International Organizations and Agreements Affecting Trade

XI. The United Nations (UN)

A. The UN is the chief international political organization.

B. The International Court of Justice, or "World Court," is the judicial branch of the UN. It only hears cases involving disputes between countries. Private persons may not directly present claims before the court.

C. The UN also has various commissions and agreements concerning trade.

XII. European Community (EC, or "Common Market")

A. The EC, which is made up of 12 European countries, has proven to be an unrivaled international organization for promoting and achieving economic unity.

B. Within the EC there is a free flow of goods, persons, services, and capital among members. The EC has various economic and political bodies for promoting free trade between members.

XIII. U.S.-Canada Free Trade Accord

A. The U.S. and Canada signed in 1988 the U.S.-Canada Free Trade Agreement, which has the effect of providing momentum and opportunities for more American businesses to explore expansion of their operations into Canada.

B. Economists have predicted that the free trade agreement will increase the gross national product for the United States by $44 billion a year.

XIV. General Agreement on Tariffs and Trade (GATT)

A. GATT is a series of over 100 international agreements subscribed to by some 90 countries, including the U.S.

B. GATT attempts to prohibit discrimination in import regulations and prevent the establishment of import quotas. It seeks to implement these goals through the mechanism of "most-favored nations" status. In other words, no country is to give special trading advantages to other countries.

XV. Other Organizations

A. The Counsel for Mutual Economic Aid (COMECON) is the Soviet-Bloc counterpart to the EC.

B. A number of other regional organizations exist that have not achieved the degree of success of the EC or COMECON.

Protecting Domestic Industries in a World Market

XVI. Restrictions on Imports

A. Imports to America have continued to swell, creating a persistent, negative balance of trade with other countries.

B. In response to this situation, Congress enacted the Omnibus Trade and Competitiveness Act of 1988, designed to obtain more open, equitable, and reciprocal foreign markets for U.S. businesses.

XVII. **Piracy and Counterfeit Goods**

A. The Paris Convention of Industrial Property provides for special relief measures with respect to articles bearing infringing marks, if action is necessary.

B. The Trademark Counterfeiting Act of 1984 provides extensive criminal penalties for product counterfeiting.

XVIII. **Antidumping Laws**

A. Dumping is the practice of selling foreign goods in one country at less than the comparable price in the country from which the goods are being exported.

B. Dumping is prohibited in the U.S. under the Trade Agreements Act of 1979. Under this act when foreign goods are being sold in the U.S. at "less than fair value" and a domestic industry is being materially injured or threatened, an additional duty (tax) will be imposed upon the goods in an amount by which their foreign value exceeds the domestic price.

XIX. **Suing Foreign Firms in the United States**

A. The Supreme Court recently has held that the plaintiff must establish "minimum contacts" between the foreign defendant and a United States forum court.

B. The plaintiff, if he wishes to sue in the United States, must also comply with the terms of the Hague Service Convention when serving the foreign defendant notice of the lawsuit.

C. The Supreme Court held in Volkswagenwerk Aktiengeseuschaft v. Schlunk that the plaintiff may also serve process on a foreign corporation by merely serving its domestic subsidiary in the United States.

XX. **Arbitration**

A. The differences among legal systems and the expense of international litigation make arbitration an increasingly used method of resolving international business disputes.

B. Several international organizations promote arbitration. One such organization is the United Nations Convention on the Recognition and Enforcement of Foreign Arbitral Awards.

C. The case of Mitsubishi Motors v. Soler Chrysler-Plymouth involved an international contract calling for arbitration of contractual disputes in Japan. The issue concerned whether matters of U.S. antitrust law could be subject to foreign arbitration. The Supreme Court ruled that the U.S. policy in favor of arbitration established that such matters could be arbitrated internationally.

XXI. **Conclusion**

A. The laws that apply to international transactions will continue to develop.

B. This chapter has provided a broad overview of selected topics of importance to the conduct of international business.

COMPLETION EXERCISES

1. International business activities generate more than _______________ of the U.S. gross national product.

2. An _______________ is commonly used in international transactions to insure that a buyer will pay for goods ordered.

3. A foreign firm will often create a _______________ in the host country to serve as the firm's legal representative.

4. _______________ concerns the transfer of intangible property rights.

5. For a foreign firm to join with a company from a host country is termed a _______________.

6. International contracts often specify that in the event of a dispute, the parties agree to use _______________ instead of the courts to settle their disagreements.

7. _______________ is the seizure of foreign-owned property by a government.

8. The _______________ doctrine provides that the courts of one country will not sit in judgment on the acts of the government of another.

9. The _______________ doctrine provides a foreign sovereign is free from lawsuits in the United States.

10. The _______________ is the judicial branch of the United Nations.

11. The _______________ is the Soviet-Bloc counterpart to the EC.

12. _______________ is a series of over 100 international agreements subscribed to by some 90 countries.

13. Economists have predicted that the free trade agreement between the U.S. and Canada will increase the gross national product for the U.S. by $_______________ a year.

14. The _______________ provides extensive criminal penalties for product counterfeiting.

15. The Supreme Court has recently held that the plaintiff must establish _______________ _______________ between the foreign defendant and a United States forum court.

TRUE-FALSE CHOICES

1. _____ The Foreign Corrupt Practices Act prohibits the giving of a bribe to any foreign official for the purpose of influencing any act or decision.

2. _____ The international legal environment consists of a body of uniform principles.

3. _____ Since legal systems differ between countries, it is important for domestic companies to retain legal counsel when dealing in foreign legal systems.

4. _____ Unauthorized use of intangible property rights is a major international problem.

5. _____ Among industrialized countries, Canada most notably restricts foreign investment to joint ventures.

6. _____ In the U.S., expropriation is called nationalization.

7. _____ The Foreign Assistance Act directs that the act-of-state doctrine shall be applied (under most circumstances) when property is confiscated in violation of international law.

8. _____ The Foreign Sovereign Immunities Act rejects sovereign immunity for commercial acts carried on in the United States that have direct effects in this country.

9. _____ The International Court of Justice is also called the World Court.

10. _____ The EC is made up of 12 European countries.

11. _____ GATT seeks to implement its goals through the mechanism of "most-favored nations" status.

12. _____ Dumping is prohibited in the U.S. under the FCPA.

13. _____ Foreign firms that violate domestic antitrust law may not be subject to domestic antitrust enforcement.

14. _____ Arbitration is an increasingly used method of resolving international business disputes.

15. _____ In general, foreign judgments are not enforceable in this country.

MULTIPLE CHOICE SELECTIONS

1. The international legal environment consists of all of the following except:

   a. The laws of other countries.
   b. Bilateral and regional agreements.
   c. Customary international law.
   d. The Uniform International Commercial Code.

2. Intangible property include all of the following except:

   a. Exported goods.
   b. Patents.
   c. Trademarks.
   d. Copyrights.

3. In making a licensing contract, parties must be concerned about all of the following factors except:

   a. That the interpretation of all words should be agreed upon before the contract is finalized.
   b. That the contract contain a choice-of-law clause.
   c. That the parties agree to use arbitration instead of litigation.
   d. That the parties engage in eminent domain.

4. Select the <u>incorrect</u> statement. The Foreign Corrupt Practices Act:

   a. Prohibits the bribing of foreign officials to enable a company to obtain business.
   b. Permits the payment of a foreign customs official to help a company get its shipment easily into a foreign country.
   c. Regulates a company's accounting practices.
   d. Allows for criminal fines up to $1 million.

5. Select the <u>incorrect</u> statement:

   a. OPIC is a combination public and private agency.
   b. Several international organizations promote arbitration.
   c. The FCPA was passed following disclosure of payments by domestic firms to officials of foreign governments.
   d. The Webb-Pomerene Act's exemption applies as long as conduct does not restrain trade overseas.

Chapter 14

DISCUSSION ANALYSIS

Discuss the process used in international transactions to insure that a foreign buyer will pay for goods ordered.

Chapter 15

Worker Protection

STUDY GUIDE AND OUTLINE

I. **The Occupational Safety and Health Act**

A. Congress adopted the Occupational Safety and Health Act (OSHA) in 1970 to ensure safe and healthful working conditions.

B. OSHA requires employers to furnish each employee a place of employment that is free from hazards likely to cause death or serious physical harm to the employee. Employers must also comply with standards established under the act by the secretary of labor. This is done through an agency called the Occupational Safety and Health Administration (also known as OSHA).

C. The most significant aspect of OSHA is its approach to enforcement by unannounced inspections. Inspections of businesses may be made either on the initiative of OSHA itself or upon the request of an employee.

D. If an inspection reveals a violation, the employer receives a citation. If the violation presents a threat of immediate harm, the secretary of labor can go into court and get an injunction to restrain the danger.

E. In Whirlpool Corp. v. Marshall the U.S. Supreme Court ruled that an employee could not be disciplined for refusing to work to protest OSHA violations when less drastic measures would not protect the employee.

F. In the 1980s OSHA had concentrated its inspections on industries that offer the greatest threat to worker health and safety. It has virtually eliminated the inspections of certain employers when the potential for danger to employees is low.

II. **Workers' Compensation Acts**

A. Workers' Compensation Acts are state legislation that impose a type of strict liability on employers for accidental workplace injuries suffered by their employees. The clear intent of these laws is to remove the financial losses of injury from workers and to redistribute them onto employers and, ultimately, onto society.

B. In the 1800's common law provided the employer with the means of escaping most tort liability by the use of the defenses of assumption of risk, contributory negligence, and the fellow-servant rule (if injury occurred because of the negligence of another employee, the negligent employee rather than the employer was liable).

C. In the early 1900's the states adopted workers' compensation acts. These acts impose liability on employers for accidental employee injuries arising out of and in the scope of employment. They abolished the common law defenses. Employer negligence is not required for recovery under workers' compensation.

D. In United Parcel Service v. Fetterman, the Virginia Supreme Court determined that a worker's injury did not arise "out of employment." The worker had injured his back while bending over to tie his shoelace. The court stated that nothing related to the workplace had caused the injury.

E. Workers' compensation boards (rather than courts) award injured employees payments for medical expenses and loss of income. The amounts of such awards are scheduled and calculated by using a percentage of wages of the employees. Also, awards usually are subject to a stated maximum. Awards for pain and suffering are not allowed.

F. Since workers' compensation laws are remedial, they are liberally interpreted under rules of statutory interpretation.

G. The exclusive remedy rule states that an employee's sole remedy against an employer for workplace injury is workers' compensation.

H. Criticisms of the state workers' compensation system:

1. Since each state has its own nonuniform statute, there are unfair inequalities of treatment between states.
2. Many statutes exclude from coverage groups such as agricultural workers, government employers, and small business employers.
3. Awards granted in most states are substantially inadequate to provide an appropriate standard of living for injured workers.

III. Federal Compensation Acts

A. The Federal Employer's Liability Act (FELA) covers railroad and other transportation workers for injuries arising out of the course of employment. This statute does not make employers strictly liable, but it greatly increases the chances of workers winning lawsuits against their employers by eliminating defendants' common law defenses. There is no maximum ceiling to the amount an employee can recover for injuries.

B. Other federal statutes, such as the Longshoremen's and Harbor Workers' Compensation Acts (the Jones Act), award commission for employee injuries in the same manner as state workers' compensation laws.

IV. Wages and Hours of Work

A. Statutes setting minimum wages per hour and maximum hours of work exist on both the state and the federal level.

B. The federal statute regulating wages and hours is the Fair Labor Standards Act (FLSA).

C. At the time of this writing, the minimum hourly wage set by federal law is generally $3.35 per hour. The standard workweek is 40 hours, with overtime pay at a rate of not less than one and one-half times the employee's regular rate of pay. FLSA does not require overtime pay for weekend or holiday work.

D. Categories of persons who are not presently covered by the FLSA include professionals, managers, outside sales persons, and certain workers employed by small farms and small businesses. In addition, messengers, handicapped workers, and full-time students may be paid lower than minimum wages provided the employer obtains a special certificate.

E. In Donovan v. Trans-World Airlines a federal court ruled that FSLA minimum wage requirements do not apply to individuals training to be flight attendants when the employer gains no benefit from the training itself.

F. Besides its wage and hour provisions, the FLSA contains sections that regulate the employment of child labor outside of agriculture:

1. The employment of 14 and 15 year olds is limited to certain occupations such as sales and clerical work outside of school time. Children under 14 may not be employed, except for a few jobs that are specifically exempt.
2. The basic minimum age for employment is 16 for any nonhazardous work.
3. For hazardous work the minimum employment age is 18.

G. The government may fine and imprison employers for violating the FLSA. Employees may sue employers civilly for unpaid wages for overtime compensation plus attorney's fees and costs.

V. Unemployment Compensation

A. Unemployment compensation is a federal-state program that provides payments for temporary periods for workers who are unemployed through no fault of their own.

B. The Social Security Act of 1935 imposes a federal tax on wages paid by all employers who are not exempt. Today, the basic standard for federal employment law imposes a tax on the first $7,000 of wages at a 1985 rate of 6.2 percent. Up to 90 percent of this may be deducted for amounts paid to a state unemployment compensation fund.

C. Certain businesses are exempt from payment of unemployment compensation tax, for example, certain small farming operations.

D. The maximum during which unemployment compensation benefits are payable varies from state to state and generally has ranged from 26 to 39 weeks. All states have adopted experience rating systems that excuse employers who have a good record of maintaining stable employment from paying part or all of the state unemployment tax.

E. Generally, a worker is disqualified for workers' compensation if he or she refuses other employment that is suitable, was discharged for proper cause, or quit work voluntarily. In Wimberly v. Labor and Industrial Relations Comm. of Missouri the U.S. Supreme Court decided that Missouri unemployment compensation law did not violate the Federal Unemployment Tax Act, which requires that "no person shall be denied compensation under ... state law solely on the basis of pregnancy ...." The state determined that a woman had left employment voluntarily when she left due to her pregnancy, and it denied her unemployment compensation.

VI. Social Security

A. Social Security is a federal program for providing income when a family's earnings are reduced or stopped because of retirement, disability, or death.

B. The Social Security law requires that during their working years, covered employees, their employers, and self-employed persons must pay social security taxes to the federal government. Employers must deduct their employees' share of the contribution to the Social Security system from their wages, match those payments, and send the combined amount to the IRS. Self-employed persons pay their tax each year when filing their individual income tax returns.

C. For 25 percent of all employees, Social Security tax is larger than federal income tax, and for small businesses it is the largest federal tax.

D. At present, the Social Security system appears underfunded, in spite of the fact that the amount of wages subject to tax, as well as tax rates, have increased dramatically in recent years. In response to this problem, Congress in 1983 amended the Social Security Act to raise the retirement age for receiving full benefits beginning in the year 2000.

VII. Private Pension Plans: Incentives and Protection

A. Economic security in retirement has been a national policy goal for much of the century. Encouragement of private pension plans is part of this policy. Some 60 million employees are currently covered by private retirement plans.

B. A major financial incentive to formation of private pension plans is favorable income tax treatment. If an employer has begun a qualified pension plan, it can claim income tax deductions for contributions made to fund the plan, and fund earnings from investments are not taxable.

C. In 1974, Congress passed the Employee Retirement Income Security Act (ERISA) to protect employee rights in private pension plans.

D. ERISA applies to both defined benefit plans and defined contribution plans.

1. Defined benefit plans usually guarantee employees a certain retirement income based on years of service and salary level.
2. Under a defined contribution plan, employers contribute a percentage of employees' pay to the pension fund. Retirement income is determined by the total of these contributions plus investment return. The majority of employers favor this type of plan.

E. An important provision of ERISA requires plan termination insurance coverage for all defined benefit plans. The federal Pension Benefit Guarantee Corporation provides this insurance in return for premiums paid by employers with defined benefit plans.

F. ERISA states that employer contributions to pension plans must vest in employees under one of several standards.

G. To avoid much of the expense in recordkeeping requirements of regular pension plans, employers may set up simplified employee pensions. Employers can contribute up to a specified amount of an employee's income in an individual retirement account (IRA). Contributions to such plans are not taxable to the employees until they begin drawing from the account in retirement, which can begin anytime after age 59 1/2 without penalty.

H. Individuals may also set up and contribute to their own IRAs.

I. Expensive paperwork and pension plan insolvency are two major problems that ERISA faces in the coming years.

VIII. Workers' Privacy

A. Individual privacy is such an important part of individual freedom that both legal and ethical questions regarding privacy are bound to multiply in the computer age.

B. The 1988 Employee Polygraph Protection Act generally forbids private employers from using lie detector tests while screening job applicants.

C. Public employees are protected from some drug testing by the fourth amendment's prohibition against "unreasonable searches."

IX. Trends In Worker Protection: Limitations on Employment-at-Will

A. In 1988 Congress passed the Worker Adjustment and Retraining Notification Act, which specifies circumstances under which employers must give advance notice of plant closings or layoffs.

B. Historically, unless employees were under contract, employers were able to discharge them without reason at any time. This is called the employment-at-will doctrine.

C. Today the federal labor laws, the civil rights acts, and several other federal statutes limit an employer's right to discharge an employee.

D. Today, the courts have also begun limiting the at-will doctrine. Exceptions limiting the at-will doctrine include:

1. When employers discharge employees for performing an important public obligation such as jury duty.
2. When employers discharge employees for reporting the employers' alleged violations of law.
3. When employers discharge employees for exercising certain statutory rights, such as the right to workers' compensation.

E. Increasingly, courts imply contractual limitations on employers' rights to discharge employees at will because of what is written in employee handbooks. In Small v. Spring Industries, Inc. the South Carolina Supreme Court ruled that an employer's "four-step disciplinary process," mentioned in the employee handbook, contractually bound the employer. The employer thus breached an implied contract with an employee who was fired without the employer's having followed the four-step process.

F. Limitations on the employment-at-will doctrine may be part of a trend that could lead ultimately to some type of broad, legally guaranteed job security.

COMPLETION EXERCISES

1. The _______________ tries to ensure safe and healthful working conditions for employees in the United States.

2. The most significant aspect of OSHA is its enforcement by _______________.

3. A major change in OSHA administration in the 1980s has been a careful _______________.

4. Workers' compensation acts impose liability on employers for accidental employee injuries arising _______________.

5. The _______________ rule states that an employee's sole remedy against an employer for workplace injury is workers' compensation.

6. _______________ covers railroad and other transportation workers for injuries arising out of the course of employment.

7. The minimum wage law was established by the _______________.

8. The _______________ generally prohibits private employers from using lie detectors to screen job applicants.

9. Eighteen is the minimum age for employment in occupations that are _______________.

10. All states have adopted _______________ that excuse employers who have had a good record of maintaining stable employment from part or all of the state unemployment tax.

11. The _______________ specifies circumstances under which employers must give advance notice of plant closings or layoffs.

12. If an employer has instituted a _______________, it can claim income tax deductions from pension funding contributions.

13. Under ERISA employers seem to favor _______________ pension plans.

14. There are substantial penalties for withdrawing pension funds from an IRA before the age of _______________.

15. An employer's ability to discharge an employee at any time is called the _______________ doctrine.

TRUE-FALSE CHOICES

1. ______ If an OSHA violation presents a threat of serious or immediate harm, the secretary of labor can go into court and get an injunction to restrain the danger.

2. ______ During the 1800's employers had strict liability to employees for most work-related injuries.

3. ______ State workers' compensation laws usually set a maximum on the amount an injured worker may recover.

4. ______ The Federal Employer's Liability Act holds employers strictly liable to employees for injuries that arise out of the course of employment.

5. ______ Workers' compensation statutes today have abolished contributory negligence, assumption of risk and fellow-servant defenses in workers' compensation cases.

6. ______ Under rules of statutory interpretation, workers' compensation laws are liberally interpreted.

7. ______ The FLSA entitles workers to be paid one and one-half times the employee's regular rate of pay if he or she works more than 40 hours in a seven-day week.

8. ______ All workers are covered by the FLSA.

9. ______ Children under age 14 may not be employed, except for a few jobs that are specifically exempt from the FLSA.

10. ______ If an employee is fired for proper cause, the employee is not entitled to receive unemployment compensation.

11. ______ Most states allow workers to receive unemployment compensation if they are on strike because of a labor dispute.

12. ______ Congress has raised the retirement age for receiving Social Security benefits beginning in the year 2000.

13. ______ Under a defined benefit pension plan the employer contributes a percentage of an employee's pay to the fund and retirement income is determined by the total of these contributions plus investment return.

14. ______ ERISA requires plan termination insurance coverage for all defined benefit plans.

15. ______ A major problem of ERISA is the expense and time consumed by paperwork required of employers who maintain pension plans.

MULTIPLE CHOICE SELECTIONS

1. Before workers' compensation, all of the following common law defenses were available to employers except:

   a. Last clear chance doctrine.
   b. Assumption of the risk.
   c. Fellow-servant rule.
   d. Contributory negligence.

2. Some courts have refused to allow employers to dismiss at-will employees under all of the following circumstances except:

   a. When the employee is dismissed for serving on a jury.
   b. When an employee is discharged for reporting the employer's violations of the law.
   c. When the employee has a personality conflict with his or her employer.
   d. When employers discharge employees for exercising certain statutory rights.

3. Joe College was working on a summer construction job. He accidentally fell off the roof of a building and broke his legs. Select the most correct statement:

   a. Joe can receive workers' compensation.
   b. Joe can receive workers' compensation only if he was not negligent.
   c. Joe cannot receive workers' compensation if he assumed the risk of being on the roof of the building.
   d. Joe is not entitled to workers' compensation if his employer had instructed him to stay off the roof of the building.

4. Cindy, a former employee of Acme Corp., is seeking unemployment compensation. Select the most incorrect statement:

   a. She will not be entitled to unemployment compensation if she voluntarily left work.
   b. She cannot receive unemployment compensation if she was discharged for stealing her employer's merchandise.
   c. She cannot get unemployment compensation if she was laid off because of declining economic conditions.
   d. She is not entitled to unemployment compensation if she was discharged for being repeatedly absent from her work.

5. Select the most correct statement about private pension plans:

   a. Under ERISA employers with defined benefit plans must pay premiums to the Pension Benefit Guarantee Corporation.
   b. Employees have no vested rights under ERISA.
   c. Only employers may contribute to IRAs.
   d. There are few problems with the solvency of pension plans under ERISA.

Chapter 15

DISCUSSION ANALYSIS

Discuss the various limitations on the employment-at-will doctrine. What does this trend suggest for the future?

Chapter 16

Discrimination in Employment

STUDY GUIDE AND OUTLINE

I. Historical Development of Employment Discrimination Law

A. The Declaration of Independence states "that all men are created equal," but nowhere have the effects of inequity and discrimination been felt more severely than in the area of job opportunity.

B. Historically, common law permits employers to hire and fire at will, unless restrained by contract or statute. Labor laws enacted during the Depression mark the first significant federal limitation on the relatively unrestricted right of employers to hire and fire. Subsequently in the 1940's and 1950's, presidential executive orders prohibited racial discrimination in all federal contracts with private contractors.

C. However, the most significant statute eliminating employment discrimination is the federal Civil Rights Act of 1964, as amended by the Equal Employment Opportunity Act of 1972.

II. The Civil Rights Act - General Provisions

A. Today federal legislation is the main statutory force that regulates employment practices. The bulk of the government's enforcement authority comes from Title VII of the 1964 Civil Rights Act.

B. Title VII of the Civil Rights Act applies to employers with fifteen or more members, all labor unions which operate a hiring hall, and employment agencies. The 1972 amendment extended coverage to federal, state, and local governments, to governmental agencies, and to both public and private educational institutions. The Act does not apply to Indian tribes, private clubs, and religious organizations.

C. The major purpose of the Act is to eliminate job discrimination against employees based on race, color, religion, sex or national origin. The types of employer action in which discrimination is prohibited include discharge, refusal to hire, compensation, and terms, conditions, or privileges of employment. Exceptions to the act include:

1. Employers can discriminate on the basis of religion, sex, or national origin when these considerations are a bona fide occupational qualification (BFOQ). Note that the omission of race and color from this exception must mean that Congress does not feel these two factors are ever BFOQs.
2. Employers working under government security programs can deny employment to individuals who are unable to obtain security clearances.

3. Employers can establish different standards and conditions of employment if they are pursuant to a bona fide seniority or merit system.
4. The Supreme Court has held that laws which create veteran preference in hiring and promoting are immune from any attack, except where intentional racial discrimination can be proved.

E. Employment agencies are prohibited from either failing to refer or from actually referring an individual for employment on the basis of race, color, religion, sex, or national origin. Employers, unions, and agencies are prohibited from discriminating against an employee because he or she participated in an investigation under the Act, or otherwise opposed any unlawful practice.

III. Enforcement Procedures

A. The Civil Rights Act created the Equal Employment Opportunity Commission (EEOC), which has the primary responsibility of enforcing the provisions of the Act. The EEOC is composed of five members appointed by the President to serve five-year terms. They have broad administrative powers to hold hearings, examine evidence, and subpoena and examine witnesses.

B. The EEOC also has the power to file civil suits in federal court and to represent a person charging a violation of Title VII. Available remedies in such an action include reinstatement with backpay for the victim of an illegal discrimination and injunction against future violations.

C. Title VII does not preempt state fair employment laws. The EEOC must wait sixty days before initiating action where state agencies have already begun discrimination proceedings or have the power to do so.

D. An illegal discrimination charge must be filed with the EEOC within 180 days after the alleged violation, or further proceedings are barred. If a person files a charge with the EEOC and it is dismissed, notice must be given to the person and then he or she may file a civil action in federal court against the employer. Note that the Civil Rights Act does not require the EEOC to bring an enforcement suit itself within any maximum time period.

E. A Title VII plaintiff must prove that the employer's actions were illegally discriminatory. Generally, this means showing disparate impact or disparate treatment.

F. In proving disparate impact the plaintiff needs to show that the employer's policies had a disparate impact (or effect) on a group protected by Title VII.

G. In proving disparate treatment the plaintiff must convince the court that the employer intentionally discriminated against the plaintiff.

H. In Watson v. Fort Worth Bank & Trust the plaintiff Clara Watson had been denied four different job promotions by her white supervisors. The denial was based on subjective evaluation policies. The Supreme Court ruled that subjective evaluation criteria could be tested under the concept of disparate impact. Thus, intentional discrimination did not need to be shown.

IV. Discrimination on the Basis of Race or Color

A. The integration of blacks into the mainstream of American society is the primary objective of the Civil Rights Act, and Title VII is the key to open employment opportunities for blacks in occupations which traditionally have been closed to them.

B. Practices involving recruiting, hiring, and promotion of employees are often discriminatory on the basis of race, color, or national origin. Even when equally applicable to everyone, such practices are still illegal if they produce a discriminatory impact. Examples might include refusing to hire persons because of their poor credit rating; refusing to hire persons with an arrest record; and using personnel instruments such as IQ tests.

C. Title VII also prohibits discrimination in employment conditions and benefits. Allowing racial insults in work situations, maintaining all-white or all-black crews for no rational reason, and granting higher average bonuses to whites than blacks for impermissible purposes would all violate Title VII.

V. Discrimination on the Basis of National Origin

A. Discrimination against the speaking of a native language is a frequent source of Title VII suits.

B. Title VII applies to foreign companies with incorporated subsidiaries in the U.S.

VI. Discrimination on the Basis of Religion

A. Religious corporations, associations, or societies can discriminate in all their employment practices on the basis of religion, but not on the basis of race, color, sex, or national origin. Other employers cannot discriminate on the basis of religion in employment practices, and Title VII requires employers to make reasonable accommodations to the religious needs of employees whenever such recommendations would not work an undue hardship.

B. In Trans World Airlines, Inc. v. Hardison an employee refused to continue working on Saturdays for religious reasons. The employer fired him. The Supreme Court held that since all possible working alternatives would result in undue hardship on the employer's management of his other employees, the employee could be legally terminated. The court noted that Title VII does not require or permit employers to discriminate against some employees in order to enable others to observe their religious practices.

VII. Discrimination on the Basis of Sex

A. EEOC guidelines interpreting Title VII forbid:

1. Jobs classified as male or female.
2. Help-wanted ads that are designed male or female, unless sex is a bona fide occupational qualification (BFOQ).
3. Standards that limit the employment of married women but not married men. All company fringe benefits also must be dispersed on an equal basis to both sexes.
4. Forms of sexual advances or harassment that create "an intimidating, hostile, or offensive work environment."

B. In defense of alleged sex discrimination, most employers claim that such practices constitute a BFOQ. Courts construe this exception narrowly; as one court stated: "There must be reasonable cause to believe that all or substantially all women would be unable to perform safely and efficiently the duties of the job involved."

C. In Meritor Savings Bank v. Vinson a female bank employee claimed a hostile working environment and sexual harassment arose from a two-year sexual relationship she had with her boss. After requesting and being denied sick leave, she was eventually dismissed due to abuse of the sick leave policy. The Supreme Court ruled that a sexually harassing work environment alone was sufficient to violate Title VII, even though no economic discrimination could be shown.

D. Under the Pregnancy Discrimination Act of 1978, employers can no longer discriminate against women workers who become pregnant or give birth. The law covers unmarried as well as married pregnant women. All aspects of employment are covered, including hiring, firing, promotion, seniority rights, and fringe benefits.

E. The Equal Pay Act of 1963, which the EEOC enforces, prohibits an employer from discriminating on the basis of sex in payment of wages for equal work performed. Courts construe equal work not to mean identical duties but substantially equal duties.

F. Title VII also prohibits sexually discriminatory male and female pay differences, but it is broader in scope than the Equal Pay Act in that the prohibition applies even when the work performed is not "substantially equal."

Employment Practices That May Be Challenged

The use of personnel tests, height and weight standards, appearance requirements, and affirmative action plans all pose a possible risk of employment discrimination under Title VII of the Civil Rights Act.

VIII. Testing and Educational Requirements

A. Among the number of tools that employers use to help them find the right person for the right job are interviews, references, minimum educational requirements, and personnel tests.

B. These tools are often challenged as discriminatory.

IX. Height and Weight Requirements

A. Maximum and minimum height and weight job requirements may be facially neutral (apply equally to everyone), but if their effect is discriminatory (e.g., on the basis of sex), the employer must prove that such requirements are validly related to the ability to perform the job. Most size requirements dictate minimum height or weight because of the assumption that a certain amount of strength that smaller persons probably do not have is necessary for work involved.

B. In Dothard v. Rawlinson the Supreme Court determined that minimum size requirements for Alabama prison guards discriminated against women and that the defendant failed to prove such requirements, in relation to strength, were job-related. However, the court ultimately upheld as legal the discriminatory effect because being a male guard is a BFOQ in a male, maximum security prison where a large population of inmates are sexual deviates who would pose a substantial risk of injury to female guards.

X. Appearance Requirements

Employers often impose grooming standards on their employees which set male hair length or prohibit beards and mustaches. The legality of such standards is unclear since courts have ruled both for and against appearance requirements. Validity depends on the degree of discriminatory impact, which is determined on a case-by-case basis.

XI. Affirmative Action Programs and Reverse Discrimination

A. A series of presidential executive orders requires employers contracting with the federal government to take affirmative action to recruit members of priority groups which are being underused in the work force. Executive orders which require affirmative action are administered through the Labor Department's Office of Federal Contract Compliance Programs (OFCPP). The OFCPP can terminate federal contracts with employers who do not comply with its guidelines and can make them ineligible for any future federal business.

B. Reverse discrimination occurs when minorities or women with lower qualifications or less seniority than white males are given preference in employment. In United States Steel Workers of America v. Weber the Supreme Court held that Title VII does not forbid the private sector from voluntarily adopting bona fide affirmative action plans which make racial preferences but are designed to eliminate racial imbalances in the work force.

C. In Johnson v. Santa Clara County Transportation Agency the U.S. Supreme Court upheld the Transportation Agency's affirmative action plan for women. The Court ruled that it did not violate Title VII to pass over qualified men and to select a qualified woman for a road dispatcher position under an affirmative action plan.

D. The 1977 Public Works Employment Plan requires that 10 percent of the work of federally funded local public works projects be performed by minority contractors or subcontractors.

XII. Seniority System

A. Seniority systems give various types of priority to employees based on length of employment. Seniority systems often determine the calculation of vacation, pension, and other fringe benefits, and control such decisions as choosing shifts, transfers, and layoffs.

B. Under the Civil Rights Act, the fact that a seniority system has a discriminatory impact is not alone sufficient to invalidate the system; actual intent to discriminate must be proved. In Memphis Fire Dept. v. Shotts the U.S. Supreme Court ruled that a district court exceeded its powers in requiring the city of Memphis to modify layoff plans under its seniority system in order to protect certain affirmative action gains.

Other Statutes and Discrimination in Employment

The 1964 Civil Rights Act is not the only statute that attempts to eliminate employment discrimination. Various other federal and state laws prohibit discrimination on the basis of age, handicap, and race.

XIII. Civil Rights Act of 1866

A. Section 1981 of the Civil Rights Act of 1866 prohibits racial discrimination in the area of contracts. There are at least two advantages to the claimant who files a section 1981 suit:

1. There are no procedural requirements for bringing a Section 1981 suit, whereas Title VII claimants must follow a number of complex requirements about filing claims with the EEOC.
2. Section 1981 allows compensatory and punitive damages, whereas Title VII does not allow for the assessment of damages except in regard to backpay.

B. As a practical matter, plaintiffs alleging racial discrimination usually proceed under both Section 1981 and Title VII.

C. An important issue under Section 1981 concerns the meaning of race. The U.S. Supreme Court has ruled that being of Arab ancestry was a racial characteristic that brings one under the protection of Section 1981. The Court noted that in the nineteenth century (when Section 1981 was passed) the word race had a broader meaning than it does today.

XIV. Discrimination on the Basis of Age

A. Since neither the Civil Rights Act nor the Equal Employment Opportunity Act forbid age discrimination, Congress enacted the Age Discrimination in Employment Act. The act protects persons over age forty from job discrimination because of age. Certain exceptions include police officers, fire fighters, and some "bona fide" executives.

B. Maximum age standards for jobs usually fail as a BFOQ because they discriminate against older persons as a class.

C. Remedies for age discrimination include reinstatement and lost wages, but courts disagree on whether damages for psychological trauma are allowed. Note that willful violations entitle victims to double damages.

XV. Discrimination on the Basis of Handicaps

A. Under Section 503 of the 1973 Rehabilitation Act, every employer doing business with the federal government under a contract for over $2,500 must take affirmative action to hire qualified handicapped persons. This section affects about one-half of American businesses and 12 million employable handicapped persons. A handicapped person protected by the Act is anyone who has a physical or mental impairment which substantially limits a major life activity.

B. Federal contractors must make "reasonable accommodations" to handicapped employees unless it would impose an undue hardship on them.

C. Section 504 of the Rehabilitation Act prohibits discrimination against a handicapped person under any program receiving federal financial assistance. In Nassau County School Board v. Arline the U.S. Supreme Court ruled that a teacher's contagious tuberculosis could make her a "handicapped person" protected under the Rehabilitation Act.

XVI. Other Federal Legislation

A. The National Labor Relations Board has declared that employer appeals to racial prejudice in a collective bargaining representation election constitute an unfair labor practice.

B. Other federal agencies under their authorizing statutes may prohibit discriminatory employment practices. For example, the FCC has required the submission of affirmative action plans as a condition of radio and TV station license renewal.

XVII. State Discrimination Laws

Federal statutes do not preempt state anti-discrimination law. The purpose of most state law forbidding discriminatory employment practices is to ensure equal job opportunities to all persons, regardless of race, creed, or color. Generally a body known as the Fair Employment Practices Commission promulgates and enforces rules to carry out state legislation.

XVIII. Avoiding Unfounded Discrimination Claims

A. Many employers face unfounded discrimination charges made by unsatisfactory employees who have been discharged or disciplined. The best protection against such claims is a system of adequate documentation:

1. Job description - A well-written job description will help applicants eliminate themselves from positions for which they lack interest or qualification.
2. Personnel manual - Each employee should receive a personnel manual which clearly defines employee benefits, work rules, and job requirements.
3. Employee personnel files - Personnel files should include regular written evaluations of employee performance, a copy of written warnings given to the employees for unsatisfactory work, and any other pertinent information about employee work histories.

B. A system of adequate discrimination produces a "paper fortress" which allows an employer to defend effectively against unfounded job discrimination claims.

COMPLETION EXERCISES

1. The most significant federal statute eliminating employment discrimination is _______________.

2. _______________ means that federally contracting employers must actively recruit members of minority groups which are being underused in the work force.

3. _______________ discrimination occurs when minorities or women with lower qualifications than white males are given preference in employment.

4. A system of _______________ gives the employer the best protection against an unfounded job discrimination claim.

5. _______________ bans racial discrimination in the making of contracts.

6. The federal agency which considers employment discrimination claims is the _______________.

7. The "equal work" standard of the Equal Pay Act does not mean identical work; it means _______________ work.

8. Employers must make reasonable accommodations to the religious needs of employees whenever such accommodations would not create _______________.

9. An employer requiring the services of a male actor does not violate Title VII in excluding female job applicants since for the acting role sex is a _______________.

10. The illegal discrimination charge must be filed with the EEOC within _______________ after the alleged violation.

11. The major purpose of Title VII is to eliminate job discrimination based on _______________, _______________, _______________, _______________ or _______________.

12. Employers can discriminate on the basis of _______________, _______________ or _______________ when these considerations are BFOQs.

13. Federal affirmative action requirements originated in a series of _______________.

14. _______________ protects women workers who become pregnant or give birth.

15. _______________ theory does not hold an employer liable for racial discrimination if the final result of the employment practices produces an appropriate racial balance.

TRUE-FALSE CHOICES

1. _____ Title VII of the Civil Rights Act does not apply to private employers with less than fifteen employees.

2. _____ The EEOC must file a complaint of Title VII violations within 180 days of the alleged violation or be barred from further proceedings.

3. _____ Title VII and the 1963 Equal Pay Act both prohibit sexually discriminatory male and female pay differences.

4. _____ Maximum or minimum height or weight job requirements are per se violations of Title VII.

5. _____ Generally, there exist no major differences between the 1866 and 1964 Civil Rights Act.

6. _____ Damages for psychological trauma are readily available to the victim of age discrimination under the Age Discrimination in Employment Act.

7. _____ Federal equal employment legislation preempts state antidiscrimination statutes.

8. _____ A seniority plan that has the effect of discriminating on the basis of race may be legal.

9. _____ In a Title VII proceeding, the employer has the initial burden of proving that employment practices are nondiscriminatory.

10. _____ Civil rights laws apply to foreign companies which do business through subsidiaries in the United States.

11. ______ Race may be a BFOQ.

12. ______ Federal affirmative action rules require that employers with more than fifteen employees, labor unions, and employment agencies all actively recruit minority members who are being underused in the workplace.

13. ______ The law requires that federal contractors make reasonable accommodations to handicapped employees.

14. ______ Personnel tests which apply equally to all employment applicants may still be illegal.

15. ______ The best protection against unfounded discrimination claims is the paper fortress.

MULTIPLE CHOICE SELECTIONS

1. Ms. Jones, an employee of Acme, Inc., has a unique position with the firm in that her duties and responsibilities are not duplicated or shared by any other Acme employee. Nevertheless, she feels that the pay difference between her and Acme male employees, as a whole, is based on sex discrimination. Select the most correct answer:

   a. Ms. Jones has a claim under the Equal Pay Act because she is paid less than the majority of male employees.
   b. Ms. Jones has a claim under Title VII if she can show that the salary differential is based on sex discrimination.
   c. Ms. Jones would have a claim under neither the Equal Pay Act nor Title VII because there is no other similar job position held by a male.
   d. Ms. Jones has a claim under Section 1981 of the Civil Rights Act of 1866 since the alleged conduct is contractual sex discrimination.

2. A public employer provides a veteran preference. The discrimination impact on female applications is clear and conceded. Select the most correct answer:

   a. The preference violates Title VII because the BFOQ exception is inapplicable in this instance.
   b. The preference violates Title VII because all public employers must act affirmatively to recruit members of minority groups, including women.
   c. The preference does not violate Title VII because only private employers and labor unions, not public employers, are subject to its coverage.
   d. This preference does not violate Title VII because veterans can receive preferential treatment.

3. An employer uses a pre-employment test developed to test job-related skills. A minority plaintiff who has been denied a job proves that 53 percent of whites and only 19 percent of racial minority groups passed the test. Select the most correct answer:

   a. The employer would win because the personnel test is job related.
   b. The employer would win because of the "bottom line" theory.
   c. The employer would lose because, as a practical matter, EEOC guidelines prohibit personnel tests.
   d. The employer would lose if another test, which is non-discriminatory, would test job-related skills equally well.

4. According to Acme Company's seniority system, adopted in 1970 by labor and management through the collective bargaining contract, the most recently employed workers are laid off first in times of economic downturn. The plaintiff, who is a Chicano hired through a federally imposed affirmative action program, is laid off first. He claims this violates Title VII and OFCPP rules. Select the most correct answer:

   a. The plaintiff would win because Title VII expressly prohibits employers and labor unions from employment discrimination on the basis of race, color, religion, sex, or national origin.
   b. The plaintiff would win because affirmative action plans, as enforced by the OFCPP, take precedence over bona fide seniority systems.
   c. The plaintiff would lose because Title VII allows discriminatory impact, absent actual intent, produced by a bona fide seniority system.
   d. The plaintiff would win because the bona fide seniority system exception only applies to systems in existence at the time Title VII was enacted.

5. Identify the incorrect statements about Section 1981 of the Civil Rights Act of 1866:

   a. As a practical matter, the 1964 Civil Rights Act supersedes the 1866 Act. Claimants very rarely use Section 1981 as a remedy for employment discrimination.
   b. Section 1981 applies only to racial discrimination in the area of contracts.
   c. There are few procedural requirements for bringing a Section 1981 suit.
   d. Section 1981 provides for punitive damages as well as compensatory damages.

Chapter 16

DISCUSSION ANALYSIS

A. Ms. Smith, a 25 year old black female, is hired by Acme Co., under the company's affirmative action plan. Mr. Jones, a 60 year old white male, is terminated, and Ms. Smith takes his position. Mr. Jones decided to sue Acme. What laws may have been violated? What are the arguments for and against liability?

B. Ms. Smith is fired because of repeated disciplinary problems. She claims she was fired because of the impending birth of her child. What laws have been violated? What defenses are available to Acme Co.? What are the potential liabilities?

Chapter 17

Right to Union Activity

STUDY GUIDE AND OUTLINE

I. **Introduction**

A. Understand that the law encourages workers to join together and bargain as a group with employers.

B. The process of negotiation between management and unions is called collective bargaining. Since collective bargaining can be successful only if the bargaining power of the parties is equal, most laws regulating labor-management relations seek to equalize this bargaining power.

II. **Federal Laws Before 1935: The Clayton Act**

A. The Act prohibits federal courts from enjoining certain labor activities. Because of its wording, this prohibition had little impact.

B. The Clayton Act states that antitrust laws do not apply to labor unions that are carrying out legitimate labor activities such as striking and picketing.

III. **Railway Labor Act of 1926**

A. The Railway Labor Act encouraged collective bargaining in the railroad industry to resolve labor disputes that might otherwise disrupt transportation. Today, the Act also applies to airlines.

B. The Act established the three-member National Mediation Board. The Board holds representation elections to see whether workers want a union to represent them as a collective bargaining agent. The Board also hears charges of unfair labor practices identified by the Act.

C. The Board attempts to settle labor-management disputes through voluntary mediation. If mediation fails, the Act provides for procedures to stop strikes for 60 days while an emergency board attempts to bring the parties into agreement.

D. In Landers v. National R.R. Passengers Corp. the Supreme Court held that there is not an implicit right of railroad operating employees to be represented by minority unions at company-level grievance and disciplinary proceedings.

IV. **Norris-LaGuardia Act of 1932**

A. The Norris-LaGuardia Act makes "yellow-dog" contracts (those forbidding union membership) unenforceable.

B. The Act prohibits federal courts from enjoining certain labor activities such as striking, belonging to a union, picketing and paying strike benefits. An exception exists to permit injunctions where unlawful acts are threatened or committed, such as violence to persons or property, and local authorities cannot protect these persons or property. Note that the Act does not restrict state courts from issuing injunctions.

C. In Jacksonville Bulk Terminals, Inc. v. International Longshoremen's Assoc. the U.S. Supreme Court ruled that a lower federal court could not enjoin the union from refusing to handle goods shipped to the Soviet Union in violation of collective bargaining clauses guaranteeing no strikes and arbitration of all disputes.

V. The Wagner Act: General Summary

A. The purpose of the National Labor Relations Act (Wagner Act) is to promote an equality of bargaining power between workers and employers. The Act accomplishes this policy by providing employees with the legal right to bargain collectively, i.e., through a union.

B. In summary, the Wagner Act:

1. Created the National Labor Relations Board (NLRB).
2. Established a procedure, supervised by the NLRB, for holding elections to determine whether employees desired to be represented by a union.
3. Outlawed certain conduct by employers called unfair labor practices.
4. Authorized the NLRB to hear charges on unfair labor practices and to take corrective action if they were found to exist.

VI. The NLRB

A. Today, the NLRB has five members appointed by the President, who hold staggered terms of five years each. In addition, there is a General Counsel of the Board who supervises Board investigations, serves as prosecutor in cases before the Board, and is responsible for conduct of representation elections.

B. Congress gave the NLRB jurisdiction over any business "affecting commerce," with a few exceptions. Exceptions include:

1. Employees of federal and state governments.
2. Persons subject to the Railway Labor Act.
3. Independent contractors, individuals employed as agricultural laborers or domestic servants, and those employed by a spouse or parent.
4. Supervisory employees (persons with access to confidential information of the employees concerning labor relations).

C. Because of budget and time considerations, the NLRB has elected not to exercise jurisdiction in labor disputes over many small employers, e.g., retail enterprises with a gross volume of under $500,000 a year.

VII. NLRB Sanctions

A. The NLRB may exercise such sanctions as:

1. Cease and desist orders.
2. Reinstatement of employees who have been wrongfully discharged, with back pay and restoration of full seniority rights.
3. Orders requiring an employer to bargain collectively with an appropriately certified union.
4. Orders requiring that a new election be held or certifying a union as the collective bargaining agent where the union has lost an election because of unfair labor practices by management.

B. As of this writing the NLRB will no longer certify a union that loses an election simply because an employer has committed unfair labor practices during the election process.

VIII. NLRB Elections

A. In the absence of an employer's voluntary recognition of a union, the selection of a union as collective-bargaining representative is made by a majority of the employees voting "in a unit appropriate for such purposes." Elections are by secret ballot and supervised by the NLRB.

B. In NLRB v. Action Automotive, Inc. the Supreme Court ruled that in determining an "appropriate unit" the NLRB did not err in excluding from voting employees who are relatives of the owners of a closely held corporation. This was true although the excluded employees did not receive special job-related benefits.

C. Before a certification election is conducted by the NLRB, a petition for such an election must be filed with the Board. The petition must be signed by a "substantial" number of the employees. "Substantial" has been interpreted to mean that at least 30 percent of the employees involved must support the petition. If a majority of the employees vote for the union at the election, the NLRB certifies it as being the bargaining representative of all the employees.

D. Employees may withdraw authority from a previously designated bargaining representative by the same procedure that the representative was elected. However, after a valid election has been conducted by the NLRB another is not permitted for one year.

E. At the present time, unions lose the majority of certification and decertification elections. This negative trend has developed since the late 1970s.

F. A union seeking to represent employees may solicit authorization cards from them. Most of these cards request that a certification election be held.

IX. The Taft-Hartley Act: Major Provisions

A. The years during World War II represented the height of union strength and influence. By the end of the war, many felt that unions needed to be curbed. Congress passed the Taft-Hartley Act, which recognized that both parties to collective bargaining need protection from wrongful interference by the other.

B. The Taft-Hartley Act created the Federal Mediation and Conciliation Service to assist in the settlement of labor disputes. Trained mediators worked with the parties to help them resolve their differences.

C. The Taft-Hartley Act also:

1. Restricted the right of unions to require union membership.
2. Attempted to give employers freedom of speech in labor-management relations.
3. Provided for an 80-day cooling off period in strikes that imperil the national health or safety.
4. Allowed suits for breach of contract against a union.
5. Outlawed unfair labor practices by unions (see Chapter 17).

X. Union Membership and Dues

A. The Taft-Hartley Act outlaws the closed-shop but permits the union shop. In a closed-shop contract the employer agrees that it will not hire any person who is not a member of the union. In a union-shop contract the employer agrees to require membership in the union after an employee has been hired.

B. Section 14(b) outlaws the union shop in states which have adopted "right-to-work" laws. These laws prohibit agreements requiring membership in a labor organization as a condition of continued employment. Approximately 20 states have right-to-work laws today.

C. Even in states that permit union shop agreements, employees can only be required to pay union dues in order to retain employment. They cannot be discharged for failing to abide by union rules or policies. The Supreme Court in Communications Workers of America v. Beck held that only those fees and dues necessary to "perform the duties of an exclusive representative of the employees in dealing with the employer on labor-management issues" may be exacted. In Pattern Makers' League of North America v. NLRB the Supreme Court ruled that the union could not fine former members who resigned the union during a strike and returned to work.

XI. Free Speech

A. The Taft-Hartley Act guarantees employers freedom of expression as long as it contains "no threat of reprisal or force or promise of benefit." This provision gives employers limited free speech at best since if an employer predicts that awful things will happen as a result of unionization, and the employer has the power to make the prediction come true, the employer is coercing or restraining employees in joining together. Also, an employer's threats to withdraw existing benefits from employees if they unionize is not protected speech.

B. However, mere predictions and prophecies are protected. Indicating that the employer intends to fight the union in every legal way possible and warning that employees can be replaced permanently if the union calls an economic strike are examples of protected speech.

XII. Eighty-Day Cooling-Off Period

A. When the "national health or safety" is threatened, the President, through the attorney general, can get the federal court to issue an injunction ordering strikers back to work.

B. The 80-day cooling-off period allows the parties time to settle their differences.

XIII. Suits Against Unions

A. Section 301 of the Taft-Hartley Act provides that suits for breach of contract between an employer and a union can be filed in federal district court.

B. Money judgments against the union can be enforced only against its assets, not the assets of individual members.

C. Employees may sue their union and recover damages they suffer because of an illegal strike.

XIV. The Landrum-Griffin Act: As a "Bill of Rights"

A. The Landrum-Griffin Act (Labor-Management Reporting and Disclosure Act) was passed in 1959 as a result of widespread corruption in some labor unions.

B. The Landrum-Griffin Act gives union members the following rights:

1. To attend membership meetings and to nominate and vote for candidates and to have a voice in business transactions.
2. To have free expression in all union meetings and functions.
3. To vote on an increase of dues or fees.
4. To sue and testify against the union.
5. To be accorded a full and fair hearing before any disciplinary action is taken by the union.
6. To be given a copy of the collective bargaining agreement upon request.

C. In Local 3489 United Steel Workers of America v. Usery the Supreme Court held that a rule by the union limiting eligibility for local union office to members who had attended at least one-half of the regular meetings of the local for three years previous to the election violated the Landrum-Griffin Act. The rule restricted the openness of the union's political process since it eliminated 96.5 percent of the members from being candidates for office.

D. In United Steelworkers v. Sadlowski the U.S. Supreme Court upheld a union "outsider rule" that prohibited candidates for union office from accepting contributions from nonunion persons.

XV. LMRDA Reporting Requirements

A. The Landrum-Griffin Act requires each union to adopt a constitution and bylaws and to file them with the Secretary of Labor.

B. Various financial reports and other information must also be filed with the Secretary on a periodic basis.

XVI. Internal Union Activities

A. The Act requires that union elections be held at minimum regular intervals to promote union democracy. Elections must be held by secret ballot and the Secretary of Labor may void an election for misconduct.

B. The Act also makes it a federal crime to:

1. Embezzle union funds.
2. Engage in extortionate picketing, i.e., picketing to force an employer to pay money to union officials for their own personal use.

XVII. Labor Law and Government Employees

A. The clear trend in the law is to allow government employees to form unions but to deny them the right to strike. However, a few states do allow them to strike.

B. The right to strike generally is denied government workers because of their adverse effect on the public.

C. The number of public employees represented by unions will likely continue to grow.

COMPLETION EXERCISES

1. The statute which exempts union activity from the antitrust laws is the _______________.

2. Today, the Railway Labor Act covers not only the railroad industry but also the _______________ industry.

3. Contracts prohibiting union membership, which are made unenforceable by the Norris-LaGuardia Act, are called _______________ contracts.

4. The Norris-LaGuardia Act greatly restricts the use of _______________ in labor disputes.

5. The _______________ supervises NLRB investigations and serves as prosecutor in cases before the Board.

6. Before the NLRB will hold a collective bargaining representation election, it must receive a petition signed by a _______________ number of the employees in a "unit appropriate for such purposes."

7. Under _______________ agreements employers must require all employees to join the union.

8. The Taft-Hartley Act set up the _______________ to work with the parties to a labor dispute in an attempt to resolve differences.

9. The union shop is prohibited in states that have adopted _______________ laws.

10. Currently, unions have organized approximately _______________ percent of the work force.

11. Where strikes imperil the national health or safety, the Taft-Hartley Act makes provisions for an 80-day _______________.

12. When an employer does not voluntarily recognize a union, the selection of a union as collective-bargaining representative is made by a _______________ of the employees voting.

13. The years during _______________ represented the height of union strength and influence.

14. The Taft-Hartley Act guarantees employers freedom of expression as long as it contains no _______________.

15. The Landrum-Griffin Act requires each union to adopt a _______________ and _______________.

TRUE-FALSE CHOICES

1. _____ The Railway Labor Act established the NLRB.

2. _____ The Norris-LaGuardia Act prohibits state and federal courts from enjoining lawful union activities such as picketing and striking.

3. _____ Congress gave the NLRB jurisdiction over any business "affecting commerce" with a few exceptions.

4. _____ After a valid election has been conducted by the NLRB, another is not permitted for one year.

5. _____ The Taft-Hartley Act makes illegal the closed shop.

6. _____ The Taft-Hartley Act permits employers unlimited freedom of expression.

7. _____ In most states public employees are forbidden from going out on strike.

8. _____ Under the Taft-Hartley Act courts may permanently enjoin strikes which imperil the national health or safety.

9. _____ The Wagner Act contains the "Bill of Rights" for union members.

10. _____ The Landrum-Griffin Act makes it a federal crime to embezzle union funds.

11. _____ At this time, unions win a majority of certification elections.

12. _____ The Taft-Hartley Act prohibits union shop agreements.

13. _____ The number of public employees represented by unions will likely continue to decline.

14. _____ In certification petitions the term "substantial" means 50 percent.

15. _____ The antitrust laws do not apply to labor unions that are carrying out legitimate labor activities.

MULTIPLE CHOICE SELECTIONS

1. Select the most correct statement:

   a. The Clayton Act contains an effective provision prohibiting federal courts from enjoining strikes.
   b. The Norris-LaGuardia Act requires employers to bargain collectively with unions.
   c. The Taft-Hartley Act gives employees the right to work without having to join a union.
   d. The Landrum-Griffin Act permits the Secretary of Labor to void union elections under certain circumstances.

2. The Wagner Act did all of the following except:

   a. Establish a "Bill of Rights" for union members.
   b. Create the NLRB.
   c. Set forth a procedure for collective bargaining representation (certification) elections.
   d. Authorize the NLRB to hear charges of unfair labor practices.

3. Select the incorrect statement. Congress gave the NLRB jurisdiction over all of the following except:

   a. Government employees.
   b. Employees subject to the Railway Labor Act.
   c. Employees whose employers gross less than $500,000 annually.
   d. Supervisory employees.

4. The NLRB can exercise all of the following sanctions except:

   a. Cease and desist orders.
   b. Orders requiring employers to bargain collectively.
   c. Reinstatement of wrongfully discharged employees.
   d. Triple damages.

5. The Landrum-Griffin Act gives union members all of the following rights except:

   a. To attend membership meetings.
   b. To remove any union official from office by a majority vote.
   c. To sue and testify against the union.
   d. To be given a copy of the collective bargaining agreement upon request.

Chapter 17

DISCUSSION ANALYSIS

A proposed strike by the United Auto Workers threatens to shut down the nation's automobile plants. Could the Taft-Hartley Act's 80-day cooling period apply to this situation? Explain. Discuss the legal steps necessary to implement the 80-day cooling off period.

Chapter
18

Unfair Labor Practices

STUDY GUIDE AND OUTLINE

I. **Introduction**

A. Labor law makes illegal certain activities, called "unfair labor practices," by both unions and management.

B. The Wagner Act as amended declares the following to be unfair labor practices by employers:

1. Interference with efforts of employees to form, join, or assist labor organizations.
2. Domination of a labor organization or contribution of financial or other support to it.
3. Discrimination in hiring or tenure of employees for reasons of union affiliation.
4. Discrimination against employees for filing charges or giving testimony under the Act.
5. Refusal to bargain collectively in good faith with a duly designated representative of the employees.
6. Agreeing with a labor organization to engage in a secondary boycott.

C. The most important of these unfair labor practices are discussed in separate sections below.

II. **Interference with Efforts of Employees to Form or Join Labor Organizations**

A. The purpose of this unfair labor practice is to guarantee employees' rights to organize and bargain collectively without intimidation from the employer.

B. Examples of tactics which constitute this unfair labor practice include:

1. Scare tactics such as threats by employers to fire those involved in organizing employees, or threats to cut back on employee benefits if employees succeed in unionizing. Even conferring of benefits by an employer may be an unfair labor practice if given too near a collective bargaining election.
2. Company work rules that negatively affect workers' attempts to organize and join a union. Rules that prohibit wearing buttons on work clothes or forbidding solicitation on company property, or denying employees the right to leave their work stations may constitute an unfair labor practice unless the employer can establish a valid reason for such rules.

C. Filing of lawsuits by the employer may or may not be an unfair labor practice. The U.S. Supreme Court has ruled that the NLRB cannot halt the prosecution of a state court lawsuit unless the suit lacks a reasonable basis in law or fact.

D. Although an employer may predict unfavorable consequences arising from unionization, it has been held an unfair labor practice to make such predictions when the employer has the power to make them come true.

III. Interfering with Concerted Activities

A. Employers may not interfere with efforts of employees to form or join a labor union. Neither may they interfere with efforts of employees to engage in "concerted activities for mutual aid or protection." Note that protected employees do not have to be union members.

B. In Eastex, Inc. v. N.L.R.B. employees tried to distribute a newsletter in nonworking areas of a company's plant during nonworking time. The employer refused to allow distribution. The U.S. Supreme Court ruled that the law protected distribution of the newsletter as a concerted activity.

C. Concerted activities often involve the refusal to follow work rules. In one case, the employer discharged seven employees who violated the rule about leaving work without permission. The employees had walked off the job on a cold day because where they worked had no heat. The Supreme Court ruled that their discharge amounted to an unfair labor practice as an interference in the right to engage in concerted activities.

D. The right to engage in concerted activity has been expanded to cover the actions of a sole employee under certain circumstances. In N.L.R.B. v. City Disposal Systems, Inc. an employee was discharged for refusing to drive a truck that he honestly and reasonably believed to be unsafe because of faulty brakes. He asserted that he had a right to do this under his collective bargaining agreement. The U.S. Supreme Court ruled that the employee's action was protected as a concerted activity reasonably directed toward enforcement of a collective bargaining right.

IV. Discharge and Other Forms of Retaliation

A. It is clearly an unfair labor practice for an employer to fire or threaten to fire workers because of unionization. However, the issues are often more complicated. In N.L.R.B. vs. Sure-Tan, Inc. an employer was found guilty of an unfair labor practice for sending a letter to the Immigration authorities, asking them to check the immigration status of five named employees following a union certification. The court termed this a "constructive discharge."

B. When union activities may have been a "motivating factor" in an employer's discharge decision, the NLRB can find an unfair labor practice if the employer does not show convincing evidence that the discharge has been for legitimate business reasons. This is called the Wright-Line Doctrine. In N.L.R.B. v. Transportation Management Corp. the NLRB found that an employee had been discharged for union activity. The company argued that the employee was dismissed for taking unauthorized breaks and negligent performance of his duties. The U.S. Supreme Court ruled that the NLRB was correct in placing the burden of proof on the employer to show that the employee would have been fired even if not involved in union activities.

C. Note that employer retaliation for union activity can take other forms than discharge.

V. Domination of a Labor Organization

A. It is an unfair labor practice for an employer to dominate a labor organization or contribute financial or other support to it.

B. It is thus an unfair labor practice for the employer to:

1. Support a union by giving it a meeting place.
2. Provide refreshments for union meetings.
3. Permit the union to use the employer's telephone or other benefits.
4. Allow the union to keep the cafeteria or vending machine profits.

C. The purpose of this unfair labor practice is to ensure that the bargaining between unions and management is adversarial. When management dominates a union, "sweetheart" collective bargaining contracts often result.

VI. Discrimination for Union Affiliation

It is an unfair labor practice for an employer to discharge or refuse to hire an employee to encourage or discourage membership in any labor organization. Nor may the employer discriminate regarding any term or condition of employment for such purposes.

VII. Discrimination: NLRB Proceedings

A. Employers may not discharge or take other steps against employees because the employees have filed charges of unfair labor practices or have testified against their employer.

B. The main defense of an employer accused under this unfair labor practice is that he or she discharged or discriminated against the employee for some reason other than filing charges or giving testimony.

VIII. The Duty to Bargain Collectively in Good Faith

A. It is an unfair labor practice for an employer to refuse to bargain collectively with a duly certified collective bargaining agent (union). Although an employer need not agree to union demands, such conduct as the failure to make counterproposals to union demands may be evidence of bad faith. Also, refusing to meet at reasonable times and refusing to reduce agreements to writing are examples of this unfair labor practice.

B. The law divides bargaining issues into two categories:

1. Compulsory bargaining issues are those concerned with wages, hours, and other terms and conditions of employment. Management must bargain with the collective bargaining agent over these issues.
2. All other issues are voluntary bargaining issues. The parties may bargain over these issues, but the refusal by either to bargain in good faith about them is not an unfair labor practice.

C. Classifying issues as compulsory or voluntary is usually done on a case-by-case basis. In Ford Motor Co. v. N.L.R.B. the Supreme Court upheld a decision of the NLRB which determined that Ford's refusal to bargain about increases in cafeteria and vending machine prices was an unfair labor practice. The services were managed by an independent caterer, but Ford had the right to review and approve the quality, quantity, and prices of food served. The Board had taken the view that inplant food prices and services are "other terms and conditions of employment," and thus were subject to mandatory bargaining. The NLRB had ordered Ford to bargain with the union.

D. Unions are required to bargain collectively over compulsory bargaining issues under the Taft-Hartley Act of 1947. Note that neither the employer nor the union is required to make concessions in the bargaining process. If the parties fail to reach an agreement after discussing their problems in good faith, each party may take whatever steps are necessary. For example, the employer may refuse to grant a wage increase request, and the union may go on strike.

IX. Agreeing with a Union to Engage in a Secondary Boycott

A. A secondary boycott involves pressure brought to bear on an employer other than the employer with whom a union has a primary dispute.

B. The hot-cargo contract is also illegal. In this unfair labor practice it is illegal for an employer voluntarily to agree with a union not to handle, use, or deal in nonunion-produced goods of another person.

X. Unfair Labor Practices by Unions: Introduction

A. The Wagner Act prohibited unfair labor practices by management. The Taft-Hartley Act covered unfair labor practices by unions.

B. There is an unfair labor practice unions use to:

1. Restrain or coerce an employee to join a union or employer to select representatives to bargain with a union.
2. Cause or attempt to cause an employer to discriminate against an employee who is not a union member, unless there is a legal union shop agreement in effect.
3. Refuse to bargain with the employer.
4. Strike, picket, or engage in secondary boycotts for illegal purposes.
5. Charge new members excessive or discriminatory initiation fees when there is a union-shop agreement.
6. Cause an employer to pay for work not performed.
7. Picket to require an employer to recognize a union that is not currently certified.
8. Agree with an employer to engage in a secondary boycott.

C. The following sections discuss certain of these unfair labor practices in detail.

XI. Restraining or Coercing an Employee in Joining a Union

A. Most allegations of unfair labor practices filed against unions are brought under this provision. This provision prohibits such behavior as:

1. A union attempting to influence the employer in selecting its representatives to bargain with the union.
2. A union restraining or coercing employees in the exercise of their rights to bargain collectively.
3. Unions interfering with the right of employees to refrain from union activities unless required by a legal union-shop agreement.

B. In N.L.R.B. v. Savair Manufacturing Co. the U.S. Supreme Court ruled that a union committed an unfair labor practice by informing employees that those who did not sign "recognition slips" before the collective bargaining representation election would have to pay a "fine" if the union were elected to represent the workers. The Court ruled that this procedure allowed the union to buy endorsements and paint a false portrait of employees' support.

XII. Causing an Employer to Discriminate Against a Nonunion Member

A. This unfair labor practice applies when a legal union-shop agreement is in effect.

B. Even if an employee is a union member, the union may not cause the employer to discriminate against him or her for not following union rules. This unfair labor practice was designed to prevent the use of union shop as a means of intimidating employees who disagreed with union officials over their policies.

XIII. Secondary Boycotts and Other Illegal Strikes and Picketing

A. It is an unfair labor practice for a union to threaten, coerce, or restrain third persons not parties to a labor dispute for the purpose of causing the third person to cease using, selling, handling, transporting, or otherwise dealing in the products of any other producer, or to cease doing business with any other person.

B. If a foreseeable consequence of a strike, picketing or boycott is to disrupt the business of a third person, the activity is an unfair labor practice.

C. In Edward J. DeBartolo Corp. v. Fla. Gulf Coast Bldg. a union distributed handbills urging customers not to trade with any stores at a mall. The union believed that a general contractor building a store at the mall was paying employees substandard wages. The Supreme Court ruled that this distribution was an illegal secondary boycott since the handbills urged that customers not trade with any mall store.

D. Other examples of illegal secondary activity include:

1. Inducing employees of an employer to strike or refuse to use, handle, or work on any goods or to perform any services to force an employer to stop doing business with any third person.
2. Persuading an employer not to handle, use, or deal in nonunion-produced goods of another person. Such an agreement with the employer is called a "hot-cargo" contract. It is also an unfair labor practice for the employer to enter into such an agreement.

E. Examples of the unfair labor practice of illegal striking or picketing by a union include:

1. Threatening or coercing an employer to recognize or bargain with one union if another one has been certified as the representative of its employees.
2. Striking to force an employer to assign work to employees in one craft union rather than another ("jurisdictional strike").

XIV. Requiring Employees to Pay Excessive Fees

A. The unfair labor practice of preventing employees from having to pay excessive union fees was included in the law to protect employees who were required to join a union as a condition of employment by reason of a union-shop agreement.

B. Since employees have no choice about membership and no bargaining power when there is a union shop, the law requires that the dues and fees be reasonable and not discriminatory.

XV. Causing an Employer to Pay for Work Not Performed

A. This unfair labor practice is known as "featherbedding." It is quite limited in actual operation. It is designed to prevent a powerful union from forcing an employer to pay workers for doing nothing when an employer has no further use for the employees.

B. Make-work rules are not prohibited under this unfair labor practice. If the union can cause the employer to create other work for employees who are no longer needed for their former work, this is not an unfair labor practice.

XVI. Picketing When Not Certified

A. Picketing to force an employer to recognize an uncertified union is illegal in the following cases:

1. When the employer lawfully has recognized another union as the collective bargaining representative of its employees.
2. When a valid certification election has been conducted by the NLRB within the past 12 months.
3. When picketing has been conducted for a reasonable time, not in excess of 30 days, without a petition for a certification election being filed with the NLRB.

B. Under Item 3, it is not an unfair labor practice to engage in "informational" picketing. This picketing advises the public that an employer has a nonunion business. It becomes illegal only if the effect of the picketing is to persuade employees of another employer to observe the picket line. This illegal variety is called organizational picketing.

Chapter 18

XVII. **The Union's Duty of Fair Representation**

A. The labor laws state that the elected union represents all employees in a unit whether or not particular employees voted for the union. Thus, bargaining by a single employee with the employer concerning that employee's terms or conditions of employment is not permitted.

B. Because the certified union is the exclusive bargaining representative, it has a duty of fair representation in the negotiation, administration, interpretation and application of the collective bargaining agreement. An employee may sue the union and its representatives for damages resulting from breach of their duty of fair representation. For example, a union's failing to file a grievance of an employee within the time permitted by a collective bargaining agreement might give rise to a lawsuit against the union.

COMPLETION EXERCISES

1. Causing an employer to pay for work not to be performed is called ______________.

2. The ______________ Doctrine places the burden of proof on employers to prove there was a legitimate business reason for discharging an employee when antiunion bias may also have been a motivating factor in the discharge.

3. An agreement by an employer not to handle nonunion goods is called a ______________ contract.

4. Compulsory or mandatory bargaining issues concern ______________, ______________, ______________.

5. If management dominates a union or gives it financial support, there is likelihood of ______________ contracts.

6. An employer's conferring of benefits on employees shortly before a certification election may be an ______________.

7. It is an unfair labor practice to interfere with the efforts of any employees, union members or not, in carrying out ______________ activities for mutual aid or protection.

8. An employer's decision to lay off workers because of automation is a ______________ bargaining issue.

9. It is illegal for an employer to discharge an employee for filing ______________ against his or her employer with the NLRB.

10. ______________ picketing truthfully advises the public that an employer has a nonunion business.

11. If a majority of the employees in a unit vote to form a union, the union becomes the ______________ representative of the employees in that unit, even if some of them did not vote for the union.

12. Charges of unfair labor practices involving concerted activities often involve the refusal to follow ______________.

13. It would be an unfair labor practice for a business to retaliate against workers for forming a union by closing down the unionized plant and shifting work to ______________.

14. For a union to picket an employer not their own in order to force that employer to stop dealing with their employer is an example of a ______________ boycott.

15. It is illegal for a union to charge excessive dues or fees to its members when a valid ______________ agreement is in effect.

TRUE-FALSE CHOICES

1. ______ The filing of a lawsuit against employees may or may not be an unfair labor practice.
2. ______ A sole employee is not protected under the Wagner Act for concerted activity.
3. ______ It is not an unfair labor practice for an employer to provide a meeting place for the union members.
4. ______ The law requires employers (in certain instances) to favor union members in hiring employees.
5. ______ Although an employer may be required to bargain with a union, a union may not be required to bargain with an employer.
6. ______ The negotiation of fringe benefits may be a compulsory bargaining issue.
7. ______ The Wagner Act did not contain any provisions relating to unfair labor practices by labor unions.
8. ______ Employees are guaranteed the right to refrain from union activities unless required by legal union-shop agreement.
9. ______ "Make-work" rules are an unfair labor practice.
10. ______ A constructive discharge may be an unfair labor practice.
11. ______ If a foreseeable consequence of a strike, picketing, or boycott is to disrupt the business of a third person, the activity is an unfair labor practice.
12. ______ Bargaining in "good faith" over mandatory issues means that the employer and union are required to make concessions to each other.
13. ______ In general, unions and employers may contract so that employers must discharge employees who have been denied union membership.
14. ______ An activity may be, and often is, a violation of more than one particular unfair labor practice.
15. ______ A company work rule requiring there be no solicitation during working hours may be an unfair labor practice.

MULTIPLE CHOICE SELECTIONS

1. Select the most correct statement:

   a. Making threats to employees could be an unfair labor practice.
   b. Threatening to fire workers if a union wins a certification election is an unfair labor practice.
   c. An employer's support of one union over another during a certification election is an unfair labor practice.
   d. All of the above are unfair labor practices.

2. Ajax Corporation and the United Widgett Workers cannot agree on a new collective bargaining contract. Select the most correct statement:

   a. Ajax may permanently replace the workers if they go out on strike.
   b. Ajax can "lock out" the workers.
   c. The union can go out on strike.
   d. All of the above are correct.

3. The United Widgett Workers strikes the Ajax Corporation. Select the most correct statement:

   a. If the collective bargaining contract has a mandatory arbitration clause in it, the federal courts can enjoin the strike.
   b. If the strikers engage in violence which cannot be controlled by local authorities, the federal courts can enjoin the strike.
   c. If Ajax is a defense plant, the federal courts can enjoin the strike.
   d. Under the Norris-LaGuardia Act the federal courts cannot enjoin strikes.

4. All of the following are unfair labor practices under the Wagner Act except:

   a. Firing an employee for joining a union.
   b. Discharging an employee for filing an unfounded complaint against the employer with the NLRB.
   c. Refusing to bargain with the union about a decision to automate a plant.
   d. Agreeing with a union to engage in a secondary boycott.

5. All of the following are unfair labor practices by unions under the Taft-Hartley Act except:

   a. Picketing an employer where a valid representation election has been conducted 11 months previously.
   b. Inducing the employees of an employer not to handle the goods of a third party with whom the union has a dispute.
   c. Causing an employer to "make work" which is of no value to the employer.
   d. Physically blocking non-union employees from entering a workplace.

DISCUSSION ANALYSIS

Discuss why work-related rules may be unfair labor practices. May these rules serve a legitimate business purpose and still be unfair labor practices? Explain.

Chapter 19

Investor Protection

STUDY GUIDE AND OUTLINE

I. Definition of Security

A. This chapter covers the Securities Act of 1933 and the Securities Exchange Act of 1934. Also mentioned are state securities laws, often called blue sky laws. The intent underlying securities laws is to give potential investors sufficient information to make informed investment decisions.

B. The term security includes much more than corporate stock bonds. It includes any investment opportunity which is a common venture that seeks profit based on the entrepreneurial efforts of others.

C. The Supreme Court in Landreth Timber Company v. Landreth held that the sale of all of the stock of a company was a "security" within the definition of the federal securities laws, and the sale of business doctrine did not apply.

II. Securities and Exchange Commission (SEC)

A. The SEC is headed by five commissioners appointed by the President for a five-year term.

B. The SEC has both quasi-legislative and quasi-judicial power.

C. In addition to regulating sale of securities, the SEC also regulates the various stock exchanges, utility holding companies, investment trusts, and investment advisors.

III. Federal Securities Act of 1933: General Provisions

A. The Securities Act of 1933 regulates the initial sale of securities to the public. The law makes it illegal to use the mails or any other interstate means of communication or transportation to sell securities without disclosing certain financial information to potential investors.

B. If the disclosure is misleading or untrue, the 1933 act provides for possible criminal punishment, civil liability, and equitable remedies.

IV. Parties Regulated

A. Definitions

1. An issuer is the individual or business offering a security for sale to the public.

2. An underwriter is anyone who participates in the original distribution of securities by selling them for the issuer or by guaranteeing their sale.
3. A controlling person is one who controls or is controlled by the issuer, such as a major stockholder of a corporation.

B. Investors and certain others are protected under the 1933 act.

C. In Junker v. Crory a federal court of appeals ruled that a lawyer who strongly recommended a merger could be held liable as a "seller" under the 1933 act.

V. Documents Involved

A. Securities subject to the provisions of the 1933 act must be registered with the SEC prior to any sale. The registration statement discloses a variety of information about the issuer.

B. A registration statement becomes effective 20 days after it is filed unless the SEC gives notice that it is not in the proper form. Only after the registration statement becomes effective can the security be sold.

C. Before the registration statement is filed, it is illegal to sell or to offer to sell a security subject to the act. During the 20-day waiting period it is still illegal to sell a security, but it is not illegal to make an offer to sell one. Many offers during the waiting period are made in advertisements called tombstone ads. After registration becomes effective the security may be sold.

D. Any time a registered security is sold, it must be accompanied by a prospectus. Like the registration statement, the prospectus is a disclosure document. It discloses information about the security and the issuer to prospective buyers.

VI. Shelf Registration

A. The SEC now permits shelf registration of securities. Shelf registration allows companies to submit a single, comprehensive disclosure statement describing their long-term financing plans. This registration permits companies to sell securities whenever rapidly changing market conditions appear most favorable. The issuer need not prepare a new prospectus for the SEC's review every time it plans to sell new securities.

B. Companies with less than $150 million in stock held by investors not affiliated with the company cannot use shelf registration.

VII. Exemptions

A. Certain securities and certain security transactions are exempt from registration requirement.

B. Transactions by a securities dealer (as distinguished from an issuer or an underwriter) are exempt after 40 days from the first public offer. Brokers' transactions are also exempt.

C. Private sales (as opposed to public sales) of securities are exempt from registration. If challenged, the issuer must prove the sale is private and not public. In determining whether a sale is public or not, the SEC considers such things as:

1. The number of offerees.
2. Their knowledge about the company in which they are investing.
3. Whether or not the security is purchased for resale.
4. The extent to which the security is promoted.

D. Securities exempt from registration requirement include:

1. Securities subject to regulation by government agencies other than the SEC.
2. Sales of government securities.
3. Securities that are offered and sold only to persons who reside within the state residence or incorporation of the issuer.
4. Commercial paper (e.g., promissory note), with a maturity not to exceed nine months.
5. Securities issued by not-for-profit corporations.

E. Disclosure requirements are limited or eliminated for issuers who sell a limited dollar amount of securities.

1. Any business may raise up to $500,000 in capital per 12-month period without filing a registration statement or prospectus with the SEC.
2. Issuers may sell up to $5,000,000 in securities without registration during a 12-month period as long as the issuer reasonably believes there are no more than thirty-five non-accredited investors who purchase the securities. A non-accredited investor is anyone who is not a director, officer, or general partner of the issuer. Also, certain financially well-off persons and certain persons with knowledge and experience in financial matters are considered accredited.

VIII. Criminal Liability

A. The Securities Act of 1933 imposes both civil and criminal liability for violations.

B. Criminal liability:

1. A fine up to $10,000 and/or 5 years in prison for a willful violation of the act or fraud in any offer or sale of securities.
2. Fraud includes an intentional omission of material fact in a registration statement which causes it to be misleading.

C. Willful means "with intent to defraud," but it includes that the defendant deliberately ignored certain facts or recklessly stated as facts things of which he/she was ignorant.

D. In Rubin v. United States the U.S. Supreme Court demonstrated the broad application of the securities laws. The Court ruled that a pledge of stock in connection with false statements made to a bank to obtain a corporate loan was an "offer or sale" of securities.

IX. Civil Liability

A. The 1933 act imposes potential civil liability on the following persons:

1. Persons signing the registration statement.
2. Directors or partners of the issuer.
3. Accountants, engineers, or appraisers who assist in the preparation of the registration statement or its certification.
4. Underwriters.

B. These persons are civilly liable if the registration statement:

1. Contains untrue statements of material facts.
2. Omits material facts required by a statute or regulation.
3. Omits information which if not given makes the facts stated misleading.

C. To recover damages, a plaintiff-purchaser need not prove reliance on the misleading registration statement.

D. Section 12 of the act imposes liability on anyone who sells a security without an accompanying prospectus or with a misleading prospectus. Purchasers of such securities may sue for actual damages or obtain a refund of their purchase price.

E. Section 17 imposes liability for the use of an instrument of interstate communication in the offer or sale of securities when the result is:

1. To defraud.
2. To obtain money or properties by means of an untrue or misleading statement.
3. To engage in a business or practice that defrauds or deceives a purchaser. Note that this section does not apply to the private remedy of monetary damages. It applies only to injunctive relief, i.e., an order to the defendant to stop violating the section.

F. Pinter v. Dahl teaches that the Supreme Court approved the defendant's argument that the plaintiff was equally responsible for the failure to register the securities sold. The case appears to be a movement away from the traditional strict liability for failure to file the required registration statement.

G. In Aaron v. SEC the Supreme Court resolved the issue of whether Section 17 requires a showing of intent to establish a violation. The SEC had sued to enjoin a broker from aiding and abetting a violation of Section 17(a), which prohibits activities specified in E (above). The Court ruled that if the SEC accuses the defendant of employing a scheme to defraud, a showing of intent is required. If the defendant is accused of obtaining money by an untrue or misleading statement, or of engaging in a transaction that may operate to defraud a purchaser, no showing of intent is required.

X. Defenses

A. A common defense to the charge of a misleading registration statement is that the misleading or omitted facts were not material (i.e., important or significant) to an average investor's decision to purchase the security.

B. Lawsuits based on civil or criminal liability must be brought within one year after the discovery of an untrue statement or omission. In no event may a suit be brought more than three years after the sale of a security.

C. A very important defense for experts such as accountants is the due diligence defense. In effect this means that if the part of a registration statement prepared by an expert was not prepared fraudulently or with negligence, the expert is free from liability upon proving this.

XI. Federal Securities Act of 1934: General Coverage

A. The 1934 act regulated transfers of securities after the initial sale. It also regulates security exchanges, brokers, and dealers in securities.

B. As a general rule, the 1934 act requires that all equity securities held by 500 or more owners must be registered with the SEC if the issuer has more than $1,000,000 in gross assets.

C. Stockbrokers and dealers may not use the mails or any instrumentality of interstate commerce to sell securities unless they register with the SEC. They must keep detailed records of their activities and file annual reports with the SEC.

D. Issuers of registered securities must file periodic reports with the SEC and also report significant developments which would materially affect the value of the issuer's securities. Under the Reagan administration, the SEC has lessened the burden of periodic reporting requirements on many small companies.

XII. Section 10b and Rule 10b-5

A. Most of the litigation under the 1934 Act is brought under Section 10b and 10b-5.

B. Issued under Section 10b, Rule 10b-5 makes unlawful to use the mail, an instrumentality of interstate commerce, or any national securities exchange to defraud any person in connection with the purchase or sale of securities.

C. The concept of fraud under 10b and 10b-5 encompasses not only untrue statements of material facts but also omission to state material facts necessary to prevent statements actually made from being misleading.

D. Liability under 10b and 10b-5 requires proof of intent (scienter), however, not mere negligence or mismanagement.

E. Defendants in 10b and 10b-5 cases fall into four general categories:

1. Insiders.
2. Broker-dealers.
3. Corporations whose stock is purchased or sold by plaintiffs.
4. Those, such as accountants, who aid and abet or conspire with a party who falls into one of the first three categories.

F. In Basic Incorporated v. Levinson, the Supreme Court held that materiality depends on the significance the reasonable investor would place on the withheld or misrepresented information.

XIII. Insider Transactions

A. Section 16 of the 1934 act requires that insiders file, at the time of registration or within 10 days after becoming an insider, a statement of the amount of such issues of which they are the owners.

B. An insider is any person:

1. Who owns more than 10 percent of any security.
2. Who is a director or an officer of the issuer of the security.

C. Under Section 16 insiders may not profit from the purchase and sale of securities within a six-month period. This is called the short-swing profit rule.

D. Short-swing profits may be recovered by an insider's company or by the investor at whose expense an insider profited.

XIV. Nonpublic Information

A. Tippees (temporary insiders) are treated like insiders under 10b and 10b-5. A tippee is one who is tipped off to nonpublic information by an insider.

B. The Supreme Court in Carpenter v. U.S. failed to support or reject the misappropriation theory of insider trading since it was evenly divided.

C. However, a person who learns of nonpublic information from a source other than an insider is not required to reveal that information prior to trading.

D. Since 1984 the SEC has been able to seek a civil penalty of three times the illegal profit gained from insider trading.

XV. Additional Civil Liability

A. Section 18 of the 1934 act imposes liability on a theory of fraud on any person who makes or causes to be made any false and misleading statements of material fact in any document filed under the act.

B. Any injured purchaser or seller of stock can sue for damages under Section 18 upon proving defendant's intent and showing reliance on the misleading statements, and damage.

C. Section 14(e) of the 1934 act prohibits fraudulent deceptive or manipulative practices in connection with tender offers. In Schreiber v. Burlington Northern, Inc. the Supreme Court ruled that unfairness was not a manipulative practice under 14(e). During a tender offer Burlington had withdrawn one tender offer and substituted a lower one. The Court stated that a "manipulative practice" required a misrepresentation.

XVI. Criminal Liability

A. The 1934 act provides for a fine not to exceed $100,000 and/or five years in prison for willful violations of its provisions or the rules adopted under it.

B. Criminal liability is important for officers and directors. It is also important for accountants since many have been found guilty of a crime for failure to disclose important facts to shareholder-investors.

XVII. State "Blue Sky" Laws

A. Federal securities laws do not preempt state "blue sky" laws that regulate the role of securities.

B. Although a Uniform Securities Act was proposed for adoption by all states beginning in 1956, state securities laws still vary a great deal from state to state.

XVIII. Ethical Considerations

A. Many companies have developed policies recognizing the legal and ethical obligations involved in financial reporting and disclosure.

B. For instance, the Caterpillar Code of Ethics requires:

1. That employees not conceal information from management or from the company's independent auditor.
2. That employees must not use material inside information about the company for personal gain.
3. That the company will not hire persons as a means of gaining access to trade secrets of others.

COMPLETION EXERCISES

1. State securities laws are often called _______________ laws.

2. The administrative agency which regulates securities at the federal level is the _______________.

3. The Securities Act of 1933 regulates the _______________ sale of securities to the public.

4. An _______________ is an individual or business offering a security for sale to the public.

5. An _______________ is anyone who participates in the original distribution of securities by selling them for the issuer or by guaranteeing their sale.

6. Prior to selling securities subject to the 1933 Act, the issuer must file a _______________ with the FTC.

7. Offers made during the waiting period often appear in advertisements called _______________.

8. Any time a registered security is sold, it must be accompanied by a _______________.

9. _______________ allows companies to submit a single, comprehensive disclosure statement describing their long-term financing plans.

10. The person sued under Section 17 of the 1933 Act may defend by proving that he/she exercised ________________.

11. A common defense to the charge of a misleading registration statement is that the misleading or omitted facts were not _______________ to an average prudent investor's decision to purchase a security.

12. Most of the litigation under the Securities Exchange Act of 1934 is brought under Section _______________ and Rule _______________.

13. An _______________ is any person who owns more than 10 percent of any security or who is a director or officer of the issuer.

14. The short-swing profits rule forbids insiders from making profits on a purchase and sale of a security within a _______________ month period.

15. The 1934 Act provides criminal penalties for _______________ violations of its provisions or the rules adopted under it.

TRUE-FALSE CHOICES

1. _____ The term <u>security</u> is limited to corporate stocks and bonds.

2. _____ The SEC has both quasi-legislative and quasi-judicial powers.

3. _____ The Securities Act of 1933 regulates all interstate sales of securities to the public.

4. _____ The protection of the 1933 Act applies only to investors.

5. _____ Sales of securities by a dealer are usually exempt from registration requirements after 40 days from the first public offer.

6. _____ Private sales of securities are exempt from registration requirements.

7. _____ Purely intrastate sales of securities are exempt from the requirements of the 1933 Act.

8. _____ Any business may raise up to $1,000,000 in capital per twelve-month period without filing a registration statement with the SEC if it limits securities sales to accredited investors.

9. _____ A director or officer of an issuer who purchased the issuer's stock would be considered an accredited investor.

10. _____ To establish criminal intent under the 1933 Act it would be sufficient to show that the defendant recklessly stated as facts things of which he/she was ignorant.

11. _____ Accountants who assist in the preparation of the registration statement can be held civilly liable under the 1933 Act.

12. _____ In establishing a civil violation of Section 17's three provisions, it is necessary for plaintiff to show <u>intent</u>.

13. _____ As a general rule, the Securities Exchange Act requires that all equity securities held by 500 or more owners must be registered with the SEC if the issuer has more than $1,000,000 in gross assets.

14. _____ The SEC currently requires anyone with advance knowledge of a tender offer to disclose his/her knowledge prior to dealing in securities issued by the companies involved.

15. _____ Federal securities laws have preempted state "blue sky" laws.

MULTIPLE CHOICE SELECTIONS

1. The Securities Act of 1933 imposes potential civil liability on the following persons except:

   a. All persons signing the registration statement.
   b. All directors or partners of the issuer.
   c. All underwriters.
   d. All stockholders of the issuer.

2. Civil liability is imposed under the 1933 Act in all of the following situations <u>except</u> when the registration statement:

   a. Contains untrue statements of material facts.
   b. Discloses excessive risks in the investment opportunity.
   c. Omits material facts required by a statute or a regulation.
   d. Omits information which if not given makes the facts stated misleading.

3. All of the following securities are exempt from registration requirements under the 1933 Act except:

   a. Securities subject to regulation by government agencies other than the SEC.
   b. Sales of government securities.
   c. Purely intrastate sales of securities.
   d. Sales of securities by corporations whose assets do not exceed $5,000,000.

4. A director of the Acme Corporation leans that his company has made a major oil find in Alaska. This information is not generally available to the public. Later that day at a party, the director offers to buy 20,000 shares of stock from a major shareholder of Acme Corporation. The offer is accepted. Select the most <u>correct</u> statement:

   a. The director is liable under Rule 10b-5.
   b. The director is not liable under Rule 10b-5 unless the purchase of stock exceeds 1 percent of the corporation's outstanding stock.
   c. This purchase does not violate Rule 10b-5.
   d. This purchase violates Rule 10b-5 unless the major stockholder qualifies as a "controlling person."

5. Select the most <u>correct</u> statement about the Securities Exchange Act:

   a. The Act does not regulate stockholders.
   b. The Act requires issuers of registered securities to report developments that would materially affect the value of the issuer's securities.
   c. Under the Reagan administration, the SEC has increased the burden of reporting requirements on issuers.
   d. The Act provides for criminal sanctions for negligent violations of its provisions.

Chapter 19

DISCUSSION ANALYSIS

What is the primary regulatory goal of federal securities laws? Your answer should include the definition of a security and whether or not these laws limit the offering of risky investment opportunities.

Chapter 20

Consumer Protection

STUDY GUIDE AND OUTLINE

I. Who is a Consumer?

A. A consumer is a natural person who incurs debt "primarily for personal, family, or household purposes."

B. In Anderson v. Foothill Industrial Bank a Wyoming court ruled that the defendant bank did not violate the Truth-in-Lending Act's requirements for a consumer loan. The court noted that the plaintiff obtained the loan in question primarily for a commercial purpose (financing a mail-route business), although part of the loan was used to pay off a home mortgage.

II. The FTC

A. Created in 1914, the FTC is responsible for promotion of free competition through the anti-trust laws and protection of consumers through Section 5 of the FTC Act, which prohibits "unfair or deceptive acts or practices in commerce."

B. The Bureau of Consumer Protection, which is one of the enforcement arms of the FTC, issues nonbinding advisory options and industry guidelines on trade regulation issues. But the Bureau's major role is to prosecute sellers for violations of Section 5. The chief enforcement tools of the Bureau are:

1. The consent order (a party "consents" to sign an order which restrains the offensive behavior).
2. The cease and desist order (a non-consenting guilty party is prosecuted before an administrative law judge who issues the order to prohibit future violations).

III. FTC Penalties and Remedies

A. The basic penalty for FTC Act violations is a fine of not more than $10,000 per violation. Its main purpose, like punitive damages, is to prevent and deter unfair and deceptive trade practices. Fines may be assessed in three situations:

1. Violation of a consent or cease and desist order.
2. Violation of a trade regulation rule.
3. Knowing violation of prior FTC orders against other parties.

B. The FTC Act states that each separate violation is a separate offense and that a continuing violation of an order is a separate offense for each day it continues. In United States v. Reader's Digest Assoc., Inc., a court of appeals upheld a federal district court's decision that the Digest violated a consent order prohibiting it from soliciting potential subscribers with check-like documents. The court ruled that each check-like letter of several sweepstakes mailings sent to over 17 million people constituted a separate violation of the consent order. Thus it ruled proper a $1,750,000 fine.

C. In addition to fines, the FTC has broad discretion to exercise other remedies to protect consumers, such as:

1. Corrective advertising - requiring companies to run ads admitting prior errors and falsehoods.
2. Refund of money or property.
3. Public notification of trade practice violations.
4. Injunctions from federal courts to restrain violators.

IV. Traditional Trade Practice Regulation

A. Most FTC regulation focuses on deceptive trade practices. To be illegal such practices need only have a "tendency or capacity" to mislead consumers; no actual harm need be shown. Deception does not necessarily involve false statements. It only requires that some sales activity, taken as a whole, has the capacity to mislead. Thus, the truthful but misleading representations can be deceptive.

B. Examples of traditional deceptive practices include:

1. Advertising that refers to a "manufacturer's list price" which is not the customary retail price.
2. Baiting and switching techniques.
3. Failure to make necessary disclosures (e.g., nondisclosure that books sold are condensed).

V. Policy Trends at the FTC

A. During the 1970's, the FTC began broad-scale use of its rule-making powers. Many rules required sellers to disclose various facts to consumers. The FTC also developed the doctrine of advertising substantiation, which holds that advertising claims not supported by adequate, existing substantiation are unfair and deceptive even if true.

B. In the early 1980's the FTC reduced its enforcement activities substantially. This reduction was in accord with the philosophy of the Reagan administration that most trade practices will be regulated successfully by the marketplace.

C. In recent years, the FTC has grappled with advertising problems presented by radio and TV. In American Home Products Corp. v. FTC a federal court ruled that the FTC had authority to analyze "aural-visual" imagery in determining that AHP had made a deceptive claim of superiority for its aspirin product.

D. The FTC has issued new deception guidelines. It will challenge a trade practice only when the practice is likely to mislead consumers acting reasonably under the circumstances. The practice must also be "material," that is, it must potentially affect consumer purchasing decisions.

VI. Introduction to Federal Credit Regulations

Much of our consumer economy today operates on credit financing. Several consumer protection laws regulating credit financing have been passed. Major ones involve nondiscrimination in credit extension, regulation of credit reporting practices, and standardization in the reporting of credit charges.

VII. Equal Credit Opportunity Act

A. The Equal Credit Opportunity Act (ECOA) was enacted by Congress in 1975 to prevent discrimination in credit extension. The ECOA prohibits discrimination based on sex, marital status, race, color, age, religion, national origin, or receipt of welfare in any aspect of a consumer credit transaction. The ECOA, which is interpreted by the Federal Reserve Board, applies to all businesses which regularly extend credit, including retail stores and credit card issuers.

B. The primary emphasis of the ECOA is prevention of sex discrimination. With rising divorce rates and increasing numbers of women in the work force, Congress perceived a fundamental need for equal credit opportunity between the sexes.

C. In Brothers v. First Leasing a federal court ruled that ECOA applied to credit extension in consumer leases as well as in consumer sales.

D. Private remedies for violation of the ECOA are recovery of actual damages, punitive damages up to $10,000 and attorney fees. The government may also bring suit to enjoin ECOA violators and to assess civil penalties.

VIII. The Fair Credit Reporting Act

A. The Fair Credit Reporting Act (FCRA) applies to anyone who prepares or uses a credit report in connection with extending credit, granting insurance, or the hiring or firing of an employee. The Act only covers credit reports on consumers, not businesses.

B. The purpose of the FCRA is to prevent character damage because of inaccurate information in a credit report and to prevent undue invasion of personal privacy.

C. If a consumer is rejected for credit he or she has the right to be told the credit agency's name. The credit agency must divulge the content of the credit report and give the consumer opportunity to correct inaccurate information. Privacy is protected since a credit agency may sell a report only to one who has a legitimate business reason for it. In Zamora v. Valley Federal Savings & Loan Assn. an employee was being considered for a branch manager's position. The employer S&L got a credit report on her husband. A federal appeals court ruled that the FCRA did not permit obtaining a credit report on the spouse of an employee and determined that the employer obtained the report under "false pretenses." Thus the employer could be held civilly liable to the employee's husband.

D. The major limitation of the FCRA is that if a credit agency follows reasonable procedures, it is not liable to a consumer, even if it reports false information.

E. Violators of the FCRA are civilly liable to affected consumers. Potential criminal liability exists for certain willful violators.

IX. Truth-In-Lending Act

A. The Truth-In-Lending Act (TILA) authorizes the Federal Reserve Board to adopt regulations to assure a meaningful disclosure of credit terms of consumers.

B. Those who regularly extend credit to consumers must inform them fully of the cost of the credit. This requirement is accomplished through disclosure of the finance charge and the annual percentage rate.

1. The finance charge is the sum of all charges payable by the debtor to the creditor as a condition of the extension of credit.
2. This finance charge must be expressed as an annual percentage rate.

C. Theoretically, a consumer armed with information will be better able to bargain and shop for credit.

D. Violations of the Act make creditors liable to debtors for an amount equal to twice the finance charge (but not less than $100 nor more than $1,000) plus attorney's fees.

E. In Herrera v. First Northern Savings & Loan Assn. a federal appeals court ruled that a plaintiff was entitled to a $1,000 statutory penalty plus attorney's fees of $1,930. The defendant had failed to print the terms finance charge and annual percentage rate more conspicuously than other terms in the disclosure statement as required by the TILA.

F. In 1980 Congress passed the Truth-In-Lending Simplification Act. The new law states that only material non-disclosures are violations and compliance with Federal Reserve Board model disclosure forms is conclusive proof of full disclosure.

X. The Magnuson-Moss Warranty Act

A. In 1975 Congress enacted the Magnuson-Moss Warranty Act to simplify warranty terms and to protect consumers from ambiguous warranty claims. Under the Act sellers must label written warranties on consumer products costing over $15 as either "full" or "limited."

B. A full warranty provides free repair, replacement of products or refund by the seller if the warranty is breached. Implied warranties cannot be limited if the written warranty is "full."

C. A limited warranty can limit or condition the written guarantees of the seller, but all limitations must be conspicuously disclosed.

XI. State Consumer Fraud Legislation

A. All states have passed consumer protection acts often called Unfair and Deceptive Acts and Practices (UDAP) statutes. Most are modelled after the FTC Act.

B. Many states also regulate specific businesses, such as the automobile repair industry.

XII. Consumer Privacy

A. Recently the law has recognized the invasion of privacy as a tort and has declared a constitutional right of privacy. The interrelationship between consumer protection regulation and privacy laws will certainly be a major focus of concern as the evolution of consumerism continues.

B. Several federal statutes regulate the government's interference in the private lives of citizens.

1. The Privacy Act of 1974 regulates methods of governmental collection of information and places safeguards to protect confidentiality.
2. The Right of Financial Privacy Act of 1978 requires the government to notify bank depositors when it seeks to investigate bank account records.

XIII. Ethical Considerations

Both legal and ethical questions regarding privacy will multiply in this age of rapid information transfer and computers. Many state legislatures have passed privacy-related statutes. Several states guarantee workers access to job personnel files, and approximately half the states forbid mandatory lie-detector tests as a condition of employment.

XIV. Policy Trends - The Future of Consumerism

Traditionally, many consumer complaints have been useless since the expense of legal fees makes such complaints illogical to pursue. However, recent change in the marketing of legal services makes attorneys more available to consumers. Low-cost legal clinics, increased numbers of attorneys, prepaid legal plans, and legal "hotlines" all indicate that consumer litigation will continue to grow.

COMPLETION EXERCISES

1. One who purchases something for personal, family, or household use is called a ______________.

2. The chief enforcement tools of the FTC are the ______________ and the ______________.

3. The major purpose of the Truth-In-Lending Act is to require ______________ of credit terms to consumers.

4. The federal law on warranties is contained in the ______________, which requires merchants who use warranties to label them as either ______________ or ______________.

5. The Equal Credit Opportunity Act was enacted by Congress in 1975 to prevent ______________ in credit extension.

6. Credit reporting practices are regulated under the provisions of the ______________.

7. Section 5 of the FTC Act protects consumers by prohibiting ______________.

8. The basic penalty for FTC Act violations is a fine of ______________.

9. ______________ requires companies to run ads admitting prior errors and falsehoods.

10. If promotional claims are not supported by adequate existing evidence, they will be considered unfair and deceptive under the FTC's ______________ doctrine.

11. Private remedies for ECOA violations include ______________, ______________, and ______________.

12. If a credit agency follows ______________, it is not liable to a consumer, even if it reports false information.

13. Under the Truth-In-Lending Act the ______________ is the sum of all charges payable by the debtor to the creditor as a condition of credit extension.

14. Most state UDAP statutes are modelled after the ______________.

15. The ______________ requires the federal government to notify bank depositors when it seeks to investigate bank account records.

TRUE-FALSE CHOICES

1. _____ The Magnuson-Moss Warranty Act requires all manufacturers to give consumer products an express warranty.

2. _____ The number of attorneys practicing law has increased only slightly in the last twenty years.

3. _____ The Truth-In-Lending Act accomplishes its purpose through required disclosure of the finance charge and the annual percentage rate.

4. _____ Besides protection of the consumer, the FTC has the responsibility to promote competition through the anti-trust laws.

5. _____ The FTC cannot engage in rulemaking.

6. _____ In addition to assessment of fines, the FTC has broad discretion in fashioning its own legal remedies.

7. ______ The president of Acme Corp. buys a television set on credit for her home. She is not a consumer under the Truth-In-Lending Act.

8. ______ A knowing violation of a prior FTC order against another party violates Section 5 of the FTC Act.

9. ______ Truthful claims cannot be deceptive under the FTC Act.

10. ______ Under the new deception guidelines the FTC will challenge a deceptive practice only when it is "material."

11. ______ Under the Truth-In-Lending Act the finance charge must be expressed in the form of an annual percentage rate.

12. ______ Under the Magnuson-Moss Act a seller cannot limit the application of an express consumer warranty.

13. ______ The law has recognized invasion of privacy as a tort.

14. ______ Approximately half the states forbid mandatory lie-detector tests as a condition of employment.

15. ______ Violation of an FTC consent order may bring a $10,000 per day penalty.

MULTIPLE CHOICE SELECTIONS

1. Susan Consumer enters into an installment sales contract with Fleet Finance, secured by a newly purchased automobile. Two days after Susan signed the contract she notices that the printed total finance charge omits the cost of liability insurance which is a condition of the loan. The loan officer assures her that it is an unintentional mistake and will be corrected, but Susan decides she wants out of the arrangement. Select the most correct answer:

   a. Susan cannot rescind the contract under the Truth-In-Lending Act because there has been no material breach of the disclosure requirement.
   b. Susan can cancel the contract within a three day period after entering into it.
   c. Susan can rescind the contract under the tort of deceit because she believed the contract contained all material finance charges.
   d. Susan must seek statutory relief before relying on common law remedies.

2. Nonick Inc. has done extensive television advertising which claims that its razor will not nick shavers. Relying on the ads, Charles Consumer buys a Nonick razor and is nicked many times during its use. Along with many others, he complains to the FTC about Nonick's advertising. Select the most correct statement:

   a. The FTC has the power to imprison those responsible for the deceptive ads.
   b. The FTC cannot take action against Nonick's advertising because the FCC has sole jurisdiction over television advertisements.
   c. The FTC can order consumer refunds because of the deceptive advertising.
   d. Actual proof of harm must be shown before the FTC can declare this advertising deceptive.

3. Select the incorrect statement about the Equal Credit Opportunity Act:

   a. There is no private right of action under ECOA, only civil penalties assessed by the Federal Reserve Board.
   b. The primary emphasis of the Act is prevention of sex discrimination.
   c. The ECOA prohibition against marital status discrimination also applies to credit applications by unmarried couples.
   d. The ECOA applies to businesses which regularly extend credit.

4. All of the following are likely to promote consumer litigation except:

   a. Low cost legal clinics.
   b. Increased numbers of attorneys.
   c. Prepaid legal plans.
   d. Increased use of arbitration.

5. Mary is denied a job with a firm because the credit report which the firm obtained stated that the plaintiff had five outstanding liens against her property. The information is false. The credit agency that supplied the credit report is:

   a. Liable under the Right of Financial Privacy Act of 1978.
   b. Liable under the Privacy Act of 1974.
   c. Liable under the Fair Credit Reporting Act only if it used unreasonable procedures in gathering the adverse information.
   d. Not liable under the Fair Credit Reporting Act because FCRA applies to reports in connection with credit extension, not in the hiring and discharging of employees.

Chapter 20

DISCUSSION ANALYSIS

Losemore is a drug manufactured by Losemore, Inc. The manufacturer claims in its ads that the drug will cause users to lose at least twenty pounds if taken twice per day for one month. Thousands rely on the Losemore ads but few users experience the weight loss claimed by the ads. Complaints about Losemore alert the FTC which is now considering action against Losemore, Inc. Discuss how the FTC might proceed against Losemore, Inc., including what remedies or fines the FTC might ask for.

Chapter 21

Creditor and Debtor Protection

STUDY GUIDE AND OUTLINE

I. **Creditor Protection: Introduction**

A. A <u>creditor</u> is one who lends money or extends credit for goods or services.

B. Creditor protection laws benefit consumers as well as creditors. They make creditors more willing to lend money and extend credit. They also keep creditors from having to charge higher interest rates and prices to all consumers to cover the greater losses suffered because of the lack of legal protection.

II. **Artisan's Liens**

A. A <u>lien</u> is an obligation for payment of money which attaches to property as a result of statute, common law, equity, or contract. Usually, the property can be sold to satisfy the lien if the creditor is not paid.

B. <u>Artisan's liens</u> are a class of liens that protects those who store, carry, or repair the goods of another for a price.

C. Usually, an artisan's lien lasts only as long as the creditor has possession of the property. For example, a TV repair shop has an artisan's lien against your TV for the repair service that it furnishes you. If you fail to pay the shop, it can sell your TV to satisfy the lien. However, once it has released the TV back to you, it loses its lien in most states.

D. Statutes creating artisan's liens usually require the creditor to give notice to the debtor before a sale takes place. Any surplus from the sale after the debt is paid must be returned to the debtor.

III. **Mechanic's Liens**

A. Almost any contract for the improvement of real property creates a <u>mechanic's lien</u> in favor of the person who improves the property. These liens also protect those who provide services or material to contractors who improve real property.

B. Mechanic's lien statutes usually specify that a lien must be recorded within 60 to 90 days following completion of work or delivery of materials to establish priority over third parties, such as mortgages or buyers of property.

C. Persons buying real estate should always check to determine whether or not improvements have been made recently in the property. This is often the only way to determine whether mechanic's liens exist against the property.

IV. Bulk Transfers

A. The law of bulk transfers is found in Article 6 of the Uniform Commercial Code.

B. A bulk transfer is a transfer (usually a sale) out of the ordinary course of business of all or a major part of the inventory (or inventory and equipment) of a merchant.

1. Inventory is the stock that a merchant holds for resale.
2. Note that the sale must be "out of the ordinary course of business" and that it must constitute a "major part" of the inventory. Regular sales to a merchant's customers are not included within the meaning of bulk transfer.

C. Anyone who buys in bulk out of the ordinary course of a merchant's business must obtain a schedule of the inventory sold and a sworn list of the merchant's creditors. The bulk buyer must then notify the listed creditors at least 10 days before the buyer takes possession of the inventory or pays for it.

D. This notice requirement gives a merchant's creditors time to stop a bulk sale by throwing the merchant into bankruptcy or otherwise protecting themselves.

E. Should a bulk buyer fail to give the required notice, the merchant's creditors can seize the inventory property from the bulk buyer and sell it to satisfy their debts.

V. Suretyship

A. A surety is one who promises to perform some obligation upon breach or default of performance by another person. The parties to a suretyship are a debtor who owes a performance, a creditor to whom the performance is owed, and a surety who will have to perform if the debtor does not.

B. Unless they state otherwise, suretyship contracts are unconditional. This means that once the debtor fails to perform, the creditor can immediately demand performance from the surety.

C. In New Hampshire Ins. Co. v. Gruhn an insurance company entered into a surety contract, agreeing to pay "all damages suffered by any persons." The suretyship bond was to protect customers of the mortgage company. A court found the mortgage company guilty of fraud and awarded the victims $5,000 in punitive damages. An appellate court held that the insurance company did not have to pay the punitive damages, since they were awarded to punish the mortgage company and were not suffered by any victim.

D. The basic rule in suretyship situations is that any time defenses are available to the debtor, they are also available to the surety. These defenses include fraud, duress, illegality, lack of consideration, mistake, and impossibility of performance. The debtor's defenses of infancy and bankruptcy, however, are not available to the surety.

E. The surety also has other defenses. For example, if the creditor and the debtor modify their contract so as to increase materially the risk to the surety, the surety is charged from liability.

F. A surety who pays the creditor has a right of reimbursement against the debtor.

G. When there is more than one surety on a debt, the arrangement is called co-suretyship. Co-sureties share joint and several liability. This means that a creditor whose debtor defaults on a loan may recover the amount owed from either or both of the co-sureties.

H. Co-sureties have the right of contribution. If both guarantees a $20,000 loan, and the creditor collects that amount from only one of them, the one who paid can recover $10,000 from the other because of the right of contribution.

I. When a creditor destroys the right of contribution of Co-surety A by releasing Co-surety B from liability, Co-surety A's obligation to the creditor is reduced by a like extent. In Keystone Bank v. Flooring Specialists, Inc. the president and vice-president of a corporation (and their wives) signed a promissory note as personal sureties of their corporation's obligation. When the bank that held the note released the president and his wife from judgment liens against real property, the vice-president and his wife asserted that they were also released from liability. The Pennsylvania Supreme Court agreed that the release of the president and his wife affected the liability of the vice-president and his wife. It ordered the case returned to the trial court for determination of the extent to which the right of contribution had been destroyed.

J. A suretyship contract must be evidenced in writing under a statute of frauds.

VI. Secured Transactions in Personal Property

A. The subject of secured transactions concerns how a debtor puts up personal property as collateral to ensure repayment of a loan or an extension of credit.

B. Article 9 of the Uniform Commercial Code controls secured transactions. It applies only to personal property. Personal property can be subdivided into tangible, intangible, and documentary property. Important: See Table 21-2 on page 662 of the text concerning the various types of personal property.

C. Secured transactions in personal property are significant for two reasons:

1. If the debtor doesn't pay, the creditor can simply seize the personal property and sell it to satisfy the debt.
2. A secured interest in the property often gives the creditor priority over many other parties who may also want the property. These parties include judgement creditors, lienholders, trustees in bankruptcy and buyers.

D. To be enforceable, a security interest in personal property must first attach. Attachment occurs when three things are present:

1. There must be a written security agreement that is signed by the debtor.
2. The creditor must give value to the debtor. Goods sold on credit or money from a loan is the usual form of the value.
3. The debtor must have rights in the property that is collateral for the security interest. In First National Bank of Santa Fe v. Quintana the debtor had a contract to purchase restaurant equipment. He had been loaned $59,000 by the bank to get the equipment. The bank had filed a financing statement. The debtor acquired the equipment from the seller, but never paid the seller the full downpayment. When the seller repossessed the equipment, the bank sued, claiming a perfected security interest in the equipment. The court ruled that the debtor had no rights in the equipment since it had never made the required downpayments.

E. Attachment alone seldom gives a secured creditor maximum priority over others who want the secured property. Perfection must also take place. The creditor perfects the security interest in one of several ways:

1. Attachment alone gives perfection when the creditor has a purchase-money security interest in consumer goods. A purchase-money interest arises when the credit or loan extended by the creditor is used to acquire the property that is subject to the security interest.
2. Possession (as with a pawnbroker) is an alternative means of establishing perfection.
3. The last method for getting perfection is by filing a financing statement in the appropriate records office. A proper financing statement is signed by the debtor and secured creditor, gives their addresses, and contains an adequate description of the secured property.

F. Article 9 contains many rules regarding priorities of security interests. Pages 531-533 of the text give 13 examples of such priorities. It is very important that you read these pages in order to understand the subject of priorities.

G. If the debtor fails to repay a loan or pay for goods or services sold on credit, the secured creditor may repossess the collateral and sell it. The secured creditor applies the proceeds gotten from the sale of the collateral in the following order:

1. Expenses of the creditor in repossessing and selling the property.
2. Satisfaction of the debt owing the creditor.
3. Satisfaction of debt owing to holders of lessor security interests.
4. Return of what remains, if anything, to the debtor.

VII. Secured Transactions in Real Property

A. The usual method of securing transactions in real property is the real estate mortgage.

B. Usually, the real estate mortgage places a lien against the real estate purchased with the loan given. If the debtor, called the mortgager, fails to repay the loan, the creditor -- or mortgagee -- can foreclose the mortgage and sell the property to satisfy the debt.

C. The mortgage arrangement usually consists of a promissory note and a mortgage deed. The mortgagee must file the mortgage deed, which is the legal document establishing the security interest, in the appropriate records office. Failure to file and record means that the security interest is not perfected against third parties who buy the property from the mortgagor.

D. A mortgage agreement or contract must be evidenced in writing to be enforceable because of the statute of frauds.

E. Table 21-3 on page 669 in the text lists common rights and duties of the mortgagor and mortgagee. For the mortgagee, the most important right is the right of foreclosure. When there has been a default in repaying the loan, the mortgagee can cut off the debtor's rights to the property (foreclose) and sell the property to satisfy the debt. A significant right of the mortgagor is the right (or equity) of redemption. For a period of time the mortgagor can redeem the property after foreclosure upon repaying the entire debt owed, plus interests and costs, even if the property has been sold.

F. The law permits mortgagors to sell their mortgaged property.

1. Most buyers of mortgaged property assume the mortgage. An assumption of mortgage occurs when the new buyer agrees to accept liability for making the mortgage payments.
2. If a buyer of mortgaged property does not assume the mortgage, the property is still subject to the mortgage. Should the mortgagor not meet the payments, the mortgagee can foreclose against the property in the hands of the buyer.

VIII. Debtor Protection: Introduction

A. When debtors are unable to repay contractual debts, the law protects them by regulating how the debts may be collected and how debts can be erased (discharged). The law also protects debtors by limiting the interest creditors can charge on loans.

B. Note that some of the laws in the following sections protect only consumer debtors; others protect business debtors as well.

IX. Usury

A. Traditionally the law has attempted to protect debtors by limiting the amount of interest chargeable upon borrowed money. Contracts which charge more than the maximum legal rate of interest are said to be usurious. Violations of usury laws can mean possible criminal liability for forfeiture of usurious interest.

B. Since there exist so many statutory exceptions to usury legislation, little if any protection is actually given those persons who the usury laws are designed to protect.

C. Note that some usury statutes apply only to personal or consumer loans. In Radford v. Community Mortgage and Investment Corp. a Virginia court held that borrowing money for payment of personal income taxes is a personal or consumer use even if the taxes were due on money earned as a self-employed business person. The court denied the creditor the right to foreclose a mortgage on the debtor's property because the loan interest was usurious as to personal loans.

X. Debt Collection

A. Congress enacted the Fair Debt Collection Practices Act (FDCPA) in response to complaints that some debt collection agencies used techniques of harassment, deception, and personal abuse to collect debts. The FDCPA applies only to consumer debt and only to agencies whose primary business is debt collection, to lawyers who collect debts for creditors, and to the IRS.

B. The FDCPA restricts the methods which can be used by the collector in the collection process. The collector cannot:

1. Physically threaten the debtor.
2. Use obscene language.
3. Claim to be an attorney unless he or she is.
4. Threaten the debtor with arrest unless he or she is legally entitled to such action.
5. Telephone the debtor repeatedly with intent to annoy.
6. Telephone the debtor before 8:00 a.m. or after 9:00 p.m.

C. The debtor may stop all contact from the collection agency by giving written notice of refusal to pay the debt. The agency's sole remedy would then be to sue the debtor.

D. Remedies for FDCPA violations are actual damages, including damages for invasion of privacy and infliction of mental distress, plus attorney's fees. Also, the FTC can seek penalties for violations of the Act.

E. The FDCPA does not pre-empt state laws regulating debt collections. Some state laws may protect consumers from certain collection efforts by creditors as well as by third parties. In Jacksonville State Bank v. Barnwell the Alabama Supreme Court allowed a debtor to sue a bank for invasion of privacy. The bank had repeatedly harassed the debtor at work about payment of a debt.

XI. Bankruptcy

A. Liberal revision of the federal bankruptcy laws in 1978 has caused a tremendous increase in the number of declared bankruptcies. Such bankruptcies are filed voluntarily by the debtor or involuntarily by one or more creditors of the debtor. In a bankruptcy proceeding, the debtor's property will be either liquidated and the debts discharged or the debts will be "adjusted" to fit a compromise repayment schedule. The decision to adjust debts instead of seek liquidation is solely that of the debtor. An alternative to liquidation is reorganization.

B. The trustee in bankruptcy is appointed by the creditors to represent the debtor's estate in liquidation of the debtor's property. The trustee has broad powers, but he or she must disperse the debtor's property in accordance with certain classes of priority:

1. Secured property rights.
2. Costs of administering the estate.
3. Claims from the debtor's business following initiation of bankruptcy.

4. Certain wages and benefits owed employees.
5. Certain consumer deposits or prepayments.
6. Taxes.
7. General creditors.

C. Debtor's obligations which cannot be discharged in bankruptcy include:

1. Alimony and child support.
2. Intentional torts.
3. Government fines.
4. Tax liens.
5. Educational loans.

D. The Bankruptcy Act particularly affects consumers in two ways:

1. Creditors can no longer contact debtors after discharge of his or her obligations in an effort to reactivate the debt. Debt reactivation can only be done voluntarily in court by the debtor.
2. Creditors are liable for the debtor's attorney's fees if an involuntary bankruptcy petition was filed merely to harass the debtor.

XII. Additional Protection for Consumer-Debtors

A. Consumers often find it too expensive to bring lawsuits against sellers who violate contracts. If consumers have already paid for products or services, they have little choice but to sue. But if consumers have merely promised to pay (e.g., signed a promissory note), they can withhold payment when the seller breaches the contract. This is true even when the seller has sold the promissory note to a third party <u>holder in due course</u>, such as a collection agency.

B. Under the Fair Credit Billing Act a consumer can also require a credit card issuer to recredit a charge account for a disputed charge made to a seller of goods or services. The disputed charge must be more than $50 and be made within the consumer's state of residency or within a 100 mile radius of the consumer's residence.

COMPLETION EXERCISES

1. A _______________ is one who lends money or extends credit for goods or services.

2. A _______________ is an obligation for payment of money that attaches to property.

3. Almost any contract for the improvement of real property creates a _______________ in favor of the person who improves the property.

4. A _______________ is a transfer out of the ordinary course of business of all or a major part of inventory of a merchant.

5. A _______________ is one who promises to perform some obligation upon breach or default of performance by another person.

6. _______________ refers to the duty of the debtor to pay back the surety when the surety has had to pay the creditor.

7. Under Article 9 of the UCC a _______________ arises when the credit or loan extended is used to acquire the property that is subject to the security interest.

8. A proper _______________ is signed by the debtor and secured creditor, gives their addresses, and contains an adequate description of the secured property.

9. For the mortgagee of real property, the most important right is the right of _______________ .

10. In a bankruptcy proceeding, an individual debtor's property will be either _______________ or the debts will be _______________.

11. Educational loans are nondischargeable in bankruptcy unless repayment would constitute an _______________.

12. _______________ is the charging of more than the maximum legal rate of interest.

13. Harassing phone calls by a collection agency to a debtor violates the _______________.

14. After meeting certain requirements, credit card users can refuse to pay credit charges under provisions of the _______________ Act.

15. The person who controls the debtor's estate in a bankruptcy proceeding is the _______________.

TRUE-FALSE CHOICES

1. _____ Artisan's liens protect those who store, carry, or repair the goods of another for a price.

2. _____ A mechanic's lien is lost if the creditor surrenders the property to the debtor.

3. _____ A sale of most of a manufacturer's inventory in the ordinary course of its business qualifies as a bulk sale.

4. _____ Should a bulk buyer fail to give the required notice, the bulk seller's creditors can seize the property from the bulk buyer and sell it to satisfy their debts.

5. _____ Unless they state otherwise, suretyship contracts are unconditional.

6. _____ A purchase-money security interest is perfected by attachment alone.

7. _____ If a debtor fails to repay a loan or pay for goods or services sold on credit, a secured creditor may repossess the collateral.

8. _____ In applying the proceeds gotten from sale of repossessed collateral, a secured creditor first satisfies the debt owing to the creditor.

9. _____ A pawnbroker usually perfects a security interest in personal property by filing a financing statement.

10. _____ In an assumption of mortgage, the new buyer agrees to accept liability for making the mortgage payments.

11. _____ The Fair Debt Collection Practices Act applies to collection agencies whose primary business is debt collection.

12. _____ Statutory exceptions to usury legislation are few.

13. _____ The Fair Debt Collection Practices Act prohibits the debt collector from telephoning the debtor after 9:00 p.m.

14. _____ The 1978 Bankruptcy Act severely restricts the availability of bankruptcy to consumers.

15. _____ The federal Fair Credit Billing Act allows a consumer to withhold any disputed charge from credit card payments.

MULTIPLE CHOICE SELECTIONS

1. The 1978 Bankruptcy Act (select the most correct statement):

   a. Allows discharge of education loans if repayment of such loans would constitute a hardship on the debtor.
   b. Gives the trustee in bankruptcy complete power to distribute the debtor's assets in a liquidation proceeding.
   c. Allows a creditor to adjust the debtor's repayment schedule so that the monthly payment will be lower, even if this adjustment is against the debtor's will.
   d. Has encouraged the number of bankruptcies since it offers debtors liberal discharge provisions.

2. None of the following can be discharged in bankruptcy except:

   a. Alimony and child support.
   b. Tax liens.
   c. Judgement debts arising from negligence.
   d. Educational loan obligations.

3. None of the following are ways of perfecting a security interest in personal property except:

   a. Having a purchase-money security interest in consumer goods.
   b. Having a purchase-money security interest in equipment.
   c. Having a purchase-money security interest in inventory.
   d. Having a purchase-money security interest in documentary collateral.

4. As a defense for having to pay the obligation of a debtor to a creditor, the surety can raise all of the following except:

   a. Impossibility of performance.
   b. Fraud.
   c. Lack of consideration.
   d. Discharge in bankruptcy.

5. The Fair Debt Collection Practices Act prohibits all of the following except:

   a. Telephoning the debtor repeatedly with intent to annoy.
   b. Physically threatening the debtor.
   c. Claiming to be an attorney unless he or she is.
   d. Mailing the debtor more than two collection letters per week.

DISCUSSION ANALYSIS

Describe the steps necessary to attach a security in personal property. Also, discuss why it is that a creditor must perfect a security interest in order to have priority over other parties who may wish to seize the collateral.

Chapter
22

Protecting Competition

STUDY GUIDE AND OUTLINE

I. The Meaning of Antitrust

A. A trust is a fiduciary (of highest loyalty and good faith) relationship concerning property. One person, known as the trustee, holds legal title to property for the benefit of another, known as the beneficiary. In the last part of the 19th century, the trust was used to gain monopolistic control of different types of businesses.

B. The first statutes attempting to control monopolistic businesses were enacted about the time this trust device was popular. Thus, these laws were called antitrust laws, although they protected the public from many types of restraints of trade.

C. The next three chapters deal with the major antitrust statutes:

1. The Sherman Act.
2. The Clayton Act.
3. The Federal Trade Commission Act.

II. Statutes Involved

A. The basic antitrust statute, passed in 1890, is the Sherman Act. It attacks two types of anticompetitive behavior:

1. Section 1 covers contracts, combinations, and conspiracies in restraint of trade.
2. Section 2 prohibits monopolies and attempts to monopolize any part of interstate or foreign commerce.

B. In 1914, Congress decided that the Sherman Act was too general and that it needed to be made more specific. It passed the Clayton Act. Specific sections of this act cover price discrimination, tying and exclusive dealing contracts, treble damage suits, mergers, and interlocking directorates.

C. Also in 1914, Congress passed the Federal Trade Commission Act. The FTC enforces certain of the other antitrust laws and has its own power to regulate "unfair methods of competition" under Section 5 of the FTC Act.

III. Exemptions to the Sherman Act

A. There are numerous business activities that are exempt, wholly or partially, from the Sherman Act:

1. There are various statutory exceptions made for certain activities by insurance companies, farmers' cooperatives, shipping, milk-marketing, and investment companies.
2. The normal activities of labor unions are exempt.
3. Activities required by state law are also exempt.

IV. The State Action Exemption

The "state action" exemption was created in the famous case Parker v. Brown. It held that the Sherman Act does not cover the sovereign action of a state that chooses to replace competition with regulation under certain circumstances:

1. The state itself, and not some private or semipublic group, must require the action that otherwise violates the Sherman Act.
2. The state action exemption applies only when state action announces a clear policy of replacing competition with regulation.
3. The state must also actively reexamine, supervise, and regulate the anticompetitive conduct.

V. The Noerr-Pennington Doctrine

A. This doctrine exempts from the antitrust laws concerted efforts to lobby government officials regardless of anticompetitive purposes.

B. The Noerr-Pennington Doctrine is based on the free flow of information and the First Amendment right to petition government.

VI. Sanctions: The Criminal Sanction

A. Violation of the Sherman Act is a federal crime punishable by up to a million dollar fine for a corporation, a fine of up to $100,000 for an individual, and/or up to three years imprisonment.

B. In criminal prosecutions antitrust defendants frequently plead nolo contendere (no contest). This plea allows the judge to sentence just as if the defendant had pleaded or been found guilty. In spite of this fact, many defendants plead nolo contendere because:

1. They save considerable litigation expense.
2. Plaintiffs in civil suits cannot introduce this plea to establish a violation of the Sherman Act. If a defendant has pleaded or been found guilty in a criminal case, it is usually easy for private civil plaintiffs to recover substantial damages.

C. The major use of the criminal sanction is in price-fixing cases. Increased numbers of defendants have been prosecuted in price-fixing cases in recent years.

VII. The Injunction

A. The Sherman Act empowers courts to grant injunctions at the request of the government or a private party that will prevent and restrain violations of its provisions.

B. Under the Clayton Act private parties who are threatened with antitrust injury can sue to get an injunction against the party who threatens the injury. In Cargill, Inc. v. Monfort of Colorado, Inc. the U.S. Supreme Court ruled that loss or damage due to increased competition resulting from purchase of one company by another did not constitute the threat of antitrust injury to a competitor.

VIII. Triple Damages

A. Private victims of Sherman Act violations may sue in a civil action to collect three times the damages they have suffered (triple or treble damages), plus court costs and reasonable attorney's fees.

B. Antitrust law also authorizes the attorney general of a state to file triple damage suits on behalf of the citizens of the state.

C. In Texas Industries, Inc. v. Radcliff Materials, Inc. the U.S. Supreme Court ruled that a defendant in a triple damage suit had no right to bring other defendants into the suit to attempt to make them contribute in paying possible damages.

IX. The "Illinois Brick" Doctrine

A. This doctrine concerns who in a chain of distribution can recover triple damages for an antitrust violation.

B. In Illinois Brick Co. v. Illinois the U.S. Supreme Court ruled that only an immediate purchaser injured by price fixing can sue a defendant for triple damages.

C. In Blue Shield of Virginia v. McCready, however, the Supreme Court ruled that a plaintiff could sue Blue Shield and a psychiatric society for conspiring to exclude psychologists from receiving compensation under Blue Shield. The suit was brought by a patient who had been denied compensation under Blue Shield for psychological services.

X. Proof of Sherman Act Violations

A. Plaintiffs seeking triple damages must show that the alleged anticompetitive activity has a substantial effect on interstate commerce.

B. Difficulties may arise in proving existence of a contract, combination or conspiracy among competitors. There must be direct or circumstantial evidence that reasonably shows the parties intended to commit an unlawful act. In most cases this issue is left to the jury.

C. However, the U.S. Supreme Court in Monsanto v. Spray-Rite Service Corp. ruled that a price-fixing agreement cannot be inferred solely from the fact that other dealers or distributors of a supplier complained about a competitor and that the competitor was terminated by the supplier. Other evidence of a conscious conspiracy to restrain prices is required. In this case there was sufficient additional evidence to warrant a jury's finding of illegal conduct.

XI. The Rule of Reason and Per Se Illegality

A. The rule of reason as applied to the Sherman Act was announced in the case of Standard Oil Co. v. United States. It held that restraints of trade and attempts to monopolize were illegal only if they were unreasonable. Joint ventures and vertical non-price restraints are examples of activities which are illegal only if unreasonable.

B. Agreements which are per se illegal have been declared illegal without reference to their reasonableness or their impact on competition. A showing that this type of agreement exists is sufficient to establish its illegality. Examples of per se illegal agreements include:

1. Price fixing (this includes horizontal price fixing, i.e., price fixing between competitors, and vertical price fixing, i.e., price fixing between a manufacturer or wholesaler and a retailer concerning the price at which the retailer will resell goods).
2. Agreements between competitors to divide territories (horizontal division of markets).

3. Agreements to limit production.
4. Group boycotts (agreements not to do business with someone or to put pressure on someone not to do business with a third party).

C. In Catalano, Inc. v. Target Sales, Inc. the Supreme Court ruled unlawful per se a conspiracy to restrain trade by refusing to sell beer unless plaintiff retailers paid cash in advance or at the time of delivery. The Court noted that extending interest-free credit for a period of time is equivalent to giving a discount equal to the value of the use of the purchase price for that period of time. Thus, an agreement to terminate the practice of giving credit is a type of price fixing.

XIII. **Enforcement**

A. The Department of Justice alone has the power to bring criminal antitrust cases.

B. The Department of Justice shares power with the FTC and private parties in civil cases.

COMPLETION EXERCISES

1. A _______________ is a fiduciary relationship in which one person holds legal title to property for the benefit of another.

2. The case of _______________ created a state-action exemption to the Sherman Act.

3. Persons injured by another's violation of the Sherman Act can collect _______________ the damages they have suffered.

4. To help prevent civil suits for triple damages, criminal defendants in an antitrust case often plead _______________.

5. Practices like price fixing that are plainly anticompetitive are said to be illegal _______________.

6. To have standing to sue under the Sherman Act, a plaintiff must be _______________ injured.

7. The Supreme Court has ruled that a defendant who owes antitrust damages is not entitled to a _______________ from coconspirators.

8. In a criminal antitrust prosecution a corporation may be fined up to _______________; an individual may be fined up to _______________ and imprisoned up to _______________.

9. Concerted efforts to lobby governmental bodies are exempt from the antitrust laws under the _______________.

10. The basic statute in the antitrust area is the _______________ Act.

11. Antitrust law authorizes the _______________ of a state to file triple damage suits on behalf of the citizens of the state.

12. To be illegal under the antitrust laws, anticompetitive activities must have a _______________ on interstate commerce.

13. The _______________ was announced in the case of Standard Oil Co. v. United States.

14. The Sherman Act empowers courts to grant _______________ at the request of the government or a private party that will prevent and restrain violations of its provisions.

15. When two competitors engage in price fixing, it is called _______________ price fixing.

TRUE-FALSE CHOICES

1. ______ There are numerous business activities that are exempt from the Sherman Act.

2. ______ Acceptance of a nolo contendere plea can save considerable litigation expense.

3. ______ In triple damage suits courts have generally restricted the right of recovery to direct purchasers.

4. ______ Evidence of a nolo contendere plea may be introduced as evidence in a private triple damage case.

5. ______ The rule of reason was announced in the case of Parker v. Brown.

6. ______ Under the Sherman Act an individual who violates antitrust law can be fined by up to $1,000,000.

7. ______ The Sherman Act was made more specific by the Clayton Act.

8. ______ Successful triple damage plaintiffs can recover not only triple damages but also court costs and reasonable attorney's fees.

9. ______ Everyone in the chain of distribution who is injured by an antitrust violation can sue for triple damages.

10. ______ In antitrust cases, the issue of the presence of illegal joint behavior is usually left to the jury.

11. ______ The concept of per se illegality simplifies proof in antitrust cases.

12. ______ The Department of Justice is the only governmental body with power to enforce the antitrust laws.

13. ______ When an antitrust case is settled by a consent order, the defendant need not admit a violation of law.

14. ______ Agreements to limit production are per se illegal.

15. ______ Only the Department of Justice can bring criminal antitrust prosecutions.

MULTIPLE CHOICE SELECTIONS

1. Under certain circumstances all of the following businesses have antitrust exemptions except:

   a. Insurance companies.
   b. Farmers' cooperatives.
   c. Textile companies.
   d. Shipping.

2. Select the incorrect statement. The state action exemption applies only when:

   a. The state is acting in its sovereign capacity.
   b. State action implements an announced policy of replacing competition with regulation.
   c. Any state law has an anticompetitive effect.
   d. The state actively reexamines the anticompetitive conduct.

3. All of the following can enforce the antitrust laws except:

   a. The Department of Labor.
   b. The Department of Justice.
   c. The FTC.
   d. Private parties.

4. Atlantic Inc. conspires with its competitors to rig bids submitted on an interstate highway project. If caught (select the most correct statement):

   a. Atlantic cannot be prosecuted since the Sherman Act does not apply to construction services.
   b. Only the corporation may be prosecuted. Atlantic's president, who submitted the bid, cannot be held responsible for the corporate act.
   c. The responsible individuals within the corporation could be sent to jail for up to three years.
   d. Atlantic could receive a fine of up to $100,000.

5. Select the incorrect statement concerning the rule of reason:

   a. The rule of reason is stated in Section 1 of the Sherman Act.
   b. The rule of reason prohibits restraints of trade only when they have an unreasonable impact on competition.
   c. The rule of reason was established by the Supreme Court.
   d. The rule of reason applies to all restraints of trade which are not per se illegal.

Chapter 22

DISCUSSION ANALYSIS

Discuss the penalties and remedies that apply to Sherman Act violations. Explain why a defendant charged with criminal violations of the Sherman Act may plea nolo contendere. What is the effect of this plea?

Chapter 23

Sherman Act Enforcement

STUDY GUIDE AND OUTLINE

I. Activities in Restraint of Trade

A. Section 1 of the Sherman Act prohibits contracts, combinations, and conspiracies in restraint of trade. This section forbids certain joint behavior.

B. An express agreement is not required to violate Section 1. Illegal restraints of trade may be implied from conduct.

C. Potentially illegal restraints of trade are almost without limit. However, the following sections discuss certain common restraints of trade.

II. Price-Fixing

A. Price-fixing agreements among competitors are illegal per se. It is no defense that prices fixed are fair or reasonable. It is just as illegal to fix a low price as it is to fix a high price. Section 1 applies to prices fixed for both goods and services.

B. In Goldfarb v. Virginia State Bar the Supreme Court decided that a minimum fee schedule for lawyers violated Section 1 as price fixing. The Court dismissed claims that:

1. Price fixing did not apply to a learned profession.
2. The fee schedule was purely "advisory."
3. There was not a substantial impact on interstate commerce.
4. The fee schedule was protected under the Parker doctrine as state action.

C. In National Society of Professional Engineers v. United States the Supreme Court ruled that an ethical standard set by the Society violated Section 1. The standard prohibited the engineers who were members of the society from engaging in competitive bidding. The Court refused to consider the claim that competitive bidding might promote dangerous construction on big engineering projects and determined that the standard of ethics violated the rule of reason.

III. Resale Price Maintenance: Vertical Price-Fixing

A. Resale price maintenance schemes are a form of vertical price fixing. Under these agreements manufacturers specify minimum retail prices for their products. Courts and Congress have held these agreements per se illegal.

B. The Colgate Doctrine recognizes the independent action by a manufacturer to achieve the effect of resale price maintenance is legal. For example, it is legal for a manufacturer to announce its resale price suggestions in advance and refuse to deal with retailers who fail to comply. Violation of Section 1 requires concerted (joint) behavior.

C. Manufacturers sometimes use consignment contracts to maintain retail resale prices. In a consignment contract the manufacturer keeps title (ownership) to goods while putting them in the possession of the retailer. The manufacturer specifies the retail sale price.

D. In Simpson v. Union Oil Co. the Supreme Court ruled illegal Union Oil's gasoline consignment plan. The Court noted that Union Oil retained "ownership" of the gasoline in name only, placing all risk of loss on its retailers.

IV. Other Vertical Restraints

A. Sometimes one competitor complains to a manufacturer about the conduct of another competitor, especially when that conduct consists of lowering prices to the extent that the complainant cannot compete.

B. In 1988 in Business Electronics Corp. v. Sharp Electronics Corp., the Supreme Court held that a vertical restraint is not illegal per se unless it includes some agreement on price or price levels.

V. Concerted Activities by Competitors

A. Concerted activities among competitors take a variety of forms. Some of these activities are subject to rule of reason. Other are per se illegal.

B. In United States v. Container Corp. of America the Supreme Court held that an exchange of price information between corrugated container manufacturers led to price uniformity and was per se illegal. The Court distinguished cases where a simple exchange of price information might have no effect on the market or where it was necessary to prevent fraud.

C. In National Collegiate Athletic Asso. v. Board of Regents of the University of Oklahoma and the University of Georgia the Supreme Court ruled that concerted activity by NCAA members raised prices and reduced the number of televised college football games; therefore, the plan was anticompetitive and violated the Sherman Act.

VI. Agreements Relating to Territory

A. Horizontal agreements dividing up markets are per se illegal under Section 1. An example of such an arrangement would arise if the widget suppliers in a state agreed to allocate each supplier an exclusive territory.

B. A vertical territorial agreement is one between a manufacturer and a dealer or distributor. It assigns the dealer or distributor an exclusive territory, and the manufacturer agrees not to sell to other dealers or distributors in that territory in exchange for an agreement by the dealer that it will not operate outside the area assigned. Such agreements are subject to the rule of reason.

C. In Continental T.V., Inc. v. GTE Sylvania Inc. the Supreme Court held that an agreement requiring each GTE franchise to sell its television sets only from the location or locations at which it was franchised was not per se illegal, but illegal only if its impact on competition was unreasonable (rule of reason).

VII. Monopoly: The Rationale for Section 2 of the Sherman Act

A. The purpose of Section 2, which prohibits monopolies and attempts to monopolize, is to promote efficiency in private markets.

B. As Justice Black once wrote about the Sherman Act, "It rests on the premise that the unrestrained interaction of competitive forces will yield the best allocation of our economic resources, the lowest prices, the highest quality and the greatest material progress...."

VIII. Section 2 - The Approach

A. Under Section 2 monopolies, attempts to monopolize, and conspiracies to monopolize any part of interstate or foreign commerce are illegal.

1. Attempts to monopolize require proof of intent to destroy competition or achieve monopoly power.
2. Conspiracies to monopolize require proof of specific intent to monopolize and at least one overt act to accomplish a monopoly.
3. Although proof of monopoly power is not required in cases based on attempts or conspiracies to monopolize, it is often very difficult to establish the intent required in these cases.

B. Once a firm has gained sufficient control over a market (usually at least 80 percent of the market), it is called a monopoly. Monopolies are illegal when their power to control prices or exclude competition has been gained by a deliberate course of conduct. This conduct is often described as predatory. Predatory means that a firm has advanced its market share by injuring its actual or potential competitors by means other than improved performance.

C. The power to control the market, which is an essential element in establishing an illegal monopoly, is determined through the economic analysis of many factors. These factors include:

1. Market concentration.
2. Barriers to entry into the market.
3. Structural features such as market shares of other firms.
4. Profit levels.
5. The extent to which prices respond to changes in supply and demand.
6. Whether or not a firm discriminates in price between its customers.
7. The absolute size of the firm.

D. In evaluating monopolies under Section 2, courts must also decide the relevant geographic market and the relevant product market:

1. The relevant geographic market is the smallest one wide enough so that products from outside the geographic area or from other producers in the same area cannot compete with those included in the defined relevant market.
2. The relevant product market determines what product (or service) is being monopolized. For example, in a case alleging monopolization of frozen pizzas sold in grocery stores, the court would have to decide whether the relevant product market is merely frozen pizzas or if it also includes pizzas sold in restaurants which compete with frozen pizzas.
3. The more substitutes there are for a product the less likely a court is to find an illegal "monopolization." In Grinnell v. United States the Supreme Court ruled that Grinnell had a monopoly on central station hazard systems with 87 percent national control. Other alternative burglar alarm systems were not sufficiently interchangeable to be substitutes.

E. In Aspen Skiing Co. v. Aspen Highlands Skiing Corp. the plaintiff alleged antitrust injury under Section 2 by defendant. The defendant ski-lift company had discontinued a joint operation with the plaintiff ski-lift company when plaintiff refused to accept certain disadvantageous terms. Subsequently, the defendant marketed ski-lift tickets in such a way that it made it difficult for the plaintiff to compete. Plaintiff's market share declined steadily. The U.S. Supreme Court ruled that the evidence supported a jury finding that Section 2 was violated.

F. Monopolistic conduct is often described as predatory, which means a firm seeks to advance its market share by injuring its actual or potential competitors by means other than improved performance.

IX. Ethical Considerations: Formal Code of Ethics

A. Codes of ethics by professional groups have been held to violate Section 1 when they unreasonably restrain members' economic activities.

B. Whether or not a conscious decision has been made to avoid the obligations imposed by law or ethics, a group's code which violates standards established by society at large is subject to legal challenge, social criticism, or both.

X. Informal Codes of Ethics

A. A code is also established by the activities encouraged (or condoned by inaction) in the corporate hierarchy.

B. If employees who violate the law "on behalf of" their companies are treated differently from those who violate the law "against" the corporation (embezzlement), a message is being sent that criminal conduct on behalf of the company will be tolerated.

XI. Caterpillar Code of Competition

A. The Caterpillar code uses United States law to establish ethical norms for conduct throughout the world.

COMPLETION EXERCISES

1. Illegal restraints of trade may be implied from _______________.
2. Section 1 applies to prices fixed for both _______________ and _______________.
3. In _______________ the Supreme Court decided that a minimum fee scheduled for lawyers violated Section 1 as price fixing.
4. _______________ is a form of vertical price fixing.
5. The _______________ recognizes that independent action by a manufacturer to achieve the effect of resale price maintenance is legal.
6. In a _______________ the manufacturer keeps title to goods while putting them in the possession of the retailer.
7. Some concerted activities by competitors are illegal per se. The others are subject to the _______________.
8. Another name for joint business operations is _______________.
9. A _______________ agreement assigns a dealer or distributor an exclusive area in which to sell.
10. The purpose of Section 2 is to promote _______________ in private markets.

11. _______________ conduct means that a firm has advanced its market share by injuring its actual or potential competitors by means other than improved performance.

12. In evaluating monopolies under Section 2, courts must decide the _______________ market and the _______________ market.

13. The _______________ market determines what product or service is being monopolized.

14. Codes of ethics by professional groups have been held to violate Section 1 when they _______________ members' economic activities.

15. Antitrust enforcement by state government is _______________.

TRUE-FALSE CHOICES

1. _____ An express agreement is required to violate Section 1.
2. _____ Price-fixing agreements among competitors are illegal per se.
3. _____ Resale price maintenance is illegal under the rule of reason.
4. _____ Manufacturers sometimes use consignment contracts to maintain retail resale prices.
5. _____ Under certain circumstances the Sherman Act does not apply to the anticompetitive actions of states.
6. _____ Joint business operations are per se illegal.
7. _____ Horizontal division of markets is illegal under the rule of reason.
8. _____ Vertical territorial agreements are illegal under the rule of reason.
9. _____ Attempts to monopolize violate Section 2 of the Sherman Act.
10. _____ 80 percent control of a market is usually sufficient to establish a monopoly.
11. _____ The power to control the market is not essential in establishing an illegal monopoly.
12. _____ The relevant geographic market is the smallest one wide enough so that products from outside the geographic area or from other producers in the same area cannot compete with those included in the defined relevant market.
13. _____ The more substitutes there are for a product the less likely a court is to find an illegal monopoly.
14. _____ Independent action by a manufacturer to achieve the effect of resale price maintenance is legal.
15. _____ The Caterpillar code uses United States law to establish ethical norms for conduct throughout the world.

Chapter 23

MULTIPLE CHOICE SELECTIONS

1. Acme Corp. stamped its widgets with a suggested retail selling price. Acme discovered through one of its sales representatives that Realistic Retail was selling the nationally advertised widgets at one-third off the suggested price. Thereafter, Acme refused to fill the orders to Realistic. Select the most correct statement:

   a. Acme is guilty of an illegal boycott against Realistic.
   b. Acme has violated Section 1 with its resale maintenance plan.
   c. Acme's refusal to deal with Realistic does not violate Section 1.
   d. Acme's refusal to deal is legal, but only if it does not have a substantial impact on interstate commerce.

2. Select the most correct statement concerning Section 2 of the Sherman Act:

   a. To be illegal, a monopoly must be national in scope.
   b. Illegal monopolistic conduct is often described as "predatory."
   c. The more substitutes there are for monopolized products the more likely the monopoly violates Section 2.
   d. Illegal attempts to monopolize may be established without a showing of intent.

3. All of the following activities are illegal per se under the Sherman Act except:

   a. Vertical territorial restraints.
   b. Group boycotts.
   c. Horizontal division of markets.
   d. Concerted production limitations.

4. In a monopoly case all of the following factors are important except:

   a. The relevant product market.
   b. The relevant geographic market.
   c. The power to control the market.
   d. The rule of reason.

5. Select the incorrect statement:

   a. Restraints of trade may be implied from conduct.
   b. Section 1 applies only to joint behavior.
   c. Price fixing under Section 1 applies to both goods and services.
   d. Price fixing does not apply to "learned professions."

DISCUSSION ANALYSIS

At a meeting of the Treetop Trade Association, a prominent member of the association announces that economic conditions look ripe for a 10 percent price increase for the services provided by the members of the association. There is a roar of approval from the rest of the members present at the association's annual meeting. Over the next month most of the association's members raise their prices 10 percent. Analyze these facts for potential violation of antitrust law.

Chapter 24

Clayton Act and FTC Act Enforcement

STUDY GUIDE AND OUTLINE

I. **Introduction**

A. After its passage, the Sherman Act was criticized as being inadequate:

1. The Act did little to prevent practices which only tended to restrain competition.
2. The Act did not apply to situations that hurt competition but that did not actually restrain trade.
3. The rule of reason as applied to the Act required that courts decide each alleged violation on a case-by-case basis.
4. The federal courts applied the Act to labor unions.

B. These criticisms led to the passage in 1914 of the Clayton Act.

C. The Clayton Act applies to anticompetitive practices before they actually restrain trade. Although there were no criminal penalties in the original acts, the Clayton Act provided for private triple damage suits.

D. The three sections of the Clayton Act discussed in this chapter are:

1. Section 2 - Price discrimination
2. Section 3 - Tying and exclusive contracts
3. Section 7 - Mergers and acquisitions
4. Section 8 - Interlocking directorates.

E. Section 8 of the Clayton Act prohibits a person from being a member of the board of directors of two or more corporations at the same time, when one of them has assets totaling more than $1,000,000 and where elimination of competition by agreement between them would violate any of the antitrust laws.

II. **Clayton Act - Section 2: Historical Perspective**

A. Section 2 of the Clayton Act of 1914 prohibited price discrimination.

B. However, the original Clayton Act permitted volume discounts. In 1936 Congress amended the act to prohibit such discounts in most instances. The amendment was called the Robinson-Patman amendment.

III. Predatory Pricing

A. The Robinson-Patman amendment made it a crime to sell at lower prices in one geographic area than elsewhere in order to eliminate competition. This crime is termed predatory pricing.

B. Predatory pricing also includes selling below costs to drive out competitors. There are several exceptions to the prohibition against selling below costs.

IV. Price Discrimination

A. The Robinson-Patman amendment (the present Section 2) makes it unlawful for any person to discriminate in price between different purchasers of commodities of like grade and quality where the effect of such discrimination may be substantially to lessen competition or tend to create a monopoly in any line of commerce or injure competition with any person.

B. It violates the law to give an illegal discrimination or to knowingly receive one.

C. Note that Section 2 applies only to discriminatory sales of commodities (not services) of like grade and quality which may injure competition and which are in interstate commerce (rather than only affect interstate commerce).

D. Note that quality discounts which may injure competition are illegal unless they meet one of the recognized exceptions. Quantity discounts which are hidden as unearned brokerage fees, disproportionate promotional allowances, or other advantages granted to volume-purchasing customers but not to others are illegal.

E. The court in Jefferson Cty. Pharmaceutical Ass'n. v. Abbott Labs held that the sale of pharmaceutical products to state and local government hospitals for resale in competition with private pharmacies is not exempt from the proscriptions of the Robinson-Patman Act.

V. Proof Required

A. Price discrimination is not illegal per se. Only those differences in price that may adversely affect competition are prohibited.

B. A plaintiff seeking damages for a Robinson-Patman violation must prove actual economic injury arising from the violation. In J. Truette Payne Co. v. Chrysler Motors Corp. the Supreme Court remanded (sent back) the case for the lower court to determine whether the evidence of actual economic injury arising from a price discrimination was sufficient to withstand the defendant's motion for a directed verdict. The plaintiff was a former automobile dealer whom the defendant required to meet higher sales quotas than his competitors in order to obtain a bonus. The plaintiff had alleged that this amounted to an injurious illegal price discrimination.

VI. Levels of Competition

A. There are three principal kinds of Robinson-Patman cases:

1. Primary line cases usually involve territorial price discrimination -- the charging of different prices in different geographic areas to drive out direct competitors. In these cases proof of an adverse competition affect is required.
2. Secondary-level cases involve competition among customers of sellers.
3. Third-level cases occur when there is a wholesaler between the manufacturer and the retailer.

B. In Perkins v. Standard Oil Co. of California the Supreme Court held that a violation of Section 2 occurred when the defendant sold gasoline to the plaintiff at a higher price than that paid by a competitor who bought the gasoline from a wholesaler, which had bought it from another oil company that purchased it from the defendant (Standard Oil). The oil company which had purchased gasoline from the defendant had passed on its discriminatory price advantage to its subsidiary, the wholesaler, which had in turn passed the advantage on to its subsidiary, the competitor of the plaintiff.

VII. Defenses

A. There are several affirmative defenses which render an otherwise illegal price discrimination legal:

1. The cost justification defense permits price differentials based on differences in the cost of manufacture, sale, or delivery of commodities.
2. The changing conditions defense permits price differentials based on the deterioration of perishable goods, distress sales, obsolescence of seasonal goods, etc.
3. The good-faith meeting of competition defense permits sellers in good faith to meet the equally low price of a competitor.

B. Sellers may also select their own customers. Thus, for example, sellers might choose only to sell to big volume buyers.

C. Because of the complexities of determining what is cost, the cost justification defense is rarely successful.

VIII. Good-Faith Meeting of Competition Defense

A. Section 2(b) permits a defendant to prove that a price discrimination was not unlawful by "showing that his lower price or the furnishing of services or facilities to any purchaser ... was made in good faith to meet an equally low price of a competitor, or the services or facilities furnished by a competitor." The need for this defense arises when a seller has granted one of his competing customers an advantage which is not offered to the others, and the seller has done so in order to meet its own competition.

B. The standard of good faith is simply the standard of the prudent business person responding to what he or she reasonably believes is a situation of competitive necessity.

C. The good faith meeting of competition defense is available to buyers as well as sellers. In Great Atlantic & Pacific Tea Co. v. FTC the Supreme Court ruled that the A & P did not violate Section 2 by knowingly inducing and receiving illegal price discriminations from the Borden Co. The A & P had induced a price discrimination from Borden by misrepresenting that it had been offered a lower price by a competitor of Borden. The Court decided that since Borden's price discrimination was legal (meeting competition in good faith), the A & P could not be found guilty of inducing an illegal price discrimination.

IX. The Future of Section 2

A. Section 2 of the Clayton Act, as amended, has resulted in higher prices than would exist in a more competitive market, according to most economists. It is seen as partially insulating small business from competition from larger companies which can buy in volume.

B. Government enforcement of Section 2 has been limited and sporadic. The repeal of Section 2 is a possibility.

X. Section 3 - Tying Arrangements and Exclusive Dealings

A. Section 3 of the Clayton Act makes it unlawful for persons engaged in commerce to lease or sell commodities on the condition that the lessee or purchaser should not deal in the commodities or a competitor or competitors where the effect may be substantially to lessen competition in any line of commerce. Section 3 covers:

1. Typing contracts.
2. Reciprocal dealings.
3. Exclusive dealing arrangements (requirements or output contracts).

B. A tying contract is one where a commodity is sold or leased for use only on the condition that the buyer or lessee purchase a different product or service from seller or lessor.

1. Tying contracts violate Section 1 of the Sherman Act when a party has sufficient power to restrain free competition appreciably, some coercion is shown, and a "not insubstantial" amount of interstate commerce is affected.
2. Tying contracts violate Section 3 of the Clayton Act where they may lessen competition substantially or tend to create a monopoly.
3. A common form of tying arrangement is known as full-line forcing. Under this arrangement a buyer is compelled to take a complete product line from the seller in order to get the desired commodity.

XI. Reciprocal Dealings

A. A reciprocal dealing arrangement exists when one party offers to buy the other's goods, but only if the second party buys goods from the first party. If such arrangements may lessen competition substantially (e.g., as to competitors who would like to sell commodities to the parties), the arrangement violates Section 3 of the Clayton Act.

B. Such arrangements may also violate Section 1 of the Sherman Act.

XII. Exclusive Dealings

A. An exclusive dealing contract may be a requirements (needs) contract, whereby the buyer agrees to purchase all its business needs of a product from a certain seller, or it may be an output contract under which the buyer agrees to buy all of the seller's output. Such arrangements are illegal under Section 3 if they may lessen competition substantially or tend to create a monopoly. Under the Sherman Act they are tested by the rule of reason or per se illegality, depending on the circumstances.

B. Franchise contracts sometimes require franchisees to purchase certain equipment or inventory from franchisors. When it is necessary to preserve the good will and image of the franchise, such required purchases are not illegal even though they are tied to the sale of the trademarked franchise.

XIII. Ethics and Section 3

The Caterpillar Code forbids reciprocity and makes exclusive dealings rare.

XIV. The Clayton Act - Section 7: Introduction

A. A business may acquire other businesses in a variety of ways, including merger, consolidation, purchase of controlling stock interest, purchase of assets, etc. In the sections which follow all of these ways are termed merger.

B. Mergers are usually classified as follows:

1. A horizontal merger usually combines two businesses in the same field or industry.
2. A vertical merger brings together a company which is the customer of the other one of the lines of commerce in which the other is a supplier.
3. A conglomerate merger is one in which the businesses involved neither compete nor are related as customer and supplier in any line of commerce. A variety of this merger is termed a market extension merger. This special kind of merger describes an acquisition in which the

acquiring company extends its existing markets with a related new product or in a new geographical area.

C. The law of mergers is based primarily on the Clayton Act, the Sherman Act, and the Bank Merger Act.

XV. General Principles

A. The most important of the antimerger laws is the Clayton Act, Section 7.

B. The Celler-Kefauver amendment to Section 7 made illegal any acquisition of corporate assets by one corporation of another when the effect may be substantially to lessen competition or tend to create a monopoly in any line of commerce in any section of the country.

C. Congress has also amended Section 7 to apply the law to any "person," not just to corporations. Also, for Section 7 to apply the merger does not have to be of businesses engaged in interstate commerce. It is sufficient if the merger will substantially "affect" commerce.

D. The case of United States v. Von's Grocery Co. illustrates that even small increases in market concentration may be sufficient to trigger Section 7 when it is necessary to avoid trends toward market concentration. In that case the Supreme Court held that the merger of two Los Angeles grocery chains, having a combined sale of only 7.5 percent of the total market in Los Angeles, violated Section 7. The number of grocery stores in Los Angeles had decreased from 5,365 to 3,590 in the previous 13 years.

XVI. Special Doctrines

A. The potential entrant doctrine holds that Section 7 may be violated where an acquisition or merger is attempted by a firm that is a potential (though not present) competitor of the acquired company.

B. The failing company doctrine allows mergers (that would otherwise be illegal) between companies when the acquired company is failing.

XVII. Enforcement

A. Section 7 of the Clayton Act is enforced by the Justice Department, the FTC, and directly affected private parties.

B. The injunction is a major tool sought by government and individuals in the merger field.

1. Preliminary injunctions are used to prevent merger until legal issues are resolved.
2. After mergers have taken place, mandatory injunctions may require a divestiture (selling off) of a merged firm or stock assets.

C. There have been numerous merger-related triple damage suits brought by one competitor against another and by a takeover candidate against its "suitor" (the company seeking to acquire it).

D. Most cases involving Section 7 are settled by agreement.

E. Section 7 applies when a domestic firm acquires a foreign firm.

XVIII. Tender Offers

A. Many acquisitions and mergers are not the result of mutual agreement. Hostile takeovers occur as a result of tender-offers (offers to buy stock) by the acquiring firm to the shareholders of the target firm. Management often objects to such takeovers for fear of losing their jobs.

B. In order to discourage hostile takeovers, a variety of techniques have been developed. These are known as shark repellants.

C. Congress is considering whether hostile takeovers should be limited more heavily.

D. Greenmail is a form of blackmail by which individuals or companies force someone to pay them off to avoid a takeover. The white knight is another firm that makes a competing offer at a price significantly higher than the tender offer.

XIX. **FTC Premerger Notification**

A. The FTC has adopted premerger notification rules. These rules require that prior notice be given to the Justice Department and the FTC of all pending mergers over a certain size.

B. The rules cover transactions involving at least 15 percent of the acquired companies' assets or securities when the purchase value exceeds $15 million.

XX. **Justice Department Merger Guidelines**

A. In 1982, the Justice Department issued new merger guidelines. Under one of these guidelines an index known as the Herfindahl-Hirshman Index is used to test the legality of horizontal acquisitions. The index is computed by squaring the market share of each firm in a market and adding the result. If the sum is 1,000 or less, the merger probably will not be challenged.

B. Certain exceptions are noted in the guidelines for failing companies and when a merger will increase market efficiency.

XXI. **Federal Trade Commission Act: Introduction**

A. The primary antitrust function of the FTC is to prevent illegal business practices rather than to punish violations.

B. Most FTC cases are settled by consent orders. In such cases the business need not admit a law violation, but it agrees not to do the act complained of in the future.

XXII. **Unfair Methods of Competition**

A. The FTC has the antitrust power to regulate "unfair methods of competition" under Section 5 under the FTC Act.

B. Anticompetitive acts or practices that do not violate the Sherman or Clayton Acts may be restrained by the FTC as being "unfair." In F.T.C. v. Indiana Federation of Dentists a group of dentists formed a federation that adopted "work rule" forbidding its members to submit x-rays to dental insurance. Insurers required x-rays to be submitted with patient claim forms so insurers could evaluate what work was performed. The FTC sued the dentists. The U.S. Supreme Court ruled that the work rule violated Section 5 of the FTC Act as an unfair method of competition.

COMPLETION EXERCISES

1. For a seller to sell at lower prices in one geographic area than elsewhere in order to eliminate competition is termed ________________.

2. The ________________ defense permits price differentials based on differences in the cost of manufacture, sale, or delivery of commodities.

3. The ________________ defense permits sellers in good faith to meet the equally low price of a competitor.

4. _______________ price discrimination cases involve discriminatory sales to directly competing customers of sellers.

5. A _______________ contract is one which a commodity is sold only on condition that the buyer purchase a different product from the seller.

6. In a _______________ contract a seller agrees to sell everything it produces to a buyer.

7. The principal amendment to Section 2 of the Clayton Act is the _______________ amendment.

8. Section 8 of the Clayton Act prohibits certain types of _______________.

9. A plaintiff seeking damages for a Robinson-Patman violation must prove _______________ economic injury arising from the violation.

10. A _______________ merger is one in which the businesses involved neither compete nor are related as customer and supplier in any given line of commerce.

11. Section 2 applies only to discriminatory sales of _______________ of like grade and quality.

12. A _______________ merger brings together two competitors.

13. Hostile takeovers usually occur as a result of a _______________ for the stock of the target company.

14. Potential target companies often implement _______________ to discourage hostile takeovers.

15. The Justice Department uses the _______________ Index to test the legality of horizontal mergers.

TRUE-FALSE CHOICES

1. ______ The Sherman Act does little to prevent practices which only tend to reduce competition.

2. ______ The Clayton Act applies to anticompetitive practices before they actually restrain trade.

3. ______ The original Clayton Act prohibited volume discounts.

4. ______ The changing conditions defense permits price differentials based on differences in the cost of manufacture or sale of commodities.

5. ______ Other advantages, not just price advantages, granted by a seller to one competitor but not to another can violate the Robinson-Patman Act.

6. ______ Exclusive dealings contracts are per se violations of the Sherman Act.

7. ______ Full line forcing is an example of a tying contract.

8. ______ Price discrimination is per se illegal.

9. ______ The cost justification defense permits price differentials based on differences in delivery costs to competitors.

10. ______ A court will presume economic injury from a Robinson-Patman violation.

11. ______ The more narrowly the product line or geographic area is defined in a merger case, the less likely a merger is to violate antitrust law.

12. ______ Companies contemplating mergers of certain size or larger must provide premerger notification to antitrust agencies.

13. ______ A market extension merger is a type of vertical merger.

14. ______ Many acquisitions and mergers are not the result of mutual agreement.

15. ______ The degree of market concentration is an important issue in merger cases.

MULTIPLE CHOICE SELECTIONS

1. The Los Angeles Advertiser, a large metropolitan newspaper, sells advertising space to larger volume purchasers at a lower rate per inch than to smaller volume purchasers. Select the most correct statement:

   a. If they may lessen competition substantially in interstate commerce, the volume discounts violate Section 2 of the Clayton Act.
   b. These volume discounts are permitted under Section 2 of the Clayton Act.
   c. Although these volume discounts are not prohibited by the Clayton Act, they may be considered illegal under Section 5 of the FTC Act.
   d. None of the above is correct.

2. Ms. Jones sits on the board of directors of the Acme Corporation and on the board of directors of the Nadir Corporation. Select the most correct statement:

   a. Section 8 of the Clayton Act prohibits Ms. Jones from sitting on two boards of directors.
   b. It is illegal for Ms. Jones to sit on the two boards of directors only if her action constitutes an actual restraint of trade.
   c. If Acme and Nadir are competitors, Ms. Jones' sitting on both boards is illegal if one of the companies has assets of $1,000,000.
   d. None of the above is correct.

3. The Acme Corporation sells widgets to Retailer A at one price and to Retailer B at a much higher price. Select the most correct statement:

   a. This practice constitutes illegal price fixing.
   b. If Acme and the retailers are all located in the state of Illinois, Acme has probably not violated the Robinson-Patman Amendment.
   c. Section 2 of the Clayton Act makes Acme's discrimination illegal per se.
   d. Acme would be cost justified in its discrimination if it makes larger profits off volume sales.

4. Which of the following is not covered by the Clayton Act?

   a. Price fixing.
   b. Price discrimination.
   c. Interlocking directorates.
   d. Mergers and acquisitions.

5. The FTC sues to force the Acme Company to divest itself of stock in the Zenith Corporation. All of the following will be legal issues in the case except:

   a. What is the cost-benefit balance.
   b. What is the relevant product market.
   c. What is the relevant geographic market.
   d. What is the potentially anticompetitive impact of Acme's ownership of Zenith stock.

Chapter 24

DISCUSSION ANALYSIS

Reynolds Metals, a manufacturer of various metals products, including aluminum foil sold in grocery stores, acquired the Arrow Company. The Arrow Company manufactured and marketed aluminum foil only to florists. In the 5 years following the merger, Arrow's percentage of the nationwide market for foil sold to florists went from 35 to 50 percent. Arrow's competitors complained to the FTC, which sued Reynolds to force its divestiture of Arrow. Discuss the legal issues in this case.

Chapter 25

Environmental Laws and Pollution Control

STUDY GUIDE AND OUTLINE

I. The National Environmental Policy Act

A. Environmental regulation remains the single most expensive area of the government's regulation of the business community.

B. This chapter considers three basic areas of environmental regulation:

1. Government's regulation of itself.
2. Government's regulation of business.
3. Suits by private individuals.

C. The federal government not only imposes pollution control on the private enterprise system but also regulates the environmental impact of the decision-making process of its own agencies. It accomplishes the regulation through the National Environmental Policy Act (NEPA). NEPA is important to the business community since many decisions of governmental agencies affect business.

D. NEPA is divided into two titles. Title I establishes broad policy goals and imposes specific duties on all federal agencies. Title II establishes the Council on Environmental Quality (CEQ), whose role consists of gathering information, issuing guidelines, and making recommendations to the President.

E. The most important section of Title I (102(2)(c)) requires all federal agencies to prepare an environmental impact statement (EIS) "in every recommendation or report on proposals for legislation and other major federal actions significantly affecting the quality of the human environment." The EIS must be a detailed report consisting of information as to:

1. Adverse environmental effects which cannot be avoided.
2. Any irreversible commitments of natural resources.
3. Available alternatives to the proposed action.

F. The U.S. Supreme Court interpreted section 102(2)(c) in Metropolitan Edison Co. v. People Against Nuclear Energy. It ruled that NEPA does not require an agency to evaluate in its EIS the psychological effects of the risk of a nuclear power plant accident. The Court stated that section 102(2)(c) requires only that an EIS evaluate effects on the environment which means the "physical environment." The case concerned the restarting of the Three Mile Island nuclear plant.

G. The CEQ issued new regulatory guidelines in the late 1970's to help clarify the ambiguity of Section 102(2)(c).

1. The "scoping" guidelines requires that even before EIS preparation, agencies must designate which environmental issues of a proposed action are most significant. Scoping ensures that agencies give primary attention to the most important environmental matters.
2. Another guideline requires that EISs be "clear, to the point, and written in plain English." The length of EISs is limited to 150 pages.

H. Critics of NEPA and CEQ guidelines point out that the present EIS process:

1. Fails to promote effective cost-benefit analysis.
2. Is "a document of compliance rather than a decision-making tool."
3. Is many times quite useless. The environment is so complex that forecasting becomes little more than guesswork.

I. NEPA applies only to federal actions, but many states have enacted similar legislation in an effort to assist decision-making.

II. Government's Regulation of Business: Introduction

A. When most people think of environmental law, they think of the public control of private action, i.e., the government's regulation of private enterprise.

B. Federal environmental laws regulating business include the Clean Air and Water Acts, Noise Control Act, Pesticide Control Acts, Solid Waste Disposal Act, Toxic Substance Control Act, Natural Resource Conservation and Recovery Act, and the "Superfund."

III. The Environmental Protection Agency (EPA)

A. At the federal level it is the EPA which is responsible for the public control of private action as it affects the environment.

B. The formation of the EPA in 1970 recognized the problems of having many different governmental departments responsible for environmental regulation.

C. The EPA's responsibilities include:

1. Gathering information and conducting research involving pollution problems.
2. Assisting state and local governments in controlling pollution through grants, technical advice, and other techniques.
3. Advising the CEQ about new environmental protection policies.
4. Administering and enforcing federal legislation concerning air, water, noise, solid waste, toxic substances, pesticides and oxidation.

IV. The Clean Air Act: Basic Structure

A. The Clean Air Act is the key federal legislation for controlling air pollution in the United States.

B. The EPA administrator has the responsibility of establishing air quality standards and enforcing these standards according to a definite timetable. There are primary and secondary air quality standards for particulates, carbon monoxide, sulfur dioxide, nitrogen dioxide, hydrocarbons, and lead. Primary standards are those necessary for the protection of public health. Secondary standards are less strict standards aimed at controlling adverse air pollution effects such as injury to property, vegetation, and climate.

C. Implementation of the Clean Air Act is a joint federal and state effort. The states are principally responsible for enforcement of the Act, with the EPA providing standard setting, coordination, and watchdog functions.

D. Penalties for violating the Act include fines and potential criminal and civil liability.

E. The Act divides air pollution sources into two categories:

1. Stationary sources, such as steel mills and utilities, are required to reduce emissions to comply with primary and secondary standards.
2. Mobile sources, such as automobiles and other machinery, must have properly functioning pollution control equipment.

F. Polluters must meet a timetable of standards for which control technology may not exist at the time. This "technology-forcing" aspect of the act was upheld by the Supreme Court in Union Electric Co. v. EPA. An electric utility alleged that it could not continue to operate if forced to comply with the sulfur dioxide restrictions. The majority of the Court held that under most circumstances the Clean Air Act does not allow claims of technological or economic infeasibility.

G. Recognizing that "technology-forcing" produces harmful consequences in some cases, the EPA often issues compliance waivers and variances from its standards.

V. The Clean Air Act: Policy Trends

A. Recently, the EPA has moved to make its regulations more economically efficient. Techniques to achieve economic efficiency include:

1. The bubble concept, under which an entire plant is licensed to emit a certain amount of pollution rather than each point source (e.g., a smokestack) within the plant being licensed to emit pollution. This approach permits companies flexibility in coordinating pollution control plans for entire plant sites. In Chevron U.S.A. Inc. v. Natural Resources Defense Council the Supreme Court upheld the EPA's authority to approve the bubble concept, even in states where pollution exceeds air quality standards. It stated that the EPA's interpretation of "stationary source" as including an entire plant area was reasonable.
2. Emissions reduction banking, under which businesses can cut pollution beyond what the law requires and "bank" these reductions for their own future use or sell to other companies as emissions offset.
3. Under the policy of prevention of significant deterioration the EPA controls new air pollution sources in certain areas where the air is cleaner than primary and secondary standards require.

B. Delay and red tape are the most common criticisms of the Clean Air Act. The formalities of the permitting process, the rigidity of state implementation plans, and the requirement that the EPA approve even minor variations in implementation plans are contributing factors to the delay problem.

VI. The Clean Water Act

A. Business enterprise is a major source of water pollution in the United States. Almost one-half of all the water in this country is for industrial cooling and condensing purposes.

B. To protect public health against industrial water pollution and other types of water hazards, such as municipal sewage discharge, Congress enacted the Clean Water Act.

C. Like the Clean Air Act, the Clean Water Act is administered primarily by the states in accordance with EPA standards.

D. The goals of the Act are to make the nation's "navigable" waterways safe for recreational use and clean enough for the protection of fish and other wildlife. The case of Quivira Mining Co. v. EPA illustrates that the term "navigable" is interpreted quite broadly. A federal court of appeals ruled that a connection between "dry gullies" and navigable-in-fact streams allowed pollution regulation of the gullies under the commerce clause.

E. Enforcement of the act is accomplished by a permit discharge system. No polluter, including municipalities, can discharge pollutants from any "point source" (e.g., a pipe) without a permit.

F. The Clean Water Act has a two-step process for clean up of industrial waste discharges. The first step requires polluters to install "best practical technology" (BPT). Dates are set for meeting BPT and BAT (best available technology) standards.

G. Two other water pollution statutes administered by the EPA are:

1. The Marine Protection, Research and Sanctuaries Act of 1972, which requires a permit for discharging various pollutants into the seas.
2. The Safe Water Drinking Act of 1974, which sets maximum drinking water contaminant levels.

VII. The Noise Control Act

A. Excessive noise not only causes deafness but also contributes to high blood pressure, heart and liver diseases, stress, alcoholism, and emotional disturbance.

B. Congress enacted the Noise Control Act in 1972 to help reduce the ill-effects of excessive noise. The EPA sets standards that limit noise emission from newly manufactured products that constitute a major noise source (e.g., buses, trucks, motorcycles, heavy machinery).

C. The act prohibits:

1. Sale of a manufactured product that does not comply with EPA standards.
2. Removal of a noise control device from a product.
3. Use of the product after such a removal.
4. Sale of a product without a required notice of noise level.
5. Importation of a product not in compliance with prescribed noise levels.

D. Recently, the implementation and enforcement of the Noise Control Act has slowed considerably.

VIII. The Pesticide Control Acts

A. Over a billion pounds of pesticides are manufactured annually in the United States. These chemicals are necessary in controlling pests, especially insects and mice, which would otherwise jeopardize this country's position as the world's greatest agricultural producer.

B. However, the widespread use of chemical pesticides causes major environmental hazards to both wildlife and human health.

C. Federal regulation of pesticides is accomplished by two statutes: The Federal Insecticide, Fungicide, and Rodenticide Act of 1947 and the Federal Environmental Pesticide Control Act of 1972 (FEPCA). It is the duty of the EPA administrator to register those pesticides that are properly labeled, which meet claims of effectiveness, and which will not have unreasonably adverse effects on the environment. Labeling must be easily comprehensible and contain instructions that include proper cautionary information. EPA enforcement for violations of the FEPCA include authority:

1. To deny or suspend registration.
2. To halt pesticide sales or usage.
3. To require safety tests.
4. To conduct on-site inspections of pesticide manufacturers.

D. There are two chief criticisms of the FEPCA:

1. Pesticide manufacturers claim that required lengthy testing procedures delay useful pesticides from reaching the market.
2. Environmentalists allege that EPA enforcement is hypocritical because FEPCA requirements do not apply to exported pesticides.

IX. The Solid Waste Disposal Act

A. Total solid wastes produced yearly in the United States exceed 5 billion tons, or almost 25 tons for every individual in the population. Half of this amount is agricultural waste, one-third is mineral waste, and the remainder is industrial and residential waste.

B. In response to the growing problem of nontoxic waste control, Congress enacted the Solid Waste Disposal Act. Under the Act the federal role is limited mainly to providing research and technical assistance to the states for their own disposal programs.

C. State and local governments have taken a variety of approaches in response to the solid waste disposal problem:

1. Development of sanitary landfills.
2. Tax breaks and incentives for industries using recycling techniques or using recycled materials.
3. Beverage container deposit laws.

X. Toxic and Hazardous Substances: Introduction

A. One survey ranks control of toxic and hazardous chemicals first on the public's list of where the government's regulation of industry is needed.

B. Regulation of toxic chemicals falls into three categories:

1. Regulation of the manufacturer of toxic chemicals under the Toxic Substances Control Act (TSCA).
2. Regulation of toxic and hazardous waste disposal under the Natural Resource Conservation and Recovery Act (RCRA).
3. Regulation of toxic and hazardous waste cleanup under the "Superfund."

XI. Toxic Substances Control Act (TSCA)

A. Over 70,000 man-made chemical compounds are in commercial use, and over 1,000 new chemicals are being produced every year.

B. To meet the unique environmental problems posed by toxic chemicals, Congress in 1976 passed the TSCA. TSCA's primary purpose is to mandate early evaluation of dangerous toxic chemicals before they become economically important.

C. Under TSCA, the EPA has the duty to collect information from manufacturers about chemicals that present a "substantial risk" of injury to health or environment. The EPA has the authority to require testing and/or prohibit distribution of chemicals that pose an unreasonable risk to human health or environmental preservation.

D. Unlike the Clean Air Act, TSCA requires the EPA to consider economic and social factors in its implementation of standards. The Act thus recognizes the beneficial role that many chemicals play in our society today.

XII. Natural Resource Conservation and Recovery Act (RCRA)

A. In 1976, Congress amended the Solid Waste Disposal Act by the RCRA in an effort to ensure proper disposal of hazardous substances. RCRA requires a generator of toxic wastes to:

1. Determine if its wastes qualify as a hazardous substance under RCRA.
2. Transport properly such wastes to a disposal facility that has an EPA permit or license.

B. Use of a "manifest system" (an exchange of transportation receipts from toxic substances generator, through waste hauler, to final licensed disposal site, back to generator) ensures proper recording and validation of toxic waste disposal.

XIII. Comprehensive Environmental Response, Compensation and Liability Act (the "Superfund")

A. In 1980 Congress enacted the "Superfund" to regulate the cleanup process of hazardous waste dumps and spills. This Act is funded by several billion dollars collected from taxes on petroleum and chemical industries.

B. Generators and others connected with the disposal of hazardous waste are responsible for unauthorized discharges of hazardous substances. They are held strictly liable for damages. No negligence need be proved.

C. Refusal to obey a cleanup order can lead to a reimbursement suit for monies spent from the Superfund plus punitive damages of up to triple the clean-up costs. Note that the Clean Air Act and Clean Water Act also contain provisions related to government suits to recover costs related to the cleanup of toxics.

XIV. Radiation

A. Although no single statute regulates radiation pollution and no one agency has broad discretionary powers regarding such pollution, overall responsibility for radiation control rests with the Nuclear Regulatory Commission. However, the EPA does have general authority to conduct research and provide assistance in this area.

B. The Clean Air Act, the Federal Water Pollution Control Act, and the Ocean Dumping Act all contain sections applicable to radiation discharges into the air and water.

XV. Suits by Private Individuals: Introduction

A. Legal rights that give private citizens standing to sue polluters come from two basic sources:

1. Most of the environmental statutes, such as the Clean Air and Water Acts, expressly provide "citizen enforcement" provisions. These provisions give private citizens the right to sue not only violators but also any responsible federal agency that has failed to implement requirements of various environmental statutes.
2. Traditional common law theories of tort, especially the law of nuisance, arm the private citizen with remedies for injury to personal health and property.

XVI. Tort Theories and Pollution

A. A public nuisance is an act which causes inconvenience or damage to the public in the exercise of rights common to everyone. A common law private nuisance is any unreasonable use of one's property so as to cause substantial interference with the enjoyment or use of another's land.

B. Besides the law of nuisance, other tort theories are available to a private citizen in pollution cases:

1. Trespass is an intentional physical invasion of another's private property.
2. Negligence is a breach of the defendant's duty to exercise reasonable care toward the plaintiff.
3. Strict liability holds the defendant liable regardless of fault, if defendant voluntarily engages in an unltrahazardous activity, such as the use of poisons.

C. An important issue in pollution-related tort cases concerns what damages are recoverable. In Ayers v. Town of Jackson the New Jersey Supreme Court ruled that plaintiffs who had drunk water polluted with toxic chemicals from defendant's landfill could recover the damages for: (1) deterioration in the quality of life while they were deprived of running water and (2) the cost of continued medical testing. They could not recover damages for (1) emotional distress caused by knowledge they had drunk polluted water or (2) the increased risk of disease.

XVII. Trends

A. Polls suggest strong public support for continued environmental cleanup.

B. Lack of unanimous scientific opinion on many environmental issues reveals the great complexity of these issues. Disagreement over causes and solutions to "acid rain" and the "greenhouse effect" illustrates the problem. A key controversy at the heart of environmental regulation is always how much certainty of harm is required to justify regulation.

XVIII. The Dilemma of Environmental Ethics

A. Merely waiting for regulation to prohibit a business practice is not always environmentally ethical.

B. A business must ensure that it pays careful attention to potential environmental issues, even when the law does not so require. It must also share information about both environmental and economic impacts with regulators and the public.

COMPLETION EXERCISES

1. _______________ is the federal agency responsible for the public control of private action as it affects the environment.

2. _______________ is the key federal legislation for controlling air pollution in the United States.

3. The _______________ concept permits air pollution licensing for an entire plant complex instead of for each individual source of pollution within the plant.

4. Enforcement of the _______________ is accomplished by a permit discharge system.

5. Distinguished from negligence liability, liability from the law of _______________ is based upon unreasonable injury rather than unreasonable conduct.

6. The _______________ has the primary responsibility for the control of radiation pollution.

7. Surveys rank the control of _______________ as first on the public's list of where government's regulation of business is needed.

8. Air pollution standards designed to protect human health are called _______________ air quality standards.

9. _______________ produces half of this country's solid waste.

10. Congress enacted _______________ to regulate the way government makes decisions having effects on the environment.

11. _______________ requires that even before environmental impact statement preparation, agencies must designate which environmental issues of a proposed action are most significant.

12. Title II of NEPA establishes the _______________.

13. _______________ allows businesses that cut pollution beyond what the law requires, to "deposit" these reductions for their own future use.

14. Before new pesticides can be sold, they must first be _______________ with the EPA.

15. The statute which holds polluters strictly liable for damage resulting from disposal of toxic wastes at unlicensed dumping sites is the _______________.

TRUE-FALSE CHOICES

1. _____ The Federal Environmental Pesticide Control Act does not apply to exported pesticides.

2. _____ Environmental regulation is the single most expensive area of the government's regulation of the business community.

3. _____ An environmental impact statement must be prepared by federal agencies prior to appropriation requests from Congress.

4. _____ The EPA is required to consider economic and social factors in its implementation of the Clean Air Act standards.

5. _____ The Noise Control Act imposes standards on total workplace noise levels.

6. _____ Regulation of toxic and hazardous waste cleanup is primarily done through the Toxic Substances Control Act.

7. _____ The Nuclear Regulatory Commission has sole federal jurisdiction in the area of radiation pollution.

8. _____ Injunctive relief is available to a plaintiff in a common law private practice nuisance action if monetary damages are inadequate.

9. _____ Many environmental statutes grant private citizens standing to sue for enforcement of the statutes.

10. _____ Under the Superfund, the government may sue for punitive damages of up to triple cleanup costs for illegal toxic dumping.

11. _____ Generators of waste who are responsible for unauthorized discharges of hazardous substances are held strictly liable.

12. _____ The Supreme Court has ruled that the EPA has broad discretionary power to interpret the compliance requirements of the Clean Water Act.

13. _____ The Noise Control Act prohibits importation of a product not in compliance with prescribed noise levels.

14. ______ The "technology-forcing" aspect of the Clean Air Act was declared unconstitutional by the Supreme Court in Union Electric Co. v. E.P.A.

15. ______ Individual states have little participation in the implementation of the Clean Air and Water Acts.

MULTIPLE CHOICE SELECTIONS

1. All of the following are approaches of state and local governments in response to solid waste disposal problems except:

   a. Development of sanitary landfills.
   b. Beverage container deposit laws.
   c. Emissions reduction banking, which allows businesses to "deposit" excess pollution reductions for their own future use.
   d. The granting of tax breaks for industries using recycling techniques.

2. The two categories of pollution sources regulated under the Clean Air Act are:

   a. Stationary and mobile.
   b. Horizontal and vertical.
   c. Active and passive.
   d. Particulate and gaseous.

3. Crass Chemical, Inc., is guilty of improperly dumping toxic chemicals at an unlicensed dump site. Select the incorrect statement:

   a. The Superfund makes Crass strictly liable for the cleanup costs of its dumping.
   b. The Superfund provides for Crass's corporate charter to be revoked.
   c. Refusal to obey a cleanup order under the Superfund could make Crass liable for punitive damages.
   d. Superfund is funded by mandatory contributions from the chemical and petroleum industries.

4. The EPA is required to consider economic and social factors in its implementation of which of the following:

   a. Toxic Substances Act.
   b. Clean Air Act.
   c. Clean Water Act.
   d. Safe Water Drinking Act.

5. Mayor Johnson proposes an ordinance to the City Council which would create a new city park. However, an environmental group threatens to sue to require preparation of an EIS under the National Environmental Policy Act. As the City Attorney, what would be your best response to the group?

   a. The EIS requirement under NEPA is inherently ambiguous and therefore unconstitutionally vague.
   b. Proposals for legislation do not trigger EIS requirements.
   c. An EIS would be extremely expensive and its cost would greatly outweigh any benefit derived from such a study.
   d. EIS requirements under NEPA apply only to federal actions, not to actions of state and local governments.

Chapter 25

DISCUSSION ANALYSIS

Chemical, Inc., is a small corporation that produces the new pesticide BUGGONA, a highly toxic substance. The production process releases emissions of hydrocarbons into the atmosphere and discharges of lead drain into a nearby stream. During transportation of a load of defective BUGGONA to an illegal dumpsite, the truck wrecks, causing the chemical to spill into Mrs. Smith's yard, which exposes her to the toxic substance. Assuming Chemical, Inc., is on the verge of bankruptcy, what federal environmental statutes has it possibly violated? What are the potential liabilities for such violations? What importance does Chemical's impending insolvency have? Who can Mrs. Smith sue and under what legal theories?

APPENDIX: SOLUTIONS TO PROBLEMS AND EXERCISES

CHAPTER 1

COMPLETION EXERCISES

1. courts
2. Substantive law
3. Procedural law
4. civil law
5. felonies, misdemeanors
6. white-collar crime
7. Contract law
8. tort
9. Negligence
10. personal, real
11. ownership
12. possession
13. constitutions, legislation, judicial decisions, administrative regulation
14. stare decisis
15. economics, ethics, social responsibility

TRUE-FALSE CHOICES

1.	T
2.	F
3.	T
4.	T
5.	F
6.	F
7.	T
8.	T
9.	F
10.	T
11.	F
12.	F
13.	T
14.	F
15.	T

MULTIPLE CHOICE SELECTIONS

1.	d
2.	c
3.	a
4.	c
5.	d

DISCUSSION ANALYSIS

The basic sources of law in our society are constitutions (state and federal), legislation (state and federal), judicial decisions (state and federal), and rules, regulations, and decisions of administrative agencies (state and federal). In many ways the U.S. Constitution is our most basic source of law. However, judicial decisions interpret even the Constitution. And administrative agency personnel and law enforcement authorities at every level make discretionary decisions regarding the application of law. These decisions are extremely important in individual situations.

CHAPTER 2

COMPLETION EXERCISES

1. judicial review
2. judges, justices
3. fact, law
4. $20
5. grand, petit
6. grand
7. Mock, mini
8. Uniform Commercial Code
9. Marshall, Marbury v. Madison
10. history
11. interpreted (construed)
12. Case law
13. precedents
14. dicta
15. stare decisis

TRUE-FALSE CHOICES

1.	F
2.	F
3.	F
4.	F
5.	T
6.	F
7.	F
8.	T
9.	T
10.	T
11.	F
12.	T
13.	T
14.	T
15.	F

MULTIPLE CHOICE SELECTIONS

1.	b
2.	d
3.	d
4.	d
5.	a

Solutions

DISCUSSION ANALYSIS

The law is a system for ordering society. As such it must provide stability and certainty (as reflected in the principle of stare decisis), but at the same time it must provide a mechanism for orderly change (e.g., by overturning prior precedent). The statement concerning constitutional relativity reflects that through interpretation of relatively open-ended constitutional terms, the Constitution accommodates changing societal needs.

CHAPTER 3

COMPLETION EXERCISES		TRUE-FALSE CHOICES		MULTIPLE CHOICE SELECTIONS	
1.	specific performance	1.	T	1.	d
2.	maxims	2.	F	2.	b
3.	unconstitutional	3.	T	3.	c
4.	limited	4.	T	4.	a
5.	Legislation	5.	F	5.	b
6.	petition for writ of certiorari	6.	F		
7.	collect judgments	7.	T		
8.	Article III	8.	T		
9.	state	9.	T		
10.	$50,000	10.	F		
11.	state where it is incorporated, state where it has its principal place of business	11.	T		
12.	abstention	12.	T		
13.	law, equity	13.	T		
14.	equity	14.	T		
15.	contingent fee	15.	F		

DISCUSSION ANALYSIS

The phrase "justice delayed is justice denied" sums up why court congestion and delay have adverse consequences for individuals and society. If disputes cannot be legally resolved in timely fashion, parties to the disputes lose confidence in the court system and suffer financial and psychological hardship. Solutions to court congestion could include (1) making the losing party in a civil law suit pay the winner's costs, (2) reform of the contingent fee system, (3) mock and mini trials, and (4) arbitration instead of litigation.

CHAPTER 4

COMPLETION EXERCISES		TRUE-FALSE CHOICES		MULTIPLE CHOICE SELECTIONS	
1.	appellant	1.	T	1.	c
2.	standing-to-sue	2.	F	2.	b
3.	the defendant	3.	T	3.	d
4.	due process	4.	T	4.	a
5.	Extradition	5.	T	5.	d
6.	forum non conveniens	6.	T		
7.	motion for summary judgment	7.	F		
8.	discovery	8.	T		
9.	Voir dire	9.	F		

COMPLETION EXERCISES		TRUE-FALSE CHOICES	
10.	preponderance of the evidence	10.	F
11.	hearsay	11.	T
12.	law	12.	F
13.	res judicata	13.	T
14.	privileged	14.	F
15.	facts	15.	F

DISCUSSION ANALYSIS

The state court system of California has personal jurisdiction because Zenith Transport has "minimum contacts" with California, i.e., it committed a tort there. The courts of Delaware and Ohio have personal jurisdiction because of Zenith Transport's residency in these two states. Finally, the federal courts have personal jurisdiction based on diversity of citizenship.

CHAPTER 5

COMPLETION EXERCISES		TRUE-FALSE CHOICES		MULTIPLE CHOICE SELECTIONS	
1.	Federal Arbitration	1.	T	1.	b
2.	litigation	2.	F	2.	c
3.	restricted	3.	T	3.	d
4.	crime	4.	F	4.	d
5.	public policy	5.	F	5.	c
6.	outside the scope	6.	T		
7.	statutorily mandated	7.	T		
8.	de novo	8.	T		
9.	consumer complaints	9.	T		
10.	confidence, good will	10.	T		
		11.	T		
		12.	F		
		13.	F		
		14.	T		
		15.	F		

DISCUSSION ANALYSIS

The primary reasons that parties to a dispute may decide to arbitrate rather than to litigate are that arbitration saves time and expense. It can also be handled in a private setting rather than in a public courtroom.

The usual procedure for arbitration is for the parties to agree (or contract) to submit certain issues to one or more arbitrators selected by the parties. The arbitrator conducts a hearing on these issues, which can be of fact or law, and hands down a written decision known as an award. If no objections to the award are filed within a statutory period, the award becomes final and will be enforced by a court. Generally, a court will not set aside an arbitration award, even if it disagrees with the arbitrator's view of the law and facts.

CHAPTER 6

COMPLETION EXERCISES

1. separation of powers
2. Supremacy clause
3. taxation
4. import-export
5. privileges and immunities
6. full faith and credit
7. rational
8. exclusive
9. Residency requirements
10. Constitution
11. Federalism
12. President, Senate
13. contract clause
14. taxing
15. states' relation

TRUE-FALSE CHOICES

1. F
2. T
3. F
4. F
5. T
6. F
7. T
8. T
9. F
10. F
11. T
12. T
13. T
14. F
15. F

MULTIPLE CHOICE SELECTIONS

1. c
2. d
3. c
4. a
5. b

DISCUSSION ANALYSIS

Under the supremacy clause the ordinance is probably constitutional since the federal statute and local ordinance do not appear to conflict. Under the commerce and privileges immunities clauses the constitutionality of the local ordinance depends upon why the tax discriminates in favor of vessels registered under California title. It is unconstitutional to discriminate against interstate commerce or against citizens of other states. Thus, the constitutionality of the ordinance is at least questionable.

CHAPTER 7

COMPLETION EXERCISES

1. establishment clause (First Amendment)
2. press
3. Prior restraints
4. false, misleading
5. Fourth Amendment
6. Eminent domain
7. Fifth Amendment
8. Miranda warning
9. jury trial
10. due process clause
11. Procedural due process
12. equal protection clause
13. compelling
14. quasi-strict scrutiny test
15. double jeopardy

TRUE-FALSE CHOICES

1. F
2. T
3. T
4. T
5. F
6. F
7. F
8. T
9. T
10. T
11. F
12. T
13. F
14. T
15. T

MULTIPLE CHOICE SELECTIONS

1. c
2. a
3. a
4. b
5. c

DISCUSSION ANALYSIS

Yes, even though obscene material does not qualify for First Amendment protection, the outlined procedure constitutes an unconstitutional prior restraint of speech. There is heavy presumption of unconstitutionality on prior restraints because of the chilling effect they have on expression. This procedure fails to meet the three-pronged test for permissible prior restraints: (1) burden of proof on the censor, (2) the restraint must be only for a short duration, and (3) a prompt final judicial determination must be available.

CHAPTER 8

COMPLETION EXERCISES	TRUE-FALSE CHOICES	MULTIPLE CHOICE SELECTIONS
1. administrative process	1. F	1. c
2. need for experts, public protection, provision of services	2. T	2. d
3. quasi-legislative	3. T	3. a
4. preponderance of evidence	4. F	4. d
5. cease and desist	5. T	5. d
6. administrative courts	6. F	
7. Competition, Consumer Protection, Economics	7. T	
8. validity of delegation, proper use of authority	8. T	
9. exhausted remedies	9. F	
10. immunity	10. F	
11. Sunshine law	11. F	
12. Civil service	12. T	
13. Ethics in Government Act	13. F	
14. 100 billion	14. F	
15. cost-benefit	15. T	

DISCUSSION ANALYSIS

Increasing complexity of society and mutual interdependence have prompted much administrative growth in this country. More specifically, the need for experts to solve and manage problems and the inability to legislate in detail have led to such growth. Also, the increasing wealth of society has led to a philosophy of wealth redistribution in the form of services and welfare assistance which requires administrative management. In recent years tight pocketbooks and growing disillusionment with the ability of the administrative process to provide answers to complex problems has provoked considerable criticism of administrative agencies.

CHAPTER 9

COMPLETION EXERCISES	TRUE-FALSE CHOICES	MULTIPLE CHOICE SELECTIONS
1. parol evidence	1. T	1. a
2. handwritten	2. T	2. b
3. third party	3. T	3. c
4. condition precedent	4. F	4. b
5. condition subsequent	5. F	5. d
6. Complete	6. T	
7. material breach	7. T	
8. executory	8. F	
9. unilateral	9. T	

COMPLETION EXERCISES

10. void
11. voidable
12. quasi-contract
13. breach
14. offer
15. bilateral
16. accord and satisfaction

TRUE-FALSE CHOICES

10. T
11. T
12. F
13. T
14. F
15. F

DISCUSSION ANALYSIS

Contract law underlies all buying and selling agreements and many employment agreements. It brings confidence to business dealings that if one party fails to live up to an agreement, the other party can go to court to get damages. It facilitates business dealings by making parties willing to do business with one another.

CHAPTER 10

COMPLETION EXERCISES

1. strict liability
2. battery
3. truth
4. willful and wanton negligence
5. Res ipsa loquitur
6. jointly and severally
7. comparative negligence
8. Punitive
9. fellow servant doctrine
10. Lanham Act
11. structured settlements
12. trespass
13. False imprisonment
14. special relationship
15. cause-in-fact

TRUE-FALSE CHOICES

1. T
2. T
3. T
4. F
5. T
6. T
7. F
8. T
9. T
10. T
11. F
12. F
13. T
14. T
15. F

MULTIPLE CHOICE SELECTIONS

1. b
2. a
3. d
4. b
5. c

DISCUSSION ANALYSIS

Trends in torts that favor plaintiffs include the movement from negligence to strict liability in product-injury cases, the change from contributory negligence to comparative negligence, the submission of more proximate causation issues to juries, the broadening concept of duty, the development of res ipsa loquitur, and the expansion of joint tortfeasor doctrine in causation. Courts have played the dominant role in creating most of these trends.

CHAPTER 11

COMPLETION EXERCISES		TRUE-FALSE CHOICES		MULTIPLE CHOICE SELECTIONS	
1.	Privity of contract	1.	T	1.	b
2.	Caveat emptor	2.	F	2.	c
3.	negligence	3.	T	3.	d
4.	strict liability	4.	T	4.	d
5.	implied warranty of merchantability	5.	F	5.	a
6.	absolute liability, express warranty	6.	F		
7.	res ipsa loquitur	7.	F		
8.	proximate cause	8.	F		
9.	state of the art	9.	T		
10.	Assumption of risk	10.	F		
11.	defect	11.	F		
12.	indemnification	12.	F		
13.	subrogation	13.	F		
14.	statute of repose	14.	F		
15.	reasonable professional	15.	F		

DISCUSSION ANALYSIS

As a user of the defective mower, Mr. Doe's gardener in most states could sue all three sellers under strict product liability and negligence (All-City and Harold's are not likely liable for negligence, however). In a state which has extended strict liability to bystanders, Mrs. Smith would have the same protection as the gardener. Mr. Doe can recover from Harold's for the defective mower under the implied warranty of merchantability. If All-City or Harold's has to pay anyone, they can obtain indemnification from the Johnson Company.

CHAPTER 12

COMPLETION EXERCISES		TRUE-FALSE CHOICES		MULTIPLE CHOICE SELECTIONS	
1.	Subschapter S	1.	F	1.	c
2.	Partnership by estoppel	2.	F	2.	d
3.	Piercing the corporate veil	3.	T	3.	a
4.	Limited	4.	F	4.	c
5.	excess accumulated earnings	5.	T	5.	a
6.	agreement to carry on business for a profit	6.	T		
7.	Sole entrepreneurship	7.	F		
8.	limited	8.	T		
9.	in its own name	9.	T		
10.	Articles of Copartnership	10.	T		
11.	assumed name statute	11.	F		
12.	charter	12.	F		
13.	licensed	13.	T		
14.	dissolved	14.	F		
15.	closely held	15.	T		

Solutions

DISCUSSION ANALYSIS

A limited partnership might best suit this new enterprise. John and Mary could raise the needed $150,000 by selling limited partnership shares. Since the business would lose money for its first three years, the investors could deduct losses from their taxable personal income. Mary could be a salaried general partner, and John and the other investors could have the limited liability of limited partners. A Subchapter S corporation is a possibility here except for the limitation on the number of shareholders.

CHAPTER 13

COMPLETION EXERCISES	TRUE-FALSE CHOICES	MULTIPLE CHOICE SELECTIONS
1. principal	1. T	1. d
2. express, implied	2. T	2. c
3. ostensible	3. F	3. d
4. ratifies	4. F	4. b
5. reveal	5. T	5. c
6. independent	6. F	
7. material	7. T	
8. indemnify	8. T	
9. control	9. T	
10. public policy	10. T	
11. Express	11. T	
12. respondeat superior	12. F	
13. complicity	13. F	
14. fiduciary duty	14. T	
15. within the scope of employment	15. T	

DISCUSSION ANALYSIS

The sellers cannot void their contracts with Ms. Orange. Furthermore, she may assign the contracts to the chemical company. Once the chemical company's identity is known the sellers can elect to hold either the company or Ms. Orange liable in case of a breach of contract.

CHAPTER 14

COMPLETION EXERCISES	TRUE-FALSE CHOICES	MULTIPLE CHOICE SELECTIONS
1. one-third	1. T	1. d
2. irrevocable letter of credit	2. F	2. a
3. subsidiary	3. T	3. d
4. Licensing	4. T	4. d
5. joint venture	5. F	5. d
6. arbitration	6. F	
7. Expropriation	7. T	
8. act-of-state	8. T	
9. sovereign immunity	9. T	
10. International Court of Justice	10. T	
11. COMECON	11. T	
12. GATT	12. F	

COMPLETION EXERCISES		TRUE-FALSE CHOICES	
13.	44	13.	F
14.	Trademark Counterfeiting Act	14.	T
15.	minimum contacts	15.	F

DISCUSSION ANALYSIS

To insure that a foreign buyer will pay for goods ordered, an irrevocable letter of credit is commonly used in international transactions. The letter of credit comes from an issuing bank in the buyer's country. It goes to a confirming bank in the seller's country. The letter of credit guarantees that the purchase price will be paid when the seller presents a bill of lading to the confirming bank that show the goods have been shipped. The confirming bank then forwards the bill of lading to the issuing bank that enable the buyer to take possession of the goods when they arrrive.

CHAPTER 15

COMPLETION EXERCISES		TRUE-FALSE CHOICES		MULTIPLE CHOICE SELECTIONS	
1.	Occupational Safety and Health Act	1.	T	1.	a
2.	inspections	2.	F	2.	c
3.	targeting of inspections	3.	T	3.	a
4.	out of and in the scope of employment	4.	F	4.	c
5.	exclusive remedy	5.	T	5.	a
6.	Federal Employers Liability Act	6.	T		
7.	Fair Labor Standards Act	7.	F		
8.	Employee Polygraph Protection Act	8.	F		
9.	hazardous	9.	T		
10.	experience rating system	10.	T		
11.	Worker Adjustment and Retraining Notification Act	11.	F		
12.	qualified plan	12.	T		
13.	defined contribution	13.	F		
14.	59 1/2	14.	T		
15.	employment-at-will	15.	T		

DISCUSSION ANALYSIS

Courts in many states are beginning to limit the employment-at-will doctrine when important public policy reasons are present. For instance, courts have limited the at-will doctrine when (1) employers discharge employees for performing important public obligations, such as jury duty, (2) employers discharge employees for reporting the employers' law violations, and (3) employers discharge employees for exercising certain statutory rights, such as the right to obtain workers' compensation. Many courts also imply contractual obligations on employers that effectively limit employment at will. Some authorities have predicted that limitations on the at-will doctrine might be part of a trend that could lead ultimately to some type of legally guaranteed job security.

Solutions

CHAPTER 16

COMPLETION EXERCISES	TRUE-FALSE CHOICES	MULTIPLE CHOICE SELECTIONS
1. Civil Rights Act of 1964	1. T	1. b
2. Affirmative action	2. F	2. d
3. Reverse	3. T	3. d
4. documentation	4. F	4. c
5. Civil Rights Act of 1866	5. F	5. a
6. EEOC	6. F	
7. substantially equal	7. F	
8. an undue hardship	8. T	
9. BFOQ	9. F	
10. 180 days	10. T	
11. race, sex, color, national origin, religion	11. F	
12. sex, religion, national origin	12. F	
13. Executive orders	13. T	
14. Pregnancy Discrimination Act	14. T	
15. Bottom-line	15. T	

DISCUSSION ANALYSIS

A. The Age Discrimination in Employment Act protects employees over the age of 40 from age discrimination. A determination of illegality would require knowledge of why Mr. Jones was fired. Absent a valid, non-age related reason, Mr. Jones' discharge fits a classic age discrimination replacement of an older, higher paid worker with a younger one who will work for less. Potential liabilities for the employer include reinstatement and lost wages. Double damages are awarded for willful violations, and some courts permit damages for psychological trauma.

B. Title VII and the Pregnancy Discrimination Act would be violated if Ms. Smith has been fired because of her pregnancy. Acme Co.'s best defense would be a "paper fortress" documenting Ms. Smith's disciplinary problems. Potential liabilities for the employer include reinstatement of Ms. Smith, backpay award, and an injunction prohibiting future violations.

CHAPTER 17

COMPLETION EXERCISES	TRUE-FALSE CHOICES	MULTIPLE CHOICE SELECTIONS
1. Clayton Act	1. F	1. d
2. Airline	2. F	2. a
3. yellow dog	3. T	3. c
4. injunctions	4. T	4. d
5. General Counsel	5. T	5. b
6. substantial	6. F	
7. union shop	7. T	
8. Federal Mediation and Conciliation Service	8. F	
9. right to work	9. F	
10. 20	10. T	
11. Cooling-off period	11. F	
12. majority	12. F	
13. World War II	13. F	
14. threats or promise of benefit	14. F	
15. constitution, bylaws	15. T	

DISCUSSION ANALYSIS

The 80-day cooling off period can apply to this situation if the federal district court determines that the strike imperils the national health or safety. Steps necessary to implement the cooling off period are that the President must appoint an emergency board to report whether or not a strike or proposed strike imperils the national health or safety. If the board reports that it does, the President can instruct the Attorney General to seek an injunction (restraining order, back-to-work order) in federal district court.

CHAPTER 18

COMPLETION EXERCISES	TRUE-FALSE CHOICES	MULTIPLE CHOICE SELECTIONS
1. featherbedding	1. T	1. d
2. Wright-Line	2. F	2. d
3. hot cargo	3. F	3. b
4. wages, hours, conditions of employment	4. F	4. c
5. sweetheart	5. F	5. c
6. unfair labor practice	6. T	
7. concerted	7. T	
8. voluntary	8. T	
9. unfair labor practice charges	9. F	
10. Informational	10. T	
11. sole	11. T	
12. work rules	12. F	
13. other plants	13. F	
14. secondary	14. T	
15. union shop	15. T	

DISCUSSION ANALYSIS

If work-related rules interfere with efforts of employees to form a union or engage in concerted activities for mutual aid, they are unfair labor practices unless the employer can prove that the rule is reasonably necessary to further production or other goals of employment. Even if the rules achieve a legitimate business purpose, they may be unfair labor practices if they are overbroad. For instance, a "no solicitation" rule can be used to keep vendors who would like to sell to employees off the employer's premises. But the rule cannot be used to prevent one employee from soliciting another for union membership unless the employer can prove that the rule is applied only to situations where solicitation actually interferes with working.

CHAPTER 19

COMPLETION EXERCISES	TRUE-FALSE CHOICES	MULTIPLE CHOICE SELECTIONS
1. blue sky	1. F	1. d
2. SEC	2. T	2. b
3. initial	3. F	3. d
4. issuer	4. F	4. c
5. underwriter	5. T	5. b
6. registration statement	6. T	
7. tombstone ads	7. T	
8. prospectus	8. F	
9. Shelf-registration	9. T	

Solutions

COMPLETION EXERCISES		TRUE-FALSE CHOICES	
10.	due diligence	10.	T
11.	material	11.	T
12.	10B, 10B-5	12.	F
13.	insider	13.	T
14.	6	14.	T
15.	willful	15.	F

DISCUSSION ANALYSIS

A security is any investment opportunity which is a common venture that seeks profit based on the entrepreneurial efforts of others. The primary purpose of securities laws is to require issuers to disclose all information material to investment decisions to investors. These laws do not limit the offering of investment opportunities based on risk.

CHAPTER 20

COMPLETION EXERCISES		TRUE-FALSE CHOICES		MULTIPLE CHOICE SELECTIONS	
1.	consumer	1.	F	1.	b
2.	consent order, cease and desist order	2.	F	2.	c
3.	disclosure	3.	T	3.	a
4.	Magnuson-Moss Warranty Act, full, limited	4.	T	4.	d
5.	discrimination	5.	F	5.	c
6.	Fair Credit Reporting Act	6.	T		
7.	Unfair or deceptive trade practices	7.	F		
8.	$10,000 per day	8.	T		
9.	Corrective advertising	9.	F		
10.	advertising substantiation	10.	T		
11.	actual damages, punitive damages, attorneys' fees	11.	T		
12.	reasonable procedures	12.	F		
13.	finance charge	13.	T		
14.	FTC Act	14.	T		
15.	Right of Financial Privacy Act	15.	T		

DISCUSSION ANALYSIS

The FTC might proceed against Losemore, Inc., under Section 5 of the FTC Act which prohibits unfair or deceptive trade practices. It would likely ask the company to substantiate its advertising claims. Inability to do so would constitute an unfair or deceptive trade practice. Remedies available in such an instance would include the consent and desist order, corrective advertising, and consumer refunds. Fines would not be appropriate unless the company has violated an FTC rule or order.

CHAPTER 21

COMPLETION EXERCISES	TRUE-FALSE CHOICES	MULTIPLE CHOICE SELECTIONS
1. creditor	1. T	1. d
2. lien	2. F	2. c
3. mechanic's lien	3. F	3. a
4. bulk transfer	4. T	4. d
5. surety	5. T	5. d
6. Reimbursement	6. T	
7. purchase money security interest	7. T	
8. financing statement	8. F	
9. foreclosure	9. F	
10. liquidated, adjusted	10. T	
11. undue hardship	11. T	
12. Usury	12. F	
13. Fair Debt Collection Practices Act	13. T	
14. Fair Credit Billing Act	14. F	
15. trustee	15. F	

DISCUSSION ANALYSIS

Unless the collateral is in the possession of the creditor, attachment requires that (1) the debtor has signed a written security agreement, (2) the creditor has given value to the debtor, and (3) the debtor has rights in the collateral. Perfection is necessary to give notice of the security interest to potential creditors of the debtor so they will not extend credit on the same collateral.

CHAPTER 22

COMPLETION EXERCISES	TRUE-FALSE CHOICES	MULTIPLE CHOICE SELECTIONS
1. trust	1. T	1. c
2. Parker v. Brown	2. T	2. a
3. triple	3. T	3. c
4. nolo contendere	4. F	4. c
5. per se	5. F	5. a
6. directly	6. F	
7. contribution	7. T	
8. $1 million, $100,000, 3 years	8. T	
9. Noerr-Pennington	9. F	
10. Sherman	10. T	
11. attorney general	11. T	
12. substantial effect	12. F	
13. rule of reason	13. T	
14. injunction	14. T	
15. horizontal	15. T	

Solutions

DISCUSSION ANALYSIS

Under the Sherman Act an antitrust violator faces criminal penalties of $1 million if a corporation or $100,000 and/or 3 years imprisonment if an individual. Civil remedies include injunction and triple damages. Criminal antitrust violators often plead nolo contendere to avoid having private parties use evidence of a criminal conviction to establish a basis for triple damages. The nolo contendere plea allows the court to treat violators as if they had pleaded guilty.

CHAPTER 23

	COMPLETION EXERCISES		TRUE-FALSE CHOICES		MULTIPLE CHOICE SELECTIONS
1.	conduct	1.	F	1.	c
2.	goods, services	2.	T	2.	b
3.	Goldfarb v. Virginia State Bar	3.	F	3.	a
4.	Resale price maintenance	4.	T	4.	d
5.	Colgate Doctrine	5.	T	5.	d
6.	cosignment	6.	F		
7.	rule of reason	7.	F		
8.	joint ventures	8.	T		
9.	vertical territorial	9.	T		
10.	competition	10.	T		
11.	Predatory	11.	F		
12.	relevant product, relevant geographic	12.	T		
13.	relevant product	13.	T		
14.	restrain	14.	T		
15.	growing rapidly	15.	T		

DISCUSSION ANALYSIS

These facts indicate the possibility of illegal price fixing under Section 1 of the Sherman Act, which prohibits every combination, contract or conspiracy in restraint of trade among the several states. It is easily arguable that the roar of approval, followed by the raised prices, was a conspiracy in restraint of trade, i.e., an agreement to price fix. Under this analysis if the restraint would have a "substantial impact" on interstate commerce, it would violate Section 1.

CHAPTER 24

	COMPLETION EXERCISES		TRUE-FALSE CHOICES		MULTIPLE CHOICE SELECTIONS
1.	primary line price discrimination	1.	T	1.	c
2.	cost justification	2.	T	2.	c
3.	meeting competition in good faith	3.	F	3.	b
4.	Secondary line	4.	T	4.	a
5.	tying	5.	T	5.	a
6.	output	6.	F		
7.	Robinson-Patman	7.	T		
8.	interlocking directorates	8.	F		
9.	actual	9.	T		
10.	commodities	10.	F		
11.	conglomerate	11.	F		

COMPLETION EXERCISES		TRUE-FALSE CHOICES	
12.	horizontal	12.	T
13.	tender offers	13.	F
14.	shark repellants	14.	T
15.	Herfindahl-Hirshman	15.	T

DISCUSSION ANALYSIS

The usual legal issues in a merger divestiture suit are (1) what is the relevant geographic market; (2) what is the relevant product market; and (3) what is the potentially anticompetitive effect of the merger? In this instance, the relevant geographic market is national in scope. But what is the relevant product market? Reynolds argued before the Supreme Court that the relevant product market was aluminum foil in general and that Arrow controlled an extremely small fraction of the market for aluminum foil. However, the FTC argued, and the Supreme Court agreed, that the relevant product market was aluminum foil marketed to florists. Under this analysis, the potentially anticompetitive effects of the merger were magnified. Considering the trend toward concentration in the relevant product market, the enormous size of Reynolds Metals when compared to Arrow's competitors, and the loss of Reynolds as a potential entrant, the Supreme Court ruled that the merger violated Section 7.

CHAPTER 25

COMPLETION EXERCISES		TRUE-FALSE CHOICES		MULTIPLE CHOICE SELECTIONS	
1.	EPA	1.	T	1.	c
2.	Clean Air Act	2.	T	2.	a
3.	bubble	3.	F	3.	b
4.	Clean Water Act	4.	F	4.	a
5.	nuisance	5.	F	5.	d
6.	NRC	6.	F		
7.	pollution	7.	F		
8.	primary	8.	T		
9.	Industry	9.	T		
10.	NEPA	10.	T		
11.	Scoping	11.	T		
12.	CEQ	12.	T		
13.	Emissions reduction banking	13.	T		
14.	registered	14.	F		
15.	NRCRA	15.	F		

DISCUSSION ANALYSIS

Chemical, Inc., has violated the NRCRA by dumping its insecticide improperly. In addition, it has violated the Clean Air and Water Acts if its discharge of hydrocarbons and lead are unlicensed.

Chemical faces various criminal fines, and its agents face fines and imprisonment under the acts violated. If Chemical cannot afford to clean up its toxic dumpings, the government can do so under the Superfund. Chemical will be subject to punitive damages for failure to obey a cleanup order.

Mrs. Smith can sue Chemical for damages for trespass and, possibly, negligence.